Larry McMurtry and the West

An Ambivalent Relationship

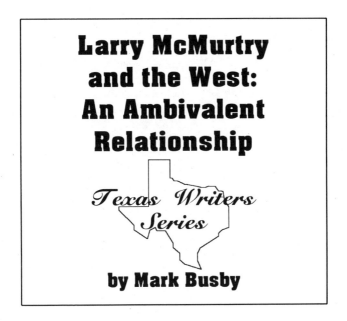

Larry McMurtry and the West: An Ambivalent Relationship

Texas Writers Series

by Mark Busby

University of North Texas Press
Denton, Texas

First printed in 1995 in the United States of America

10 9 8 7 6 5 4 3 2 1

The paper in this book meets the minimum requirements of the
American National Standard for Permanence of paper for
Printed Library Materials, Z39.48.1984.

Library of Congress Cataloging-in-Publication Data

Busby, Mark.
Larry McMurtry and the West : an ambivalent relationship
/ by Mark Busby.
p. cm. — (Texas writers series ; no. 4)
Includes bibliographical references and index.
ISBN 0-929398-34-3
1. McMurtry, Larry—Knowledge—West (U.S.) 2. Western
stories—history and criticism. 3. West (U.S.)—In literature. 4.
Ambivalence in literature. 5. Texas—In literature. I. Title. II.
Series.
PS3563.A319Z59   1995   94-47200
813'.54—dc20   CIP

For my grandfather, father, and uncle
—Arch, Jim, and Lon Busby—
who paid homage to the cowboy god riding West,
and for my son, brother, and nephew
—Josh, Steven, and Zack Busby—
who live in a different world.

Table of Contents

Preface

The purpose of this study is to examine Larry McMurtry's writing career in order to establish the significance of his relationship with his home region. My thesis is that McMurtry's writing is characterized by a deep ambivalence toward his home territory, a vacillation that cuts through his work and his attitudes about writing itself. The course of his career demonstrates his shifting attitudes that have led him toward, away, and then back again to his home territory and the "cowboy god" that dominates its mythology.

Over the years McMurtry has increasingly been perceived as eccentric, aloof, and somewhat ornery, most recently tending to avoid interviews and refusing to hit the promotion circuit. But of all the people I would like to thank for help with this project, I first need to acknowledge Larry McMurtry for generously giving the time to talk with me about his work and exchanging faxes with me, as technology continues to touch research in different ways. I would also like to acknowledge the help of the rest of the McMurtrys—Sue, Judy, and Charlie. Sue Deen and the group at the Blue Pig book store in Archer City welcomed me graciously. I would also like to thank Ken Kesey, whom Larry calls the "last wagon master," for the evening at our house in Wimberley, Texas, talking books, recalling his times with Larry, and being the merry prankster of old; and Bill Wittliff, who offered his observations on publishing and adapting McMurtry. There are also the people who engaged me in the project: my old friend Clay Reynolds, who asked me to edit a section of *Taking Stock: A Larry McMurtry Casebook* in 1989 and with whom I share a similar relationship to McMurtry's work; James Ward Lee, general editor of the Texas Writers Series, and Fran Vick and Charlotte Wright, director and editor at the University of North Texas Press, who encouraged me to do the project, kept after me to finish, and read and edited the manuscript; and a number of others who provided me with material: Patricia Bozeman, Head of Special Collections at the University of Houston; Jay Cox at the University of Arizona, for a copy of her master's study of McMurtry's sources in *Lonesome Dove*; George Hickenlooper, who provided me with a copy of his fine documentary *Picture This: The Times of Peter Bogdanovich in Archer City, Texas*; Roger Jones, my former dissertation student at Texas A&M, now at Ranger College, for supplying me with an advance copy of his revised dissertation (later published by A&M Press); Bobbie Jean Klepper, Special Collections Librarian at the University of Texas of the Permian Basin; Ken Lavender at the University of North Texas, for opening the Rare Book and Texana Collection at UNT one spring break; Steve Tatum at the University of Utah, for material on Billy the Kid; and my friend and colleague, Dick Holland, curator of the Special Collections at Southwest Texas State University, who took me through the material in the collection and talked with me often about most aspects of the project. Finally, I'd again like to thank my wife, Linda Busby, for reading and editing the manuscript with her usual incisive skill.

Over the years I have written often about McMurtry's work, and I have reviewed books for various publications. I have incorporated elements from those scattered writings in this work: *New Mexico Humanities Review*, *Texas Books in Review*, *Southwestern American Literature*, *The Houston Chronicle*, *Bryan-College Station Eagle*, *Taking Stock: A Larry McMurtry Casebook* (SMU Press), and *Western Writers* (Gale Press). I've also drawn from the introduction I wrote for a collection of short stories I edited for Corona Press, *New Growth/2: Contemporary Short Stories by Texas Writers*. Rounding up these and other sources has been a pleasant task, and I have been aided in a number of ways by my administrative assistant at the Center for the Study of the Southwest, Sharon Pogue, and by the student workers who have worked with us: Mitch Cameron, Danny Gaitan, Adrienne Moore, Dana Moore, and Hector Negrete.

Much of my discussion depends upon a double vision of the mythic appeal of Texas. As expatriate but perennial Texan Larry L. King mused about the Texas of myth in *Of Outlaws, Con Men, Whores, Politicians, and Other Artists* on one his many returns to his blood's country beyond San Angelo, it is difficult to leave the elements of Texas past:

> Never have I rounded the turn leading into that peaceful valley, with the spiny ridge of hills beyond it, that I failed to feel new surges and exhilarations and hope. For a precious few moments I exist in a time warp: I'm back in Old Texas, under a high sky, where all things are again possible and the wind blows free. Invariably, I put the heavy spurs to my trusty Hertz or Avis steed: go flying lickety-split down that lonesome road, whooping a crazy yell and taking deep joyous breaths, sloshing Lone Star beer on my neglected dangling seat belt, and scattering roadside gravel like bursts of buckshot. Ride 'im, cowboy! *Ride* 'im. . . . (67)

McMurtry too understands the pull of these ideas, and his work reflects them in numerous ways. This appeal is one of the reasons that McMurtry remains the foremost Texas writer. He also commands a wide audience because of his prolific production. Writing steadily on several projects at once, he reaches completion, and new publications appear on the horizon as regularly as the posse chasing Butch and Sundance. This abundance is a horn of plenty, but it makes it almost impossible for a critic to stay even with him, and as I write this, two new novels, *Comanche Moon,* a prequel to *Lonesome Dove,* and *The Late Child,* a sequel to *The Desert Rose*; a miniseries of *Streets of Laredo,* and a movie of *Buffalo Girls* are in stages of completion. All I can say to this is, "Write 'em, cowboy, write 'em!"

> Mark Busby
> Center for the Study of the Southwest

1

His Blood's Country

Larry McMurtry's career demonstrates the mythic pattern of escape and return. In his early books, he gained initial fame writing about the passing Southwest of the cowboy. Soon McMurtry scorned the work his critics praised and instead praised the work his critics scorned: urban novels cut off from the old Southwest. In the 1980s, however, McMurtry returned to the settings and themes he previously rejected, and the critical acclaim he previously enjoyed came back as well. In fact, both McMurtry's novels and his life demonstrate that traveling is a fundamental part of both, especially the mythical pattern of escape and return. Throughout much of his life McMurtry seems to have found his home territory an awkward, uneasy place. Like the well-cinched bucking strap on a good rodeo horse, growing up in the Southwest created productive tension between his deep love for the land that nurtured him and the equally strong repulsion at limiting aspects of his heritage.

Between 1961 and 1994 McMurtry, a prolific writer, published sixteen novels, two books of nonfiction, several screenplays, and hundreds of book reviews. Five of his novels have been made into movies, one into a television miniseries. A compulsive writer, he gets a headache if he does not complete his self-imposed task of writing at least five double-spaced pages every day— over 1800 manuscript pages a year. On volume alone, he has moved a long way from the sweatshirt he used to wear with "Minor Regional Novelist" ironically emblazoned on it: *Horseman Pass By* (1961), *Leaving Cheyenne* (1963), *The Last Picture Show* (1966), *In a Narrow Grave* (1968), *Moving On* (1970), *All My Friends Are Going to Be Strangers* (1972), *Terms of Endearment* (1975), *Somebody's Darling* (1978), *Cadillac Jack* (1982), *The Desert Rose* (1983), *Lonesome Dove* (1985), *Texasville* (1987), *Film Flam* (1987), *Anything for Billy* (1988), *Some Can Whistle* (1989), *Buffalo Girls* (1990), *The Evening Star* (1992), and *Streets of Laredo* (1993). In 1994 McMurtry published his first collaborative novel, *Pretty Boy Floyd*, written with Diana Ossana.

Growing up in Archer County, Texas, as part of a family that had ranched in West Texas for three gen-

erations, Larry Jeff McMurtry, born June 3, 1936, in
Wichita Falls, learned about southwesterners' violence,
intolerance, and puritanical attitudes as well as their
strength of character, emphasis on hard work, courage,
and what became the most important tools in his work-
shop: the power of storytelling and humor. He also
discovered what would become one of the primary
themes of his work, what he has called the one tragic
theme of the twentieth-century Southwest: the end of
a way of life signalled by the move off the land. Climbing on the roof of the barn at nights, young Larry would
sit there and look out across the West Texas prairie
and send his imagination along the way with the night
trains to Los Angeles and the eighteen wheelers pointed
toward Fort Worth.

McMurtry's grandparents, William Jefferson
McMurtry (1858–1940) and Louisa Frances McMurtry
(1859–1946), originally from Benton County, Missouri,
moved to Archer County from Denton County, Texas,
in 1889. For three dollars an acre, they bought a half-
section of Archer County land, near a good spring along
an old military road that had originally run from Fort
Belknap to Buffalo Springs and was then used as a cattle
trail. They arrived on the bluestem prairie to fight the
battle against drought and mesquite only a few years
after the battle against the Comanche and Kiowa had
been won. There the McMurtrys raised their twelve children and watched the last cattle drives headed north.

Among the nine sons was William Jefferson, Jr., called Jeff by the family, who with his wife Hazel Ruth would become the parents of Larry McMurtry and his two sisters and brother.

Growing up in Archer County provided the basis for McMurtry's work. In a lecture entitled "The American Southwest: Cradle of Literary Art," given at Southwest Texas State University in 1978 (and later published as "The Southwest as the Cradle of the Novelist"), McMurtry pointed out the importance of his family background:

> I grew up in a post-frontier mentality in Archer County in the 30s and 40s (I wasn't born until 1936), and yet my grandparents were among the very first white people in my county; and I knew, as I was growing up, numerous people who had been really, literally, in the first generation of white people in West Texas and who settled the land, and who, in settling the land, had acted upon and developed a set of values, a set of beliefs, a set of traditions and customs that really went with the frontier way of life and that were designed to insure certain things, namely survival in the first place: not only survival of the individual but, hopefully, survival of the group, survival of the settlement. (27–28)

Larry was admittedly out of place among the hard-working but anti-intellectual West Texans who lived along the area ironically called Idiot Ridge. His family found him "insufficiently mean" in a world where mean-ness meant survival, where violence against animals in the form of bronc-busting, calf-throwing, dehorning, and castrating cattle were all part of daily life. He was a "bookish boy" in a "bookless" part of the state, as he called himself in *In a Narrow Grave*.

McMurtry's parents lived on his grandfather's ranch near Windthorst eighteen miles from Archer City when Larry was born, but Hazel Ruth's desires looked toward town. A confirmed bridge player, she wanted her family to be nearer civilization, and she soon con-vinced her wiry, taciturn husband to move the family to a small white frame house in Archer City when Larry was six. Living in the small town and visiting the ranch led to his awareness that he was living on the cusp of change. In his Southwest Texas State lecture, he noted:

> I came to consciousness, really, in the 40s, and my county had been settled for about sixty years then. I grew up on the ranch, moved when I was a young boy into a small town, and formed my consciousness in the period when (a very fortunate period for the development of any novelist, I have to think) one set of val-ues and traditions was being strongly

challenged by another set of values and traditions. That is, I grew up just at the same time when rural and soil traditions in Texas were really, for the first time, being seriously challenged by urban traditions. ("Southwest as the Cradle" 30)

For a novelist, this growing chasm provided him with a wealth of material:

Out of this challenge comes the kind of conflicts that are perfect for a novelist to deal with. You see, within many families will come the kind of little dramas, changes, little rivalries of manners between the two ways of life; and rivalries of manners have always been one of the most fertile and productive things that a novelist deals with—just the difference in the way people live and the conflict of the generations. The conflict of the generations is an eternal theme that novelist after novelist— poets—have always dealt with. But when the conflict of the generations, which is natural, can be joined with such a structural and stylistic difference as exists in Texas between the country life and the city life as it developed in the '40s and the '50s, then you have something very rich, something that is often very painful

to the people that are in the process of making
the transition from one way of life to the other,
nonetheless something very rich. ("Southwest
as the Cradle" 31)

McMurtry's parents made the transition from country to town in 1942, and McMurtry's three siblings were
born after the family moved. Sue was born the year the
family moved, Judy five years after Sue, and Charlie
four years after Judy. The McMurtrys lived in a mod-
est house on Ash Street in Archer City. Larry's high
school yearbook entry suggests that he had a rather
normal life: four-year letterman in band; three-year
letterman in basketball; one-year letterman in baseball; 4-H Club officer for four years; editorial writer on
Cat's Claw staff; member of the cast of the junior class
and senior class plays; fourth-place winner in the dis-
trict mile race; second-place winner in editorial writing
(Peavy, *Larry McMurtry*, 13). In an undergraduate paper titled "An Abridged Autobiography" written when
he was "age 20 years and some months," now in the
Rare Book and Texana Collection at the University of
North Texas, McMurtry calls himself a "pure Caucasian Democrat" but says some "snobbish aunts on my
maternal side claim Scottish lairds among their pro-
genitors, while my paternal grandmother spoke
familiarly of Sitting Bull." He also wrote about his high
school experience:

In high school I did a surprising number of things mediocrely. Among these were baseball, basketball, 4-H work, tennis, track, ready writing, editorial writing, extemporaneous speech, drama, declaiming, trombone playing, and debating. Unfortunately, the area I lived in was so devoid of talented competition that by my Senior trip I was convinced I could look down my nose at Aristotle.

Actually, all these activities did serve to give me a Renaissance outlook on life that has since proved perhaps more beneficial than specialization and mastery of any one of them would have been. And I did work through regional and win 2nd in state in editorial writing. And somehow, in my spare time, I ended up salutatorian, with a 95.4 average. Let it be known, however, that my high school curricala [sic] was so easy that all this required was that I pay attention in class.

It was a small town controlled by religious fundamentalism and sexual restrictions. Football ruled, as it still does in West Texas. The time spent with his friends and acquaintances in Archer City was as important as the time spent with the family. Classmate Ceil (called Ceilie) Slack is usually acknowledged as the model for Jacy Farrow in *The Last Picture Show*, while Bobby

Stubbs provided the outline for Sonny in the first novel and later for Duane in *Texasville*. Before Stubbs's death in the early 1990s, McMurtry would inscribe books to him, always suggesting that he was the model for one character or another. Ceilie Slack lived only two blocks away from Larry, and they competed for the various school awards. Ceil's mother, a poet and painter, encouraged Larry's friendship, and he dedicated *Anything for Billy* to her and his first agent: "For Margaret Ellen Slack and in memory of Dorothea Oppenheimer. The flower of friendship never faded."

After graduating with honors from Archer City High School in 1954, he enrolled briefly at Rice University in Houston. Encountering the library at Rice became a transformative experience for the boy who had grown up in a bookless town: "When I graduated from high school and went to Rice, there was a very good library, and I read and read and read. Eventually, I, like many young writers who begin to write, started imitating. . . . You find someone you like to read so much and become curious whether you can do it, too" (*Humanities* 1). Still, he didn't stay at Rice, saying his "chief nightmare was a freshman math course (the calculi, trig., analytics) which I failed completely" ("Abridged Autobiography"). He transferred to North Texas State College (now the University of North Texas) where he studied literature and writing with Dr. Martin Shockley and Dr. James Brown, writing papers on James

Fenimore Cooper, Benjamin Franklin, Henry David
Thoreau, Mark Twain, Henry Adams, Sinclair Lewis,
John Steinbeck, Shakespeare, Samuel Butler, James
Joyce, Honoré de Balzac, Gustav Flaubert, Fyodor
Dostoevski, Albert Camus, and others. Many of these
undergraduate papers indicate directions in McMurtry's
career. His analysis of *The Adventures of Huckleberry
Finn*, for example, criticizes Huck for being "too fine,"
having "Boy Scout virtues." But he praises the prose as
being "as completely free of affectation as Huck him-
self, a prose of remarkable fluidity and naturalness."
Much of McMurtry's own early prose in *Horseman, Pass
By* and *Leaving Cheyenne* reveals his careful study of
Twain's language.

McMurtry also published fiction, poetry, and es-
says in an unauthorized literary magazine, the
Coexistence Review, and the student magazine, the
Avesta. The *Coexistence Review*, a journal on which
McMurtry worked at North Texas with Grover Lewis
and John Lewis, begins with a "Credo" attributed to
McMurtry:

> Boo! you sanforized people.
> you with TIME on your hands and LIFE
> on your ipana consciences.
> you who hate NEGROES JEWS CATHO-
> LICS NEIGHBORS VIRGINS POETRY
> TAXES

& ANYTHING ELSE THAT LACKS
UTILITY.
    you who hid JESUS with other old easter
eggs and beat your kids
    when they couldn't find HIM.
    you who believe absolutely every word of
scripture tv commercials
    the reader's digest dale carnegie billy gra-
ham and popular songs
    run on to your sleazy heaven and check
the trade in on haloes for me.
    in case I can't find a flannel suit to match
my SOUL.

It also includes a poem by McMurtry called "The
Watch Fires" with sections dedicated to James Agee,
Lester Young, Hart Crane, and Erwin Smith; a section
called "Grandad's End": a section from *Horseman, Pass
By*, in which Jesse shoots Grandad while Lonnie goes
for help. When Lonnie hears a shot and returns, Jesse
tells him that he did it "for a kind thing, Lon." Included
as well is a story called "A Springtime Red Cow" by Jo
Scott, whom McMurtry later married.
    The second issue begins with a sworn statement
by the editors affirming their loyalty for the United
States and an introductory note acknowledging that
the first issue's title and bright red cover were contro-
versial during those Cold War days and led readers to

make "assumptions and allegations that were not war-
ranted." The issue contains two poems by McMurtry,
one labeled "First Prize Winner," with a note saying it
"won first prize in a contest sponsored by a literary
magazine now defunct." Another poem titled "From 'The
Watch-Fires'" is dedicated to Jimmie Rodgers. It also
includes a draft of the "Prologue" from *Horseman, Pass
By* and a section labeled "a fragment from *Scarlet Rib-
bons*." Also included is another poem by Jo Scott, "FOR
THE COMMON DEFENSE."

The 1957 issues of the student magazine, *Avesta*,
include several of McMurtry's works: short stories "Roll,
Jordan, Roll" and "Cowman," early sections of *Horseman, Pass By*; a poem, "Yes, I Am Old"; and essays,
"Journey to the End of the Road" about the Beats, and
"Beiderbecke," about a white jazzman, which won the
$25 nonfiction award. McMurtry's story lost out to one
by a young Dallasite named Grover Lewis, his coeditor
for *Coexistence Review*, to whom the first draft of *Horseman, Pass By* is dedicated.

These were important, formative times for a young
writer. In his undergraduate "Abridged Autobiography"
he makes it clear that by age twenty he had decided to
be a writer: "I cherish fond hopes of being a writer. I
shall almost certainly make some weird combination
of writer-rancher-professor out of myself." He notes that
he has an "ever growing vocabulary" and a "definite
yen for poetic, striking imagery. My chief deficit at

present, is a lack of anything significant to say." He also notes:

> One revealing fact that might be placed on the distaff side is my antagonism to orthodox religion. Rice (where I met Julian Huxley) and the nineteenth century skeptics had a hand in this. I am agnostic, with a slight leaning toward Brahminism. I take a great deal of pleasure from spoofing religious people about some of the more obvious absurdities of their particular dogma. This is a raging controversy in my hometown even now.

McMurtry's maternal grandfather was a Methodist minister; perhaps his antagonism to religion stemmed from the closeness to organized religion at home. Whatever the source, McMurtry has treated ministers harshly throughout his career.

Despite his criticism of religion and his stated skepticism, he concluded his undergraduate autobiography by noting: "I have a great many friends. I have a bad habit of forming friendly alliances that are too deep to last. My friends and I are, consequently, occasionally prone to be disillusioned about one another. But any abiding faith I might possess is in man."

During his last two years at North Texas, McMurtry said he wrote fifty-two "very bad" short stories but burned them. Then, "in an effort to write one less appalling than the original 52," he turned to his cowboy past and wrote one story about the destruction of a cattle herd and another about a cattleman's funeral. He then decided to connect the two stories and extend them into a novel (Peavy, *Larry McMurtry*, 15; all references to Peavy hereafter are to this book rather than Peavy's articles), which he began writing in Denton toward the end of the semester shortly before receiving a B.A. in 1958. He continued writing at home in Archer City over the summer and finished it in Houston when he went to Rice for graduate school the next fall. The final page of the first draft of the manuscript of *Horseman, Pass By*, now in the Humanities Research Center at the University of Texas, reads

> Denton May 26–June 3
> Archer City June 4–Sept 6
> Houston Sept. 6–Oct. 11 (end Houston Tx. Oct. 11
>   1958)

McMurtry sent the manuscript to *Texas Quarterly*, which was then publishing book supplements, and Frank Wardlaw read it. Wardlaw sent it on to a friend in New York at Harper Brothers, who decided to publish it.

In July 1959 he married Jo Ballard Scott (his only marriage)—with whom he had a son, James Lawrence

McMurtry, named for Henry James and D. H. Lawrence. Jo was a beautiful woman, tall and long-legged, but reportedly shy and nervous. They had met in Denton when she was a student at Texas Woman's University. After their divorce in the mid-1960s, Jo went on to complete a Ph.D. in English, teach in Virginia, and write several textbooks. In 1991 James McMurtry, who has become successful as a singer-songwriter, and his wife Elena had a son, Curtis, making Larry McMurtry, once the Young Turk of Texas literature, a grandfather.

As a graduate student at Rice, McMurtry began reviewing for *The Houston Post*, and in the December 27, 1959, issue he reviewed *The Henry Miller Reader*. J. Frank Dobie read the review, clipped it out, and sent it to Frank Vandiver, then the President of the Texas Institute of Letters, with this note jotted in the margin: "Frank. This newspaper critic can think; he can write; he knows. Who is he? Better regard him for Texas Institute of Letters—A Bully New Year to You!—Frank Dobie." Just three years later, *Horseman, Pass By* won the TIL award for fiction, and this clipping ended up in the TIL files, where Dick Holland, the curator of the Southwestern Writers Collection at Southwest Texas State University found it. It is another of many ironies that Dobie, who would be the subject of McMurtry's withering attack on Texas literature nine years later, demonstrated his literary acumen and "discovered" Larry McMurtry.

McMurtry's graduate writing at Rice looked to English literature. He wrote papers on *Troilus and Cressida*; "Elizabethan Realism: Realistic Prose in England from 1525 to 1610"; "The Effectiveness of the Ode to Evening"; *Lay of Havelok*; Thomas Nashe; and "Political Satire in the First Voyage of Gulliver." His master's thesis was titled "Ben Jonson's Feud with the Poetasters: 1599–1601." These last two papers' focus on satire no doubt influenced the satirical streak that appears throughout McMurtry's career. He also wrote a long analysis on the Beats, published in the Rice literary magazine *Janus* in March 1960.

After getting an M.A. from Rice in 1960, Larry accepted a scholarship and studied creative writing at Stanford University with Wallace Stegner, as one of a remarkable group of new writers. Among the other students in Stegner's program were Peter Beagle, Wendell Berry, Australian novelist Chris Koch, Ed McClanahan, Tillie Olsen, Ernest Gaines, Robert Stone, and Ken Kesey. McMurtry was still a shy young man and did not know many in this group well, but he was close to Koch, author of *The Year of Living Dangerously*, and he connected with Kesey, the big, boisterous red-haired wrestler from Oregon, primarily because of their mutual western backgrounds. (Kesey was born in La Junta, Colorado, in 1935.) McMurtry dedicated *In a Narrow Grave* to Kesey, calling him "the last wagon-master." Their relationship became part of Tom Wolfe's recounting of Kesey's bus trip across America in 1964 in *The Electric Kool-Aid Acid Test*. The various teachers— Stegner, Dick Scowcroft, Frank O'Connor, and Malcolm Cowley—taught them to respect one another's work, Cowley reminding them that it was just as hard to write a bad book as it was to write a good one. The group has remained in close contact over the years. In a personal interview in Wimberley, Texas, in 1994, Kesey said that they all take pride in each other's success: "When Larry won the Pulitzer Prize for *Lonesome Dove*, it gloried all of us." Over the years, the members of this astonishing group continue to correspond and many send the others copies of their books.

McMurtry returned to Texas in 1961 and taught at Texas Christian University in Fort Worth during the 1961–62 academic year, where his colleague was John Graves, who had published *Goodbye to a River* in 1960. For 1963–64, he began teaching at Rice and remained there for most of the 1960s, except for 1964–65, when he held a Guggenheim for creative writing. He lived for eight months in Austin, sharing a house on Windsor Road with Bill Brammer, shortly after Brammer published *The Gay Place*.

In 1964 McMurtry and Jo separated, and, back in Houston, he was raising Jamie as a single father when his old Stanford schoolmate, Kesey, came to call. At that time raising a son as a single father was an unusual occurrence. The neighbors on Quenby Road near Rice

University in Houston had uneasily reconciled to this unusual relationship. Then in pulled this day-glo 1939 International Harvester bus crammed with the Merry Pranksters: Kesey, Neal Cassady, Ken Babbs, Ron Bevirt, Mike Hagen, who was in charge of making "the movie" of the trip, and Hagen's girlfriend, who was wrapped up naked in a blanket. In the chapter titled "The Bus" in *The Electric Kool-Aid Acid Test*, Tom Wolfe tells of Kesey's trip across the country and the visit to Houston. Out of the house came McMurtry, described by Wolfe as "a slight, slightly wan, kindly-looking, shy-looking guy" with his son, James. Wolfe continues the story:

> Cassady opens the door of the bus so everybody can get off, and suddenly Stark Naked shrieks out: 'Frankie! Frankie! Frankie! Frankie!'—this being the name of her own divorced-off little boy—and she whips off the blanket and leaps off the bus and out into the suburbs of Houston, Texas, stark naked, and rushes up to McMurtry's little boy and scoops him up and presses him to her skinny breast, crying and shrieking . . . while McMurtry doesn't know what in the name of hell to do, reaching tentatively toward her stark-naked shoulder and saying, 'Ma'am! Ma'am! Justa minute, ma'am!' (Wolfe 90)

Recalling the visit in 1994, Kesey remembers the Houston trip fondly, saying that Larry would pull Jamie back, while gently calling Stark "Ma'am," and "Stark would pull in the other direction." For years, until her death in 1993, Kesey kept up with "Stark," and they would laugh about the Houston visit.

Among the nearby neighbors were Bill Hobby, later to become the lieutenant governor of Texas, and Diana Hobby, then the book editor for *The Houston Post*. Diana had told McMurtry that she wanted to meet Kesey when he came to town and asked Larry to call her when Kesey arrived. After things settled down, he called and she rode her bicycle over to meet the author of *One Flew Over the Cuckoo's Nest*. Meanwhile the Pranksters, proud of the bus called Further, had gotten out the day-glo hues to touch up the paint job. When Diana got ready to leave, she went out to retrieve the bicycle she had left leaning against a tree and discovered that it too had gotten the day-glo treatment. She wrote me in 1994: "My old bicycle still survives, still proudly painted."

McMurtry had moved back to Houston to teach literature and creative writing at Rice. Among his students was Gregory Curtis, later to become editor of *Texas Monthly*, who recalled that McMurtry's teaching style could best be called "polite discouragement." Ambling into class in boots and jeans, McMurtry exhibited little interest in students' work. (Curtis remembered that McMurtry once mentioned that he liked one of Curtis's titles). Still, McMurtry inspired his students by example. He told them about his own work, and he demonstrated that he read constantly and eclecticly, passing out long reading lists divided into categories such as "Classics," "Cartoon," "Travel," "Varied Delights," and others (Curtis 6). At the same time McMurtry worked at a shop called The Bookman and established a life-long passion for book collecting, which required scouting through junk and secondhand stores and estate sales all over Houston, and later, the country.

In 1969, McMurtry again left Texas physically, and he left Texas as the subject of his fiction, too. He moved to Waterford, Virginia, a town forty miles northwest of Washington, and for most of the 1970s lived there with his son James and his dog Franklin. Later he moved into Washington, bought a 1967 gunboat gray Cadillac, and lived above the rare book store, Booked Up, that he and Marcia McGhee Carter had opened near her home in Georgetown. As Patrick Anderson explains, "Larry had come to the Washington area because of his romance with Marcia McGhee Carter, the elegant daughter of Texas oilman-diplomat George McGhee. . . . [A]lthough their romance faded they continued as partners and close friends" (27).

He taught briefly at George Washington and American Universities and continued to cut his ties to Texas by taking shots at his home state. In a 1975 essay in *Atlantic*, "The Texas Moon and Elsewhere" he scanned the Texas horizon and found it blighted, saying Texans were limited by the wornout myth of the cowboy with its unhealthy emphasis that stifles emotion, articulateness, and community. He blasted Austin as a "third-rate" town.

In Virginia and then Washington, McMurtry continued his pattern of hard work, describing his best and worst trait as "doggedness." He became friends with columnist Joseph Alsop and with Colorado Congressman Timothy Wirth and his wife Wren. Friendships with Peter Bogdanovich and Cybill Shepherd began during the filming of *The Last Picture Show* in 1971. McMurtry wrote the screenplay while living in Virginia. He would send his daily drafts by Air Special and review them with Bogdanovich by telephone. In Bogdanovich's *Daisy Miller*, in which Shepherd played the title role, McMurtry's son James played the younger brother. McMurtry became a famous junk food addict, fond of pizza rolls, fritos, pork rinds, and peanut patties, a trait which may have led the once slim writer to gain weight and develop heart problems in his fifties. Even though he lived out of state, he maintained the family ranch in Texas as his permanent address, and he returned to the state often for business and, in 1977, when his father died.

The summer of 1978 found him in Archer City

again, where he spent much of his time at the Dairy
Queen on Highway 79, just south of town. He was also
reading and contemplating the work of literary critic
Walter Benjamin, especially his work on the importance
of the storyteller. As a result, McMurtry began writing
a long piece titled "Walter Benjamin at the Dairy
Queen." The eighty-three-page manuscript, unfinished
and unpublished, now in the Southwestern Writers
Collection at Southwest Texas State University, indicates how McMurtry continued to be pulled in several
directions as he considered his home town, his calling
as a novelist, and the nature of storytelling. Sitting and
listening to the talk in the Dairy Queen, he realized
that DQs functioned as a community center, and he
also concluded that few real storytellers came in for a
Dilly Bar. He also noted Benjamin's distinction between
storytelling, which is a communal experience, and novel
writing, which is isolating, and he asks: "How is it that
I, who grew up in a family of accomplished story tell-
ers, should have ended up married to a form that travels
in the opposite direction of the story telling?" He then
provides his own answer:

> I left the county, which is to say the commu-
> nity of talkers, and went to the university, soon
> to be lost in a community of readers, people
> who had embraced and become dependent on
> the book. One obvious consequence of a depen-

dence on the book is that, gradually, one loses one's voice.

But now back in the DQ, he realized that television had replaced the traditional storyteller, and that most of the conversation there was about the weather and ephemeral contemporary events: "No one at the DQ was disposed to regard Archer County's past as a source of mystery or myth." The thoughts led him to contemplate Archer County's history as it prepared for its centennial celebration in 1980, and he recalled Captain Randolph Marcy's visit to the area in 1845, Satanta's trial in Jacksboro in 1871, the oil boom of 1925, a human fly's thwarted scaling of the courthouse, and a helicopter visit by Lyndon Johnson. Obviously, the Texas prodigal was deeply involved in examining his connections to home, connections that would be more directly dramatized in the novels to follow.

But in 1981, he created another flap on the Texas literary scene with a speech titled "Ever a Bridegroom" delivered at the Fort Worth Art Museum and published later in *The Texas Observer*. There McMurtry again found the Texas literary scene wanting and managed to anger almost everyone in Texas. He also began traveling around the country more than he did during the 1970s when he had young James's daily welfare to keep him in Washington. He maintained apartments in California for his filmwriting connections and in Arizona, after developing a close friendship with the Native American writer Leslie Silko. But his health suffered, as he developed what was then called "valley fever," a debilitating condition that enervated him.

McMurtry's writing during the period from 1976–1983 suffered. He worked sporadically on a traildrive novel that had begun as a screenplay, and he wrote novels set outside of Texas. The last one, *The Desert Rose*, marked a turning point in Larry McMurtry's career. With this book he regained the enthusiasm for writing he had lost writing *Somebody's Darling*. With his renewed energy, he returned to the traildrive novel— and to Texas as both a part-time home and the subject for his fiction. He soon finished the novel he had been tinkering with for years, *Lonesome Dove*, and it was published in 1985. He was at a writers' conference in Uvalde, Texas, when he learned that he had won the Pulitzer Prize.

After years of an uneasy relationship with McMurtry following his unfavorable characterization of his hometown, even Archer City embraced him. The Chamber of Commerce declared a Saturday in October, 1986, "Larry McMurtry Day," and 400 of the 1900 residents turned out to stand in the rain to attend a reception for him at the Country Club. He told them:

> I have to tell you that this award moves me more and surprises me more than winning the

Pulitzer Prize. It's one thing to write a book that appeals to the taste of the people on the prize committee. It's harder to earn the respect of people who know you. The myth is that small towns in America don't care about their writers and are small minded and intolerant. But here I am, a writer being honored by his hometown. In a sense, you have all helped me with this award. I don't know if I have ever used a literal event that has happened in this town, but what I have used are the intimations and hunches you have given me. (quoted in Curtis 6)

McMurtry's effect on Archer City is one of the greater ironies of his life. After excoriating his hometown in *The Last Picture Show* and portraying it as small-minded and "bookless" in *In a Narrow Grave*, McMurtry and his family have transformed the small county seat of Archer County into a literary oasis in the middle of dry, mostly flat cattle and oil country. For a while in the 1980s McMurtry also alternated living in Washington and Texas, but he then moved back to Texas full-time. He renovated the Archer City golf course clubhouse for his residence—lovingly called the Mansion by the staff at the Blue Pig—mainly to hold books, although it also houses his skull collection. He helped install his sister Sue Deen as the proprietor of the Blue

Pig Book Shop in his hometown. Originally in a single building, the Blue Pig expanded into a building next door called the Annex, and into a large former grocery store across the street whimsically named "The Blue Pig Too" when McMurtry closed his Booked Up stores in Dallas and Houston in 1993. The Houston store was managed by Silko's son Robert Chapman, who moved to Archer City to work when the Houston Booked Up closed. In 1994 Harlan Kidd took over as manager, and the various buildings became "Booked Up." The bookstore complex is just south of the title company managed by Larry's younger sister Judy. He has been regarded as something of an eccentric by refusing to use air conditioning either in the Mansion or when driving around in a rented Cadillac, but the allergies that developed after his bout with valley fever make breathing air conditioning uncomfortable.

As usual, his life called him beyond his hometown. In 1989 he was elected to succeed Susan Sontag as president of the American Center of PEN, the first non-New Yorker to head the writer's organization since Booth Tarkington. As he does with all projects, McMurtry threw himself into PEN's activity. Normally a shy person, McMurtry was called upon to speak out against censorship. He was especially vocal in support of Salman Rushdie, who was condemned to death by the Ayatollah Khomeni for writing *The Satanic Verses*. Being PEN's president was a stressful position. McMurtry had to fly in and out of New York over eighty times during those two years as PEN president. The stress, along with a lifetime of poor eating and exercise habits, took a toll.

After the PEN position ended in June 1991, McMurtry began working on *The Evening Star* and completing renovations on the house in Archer City. After a day of moving boxes of books into the house, McMurtry drove the eighteen miles back to the ranch and slept fitfully. The next morning he drove himself to his doctor in Wichita Falls, who told him that he was having a heart attack. Even though his doctor contended that he needed an operation immediately, McMurtry insisted on finishing his novel. Then in December, he went to Johns Hopkins Hospital in Baltimore and had a quadruple heart-bypass operation that many feared (and others hoped) would slow his writing career, but the appearance of *Streets of Laredo* in 1993 indicated that he had returned to writing form, though perhaps with a darker vision.

He told Malcolm Jones of *Newsweek* that although he recovered quickly from the operation, he began to feel empty:

> I went about the physical recovery very quickly and went about my life doing the things I had done—running bookshops, writing screen- plays, writing fiction, traveling, lecturing, etc.

And it just sort of gradually emptied out of content, until it was like a ghost doing these things,
not me at all, until there was nothing but an
outline. (52)

However, when he turned to writing the novel, the words
just tumbled out.

Some of his friends were worried about him after
the operation and the dark vision of *Streets of Laredo*.
The dust jacket photograph revealed a thinner, grayer
man. Indeed, he had suffered the usual post-operative
depression, and it had taken him some time to recover.
Ultimately, he had written himself out of depression.
When he finished, he told friends and family that he
was saddened by completing it because it had given his
life a focus that he lacked until he settled on a new
project. But he accepted his doctor's restrictions and
began exercising on a treadmill regularly. He also received support from his companion, Diana Ossana,
whom he met in Tucson in the mid-1980s.

In 1993, the death of McMurtry's agent, Irving
"Swifty" Lazar, who had represented him for several
years, led to new arrangements that included Ossana.
Soon, McMurtry retained a new agent, Andrew Wylie,
to deal with Simon and Schuster and his editor there
for over twenty years, Michael Korda. McMurtry was
described by *The New York Times* (February 2, 1994)
as a "hot commodity," primarily because of the popular-

ity of *Lonesome Dove*, in both book and miniseries, and the television sequel *Return to Lonesome Dove*. Wylie renegotiated McMurtry's contract, which calls for four new books, including *The Late Child*, a sequel to *The Desert Rose*, published in 1995, and two new books to be written collaboratively with Ossana. Their first collaborative book is *Pretty Boy Floyd*, begun originally as a screenplay.

McMurtry describes their working style as fully collaborative: "I write five pages early, Diana makes them ten, a little later. My narrative is spare, she expands it. It is a full collaboration, meaning the division of labor is as equal as equal can be. We work on it together, and we work on it separately, as well. We researched it together." Thus, it seems clear that Larry McMurtry will continue to work and be a major voice in Texas, southwestern, and American fiction into the twenty-first century.

McMurtry grew up on a ranch and learned the ranch work ethic, where every day began early and ended late. As a student, writer, and book dealer, McMurtry approaches his work with an intense stubbornness that forces him to produce. He publishes profusely, not for the sake of money or fame. His large house reveals more about his need for more space for books than about pretention. His wardrobe, for example, has changed little over the years—Levi's, faded and frayed blue chambray work shirt usually with ink stains on the pocket, and boots. Occasionally he'll add a sport coat for speaking engagements. Over the years he has changed from the slim, bespectacled, bookish-looking academic with shocks of unruly dark hair, to a jowly, heavier man. After his operation, he lost weight, and the dark hair turned gray. But he has never been especially concerned about his appearance or about fame. Instead, he is concerned about production, about using time wisely, about working steadily and doggedly, and trying, as many of his characters do, to fool time. In the process, he has become the best-known Texas writer of the twentieth century. If, as he claims, Texas has never produced a Faulkner, it has produced a Larry McMurtry, whose Thalia and Hardtop County have become as recognizable to Texas readers as Faulkner's Jefferson and Yoknapatawpha County. Early in his writing career, someone gave him a sweatshirt that read "Minor Regional Novelist." But he lost it in a laundromat during one of his many moves, and his career has removed the label forever.

2

Escape, Ambivalence, and Return

Escape and return, leaving and returning, looking-to-leave, longing-to-return—the various versions of this "double *dicho*" characterize much of McMurtry's life and writing. McMurtry set up part of this pattern in the introduction to his first essay collection, *In a Narrow Grave* (1968), recalling a poem by Cavafy based on a scene in Shakespeare where Hercules abandons Marc Antony and the guards hear a strange music to mark the god's passing. As he listened to the wind blowing along the Brazos and across the Llano Estacado, McMurtry found "the music of departure . . . faint, the god almost out of

31

hearing," and he speculated on the god then abandoning Texas: "Sometimes I see him as Old Man Goodnight, or as Teddy Blue, or as my Uncle Johnny . . . but the one thing that is sure is that he was a horseman, and a god of the country" (xvii).

Throughout his long career, McMurtry has examined the disappearance of this cowboy god and the frontier that was his range. His books have concentrated on both the actual golden days of cowboying and trail driving, the transitional time between the early rural life and the new urban one, and the twentieth-century urban world that searches for values to replace the old ones that have disappeared. In all his work, McMurtry approaches these subjects with a "contradiction of attractions" that produces an "ambivalence as deep as the bone" (*In a Narrow Grave* 141), which he acknowledged in 1994 still characterizes his attitude toward home. Through a creative process that draws from his wide reading and background, McMurtry has produced novels, essays, and screenplays that draw their creative tension from his deep ambivalence about the frontier myth, initiation, the modern world, the pursuit of happiness, writing and art, and other themes. These themes affect the structure, style, and symbols and images of all his work.

Creative Process

McMurtry carefully described his method of writing in a 1979 interview with Patrick Bennett, published in *Talking with Texas Writers*. McMurtry called writing a novel "a process of discovery" and noted that he starts with the end of the novel:

> My novels begin with a scene that forms itself in my consciousness, which I recognize as a culminating scene. I can tell that the scene ends something, like the closing of the picture show in a small town, which is a kind of natural symbol. Often this scene will refine itself in very high definition before I write a word. It's been to the point where I see the people, and I hear the conversation, and I know what the last words are going to be, and I know that something's ended. I don't know exactly what's ended, and the writing of the novel is the process in which I discover how these people got themselves to this scene. I usually simply go back arbitrarily a year or two years at a time, or whatever, with the characters that I have, and the scene, and sort of work toward it. I get tremendous surprises. People pop in that I had not expected, who aren't in the final scene perhaps, totally surprising characters. Sometimes

novels zig to the left or zig to the right as I go
through them, but I've always ended up at the
final scene. I've never missed. So far I've always ended up with exactly what I thought I
would end up with, although not always with
the exact kind of book I thought I'd have. I don't
prejudge that. The final scene contains, sort
of, the thematic resolutions of whatever story
you're telling. Then I go back to find the story;
I'm perfectly comfortable with that. Of course,
I have written several hundred pages with the
final scene in sight, and I can see that certain
things are going to have to happen. I probably
could outline the last quarter or third of the
book if I really wanted to. But I very seldom
do. (22–23)

Once he has this clear vision of where the novel
will lead, he then begins selecting the names for the
characters who will people the book. For that purpose
he collects names of people and places that interest him:

If I spend any time on anything, it's naming
my characters and naming the places where
they live, things like that. I think personal
names are very important, and you want to
have the right names. If I jot anything down,
it will be a list of names. Maybe I won't use

half of them, and maybe they won't get attached to the characters that I think they will get attached to, but I'll always do that. (Bennett 23)

He writes every day. Early in his career he set a goal of five pages a day, writing early in the morning, but in most of 1994, with several projects underway at the same time, he typically produced fifteen to twenty pages daily, writing some in the mornings and evenings with time in between for his book and antique store activities. Working on several projects at one time is a strategy he adopted in the late 1970s, when his enthusiasm for writing flagged. When he lost interest in one project, he would turn immediately to another one. Throughout the creative process, McMurtry returns both to his personal history growing up on and near a ranch in northwest Texas and to his extensive literary past.

Influence

As much as any writer of his generation, McMurtry draws from his regional experience for theme, character, setting, and story. An inveterate reader and moviegoer, McMurtry has absorbed the history, literature, and popular culture of the region. He told an interviewer in 1989:

> My writing comes as much out of the place as
> it does out of anything else. It's a particular
> place that I'm trying to describe and render;
> so, there is a bit of a clash. . . . It's literary
> commonplace that you reach the universal
> through a close attention to particulars, that
> are not universal. You reach what is common
> in human experience through attention to what
> is local. Great writers will do that. ("A Novel-
> ist" 2)

Of the many books about the old Southwest that
McMurtry has read and absorbed over the years, among
the most important are J. Evetts Haley's *Charles
Goodnight: Cowman and Plainsman* and Teddy Blue's
We Pointed Them North. (Blue's real name was E. C.
Abbott and the book was written with Helena Huntington Smith). Goodnight has appeared in several of
McMurtry's novels; his story is important to *All My
Friends Are Going to Be Strangers*, and he is an important character in *Streets of Laredo*. Further, the story
of how Goodnight promised to bring Oliver Loving's body
back for burial in Texas, as told by Haley, is the basis
for Gus and Call's relationship in *Lonesome Dove*.

Another influential character in Haley's biography
of Goodnight is Bose Ikard, Goodnight's black companion, whose story becomes the basis for Josh Deets in

Lonesome Dove. Goodnight held Ikard, according to Haley, in greatest esteem:

> He was a good bronc rider, an exceptional night herder, good with the skillets and pans, and according to his boss, "surpassed any man I had in endurance and stamina. There was dignity, a cleanliness, and a reliability about him that was wonderful. He paid no attention to women. His behavior was very good in a fight, and he was probably the most devoted man to me that I ever had. I have trusted him farther than any living man. He was my detective, banker, and everything else in Colorado, New Mexico, and the other wild country I was in. The nearest and only bank was at Denver, and when we carried money I gave it to Bose, for a thief would never think of robbing him—never think of looking in a negro's bed for money." (242)

When Bose Ikard died, Goodnight erected the following headstone for him:

BOSE IKARD

Served with me four years on the Goodnight-Loving Trail, never shirked a duty or disobeyed an order, rode with me in many stampedes,

participated in three engagements with
Comanches, splendid behavior. (Haley 243)

In *Lonesome Dove*, Call erects the following headstone for Deets:

JOSH DEETS
SERVED WITH ME 30 YEARS. FOUGHT IN
21 ENGAGEMENTS WITH COMMANCHE
AND KIOWA. CHERFUL IN ALL WEATHERS,
NEVER SHERKED A TASK. SPLENDID BE-
HAVIOR. (808)

From Teddy Blue's *We Pointed Them North,*
McMurtry learned of a different West from the asexual
one described by J. Frank Dobie. Blue was a drinker
and rounder who told of the women along the trail when
he rode it in the 1880s. Blue's language and realistic
picture of the West became a strong influence on
McMurtry, who set out to debunk the mythic, romantic
West, with its larger-than-life heroes and women on
pedestals. McMurtry has so far named two characters
"Teddy Blue." One, although he never actually appears,
is a hippie who lives on Perry Lane in San Francisco in
All My Friends Are Going to Be Strangers; and the other,
loosely based on the historical figure, appears in *Buffalo Girls* as a friend of Calamity Jane and the lover of
Dora Dufran. He breaks Dora's heart by marrying the

half-breed daughter of the great cattle king, Granville Stuart.

Beyond the language and tone, McMurtry borrowed some specific details from *We Pointed Them North* for *Lonesome Dove*, especially in the section concerning Jake Spoon's ill-fated connections with the Suggs brothers and their murderous black companion, Frog Lip. Teddy Blue tells a similar story of a mean black man who joined some would-be trail cutters surnamed Olive. The Olives hired an African American that they called "Olive's bad nigger, because he was a gunman and fighter himself." Blue's description provides a good example of his language:

> The Olives used to send him ahead to talk turkey to the settlers; where one of these fellows had taken up a homestead on good water, not to work it you understand, but just so he could charge the trail herds a big fee. They were doing that all along the trail, especially in Kansas; it was just a graft, but a lot of the bosses would pay what they asked rather than have trouble. The Olives never would. They would send Kelly, and that big black boy with his gun would sure tell them punkin rollers where to head in at. He'd roll up his eyes like a duck in a thunderstorm and grit his teeth—Lord, he could play a tune with his teeth. (34)

One of the Olive brothers is killed, and the other one, Print, performs an act of vengeance on the two settlers who were responsible: "Print followed them up when they was on their way to trial, took them away from the sheriff, and hanged them to a lone elm tree near Plum Creek. It was told afterwards that he poured coal oil on them and burned them alive" (34).

In *Lonesome Dove*, when Dan Suggs comes upon two settlers plowing, he shoots them first, hangs them, and then splashes coal oil and sets fire to the bodies. In *Streets of Laredo* Mox-Mox the Manburner is a re-embodiment of the psychopathic Dan Suggs. While Teddy Blue defends Print Olive, McMurtry transforms him into a cold killer. By drawing from the real history of the range and transmuting history into fiction, McMurtry thrusts the particulars of a place's history into the higher arena of universal truth. As Chief Bromden, Ken Kesey's narrator in *One Flew Over the Cuckoo's Nest*, says, "All of this is true even if it didn't happen."

In *Larry McMurtry and the Victorian Novel*, Roger Jones concentrates on the importance of nineteenth-century Victorian novels to McMurtry's style, character development, and themes. Jones notes:

> In his attempts to reconcile the reader to experience, and thus give his art a religious

function, McMurtry was inspired by the Victorians' treatment of three major themes: the problem of reconciling the needs of the individual with those of society, the growing conflict between civilization and nature in an industrial age, and the attempt to find a basis for spirituality in a world without God or faith in organized religion. (4)

To support his point, Jones quotes McMurtry's interview with Bennett in which McMurtry says, "I was more influenced by nineteenth-century writers than by twentieth-century writers. . . . Oddly enough, I think my main influences were not American writers. I think they were probably George Eliot, Thomas Hardy, Tolstoy, and the Russians and the French. I read a lot of Balzac, Stendhal" (Bennett 17). McMurtry also told Bennett: "Of American writers, I suppose Faulkner hit me the hardest; I didn't much like the nineteenth-century Americans. I still don't somehow" (17). But he acknowledged that among the other American writers who have been especially influential are the Beat Writers. As a student, McMurtry wrote two essays about the Beat generation, and he commented especially on Jack Kerouac's *On the Road* as a significant influence, especially for its emphasis on the journey. Other Texas writers have also been influential, as the next chapter's discussion of J. Frank Dobie, Walter Prescott Webb, and

Roy Bedichek in *Lonesome Dove* indicates. It also seems clear that McMurtry was influenced by the trail drive novels of Andy Adams, Benjamin Capps, and Robert Flynn, as well as trail drive films. Through a creative process that draws from a variety of sources, McMurtry concentrates on a number of themes that reveal the creative tension produced by his ambivalence about his home country and its connection to frontier mythology.

Theme

Ambivalence

In his luminous work "Take My Saddle from the Wall: A Valediction," the last essay in *In a Narrow Grave*, McMurtry points out that his attitude toward his home state is marked by ambivalence:

> The reader who has attended thus far will have noticed a certain inconsistency in my treatment of Texas past and present—a contradiction of attractions, one might call it. I am critical of the past, yet apparently attracted to it; and though I am even more critical of the present I am also quite clearly attracted to *it*. Such contradictions are always a bit awkward to work with. . . . What in this book appear to be inconsistencies of attitude are the manifestations of my ambivalence in regard to

Texas—and a very deep ambivalence it is, as
deep as the bone. Such ambivalence is not help-
ful in a discursive book, but it can be the very
blood of a novel. (141–42)

Indeed, it is this deep ambivalence that characterizes
Larry McMurtry's body of work—ambivalence toward
Texas and the West, toward the values of the past and
the mythic world of the cowboy god he grew up paying
homage to, and toward writing and artistic production.
Ambivalence, being drawn at the same time toward two
almost opposing forces such as civilization and wilderness, is central to the southwestern legend, and it
appears forcefully in many Texas writers' works. J.
Frank Dobie's *A Vaquero of the Brush Country*, for example, laments the end of open country and at the same
time acknowledges that human greed made barbed wire
necessary. Katherine Anne Porter's ambivalence also
cut deep as she struggled to get away from Texas and
yet returned to it again and again in stories that often
tried to appear to be about somewhere else.

As Louis Cowan notes in "Myth in the Modern
World," the Texas frontier experience produced deep
feelings of uncertainty:

Texans from the beginning were confronted
with a dual consciousness: were they transplanted Americans or a new breed? Should they

look to the aristocratic landed gentry for their
ideals or to Rousseau's noble savage? Should
their allegiance be with the Anglo-Saxon or the
Spanish culture? Should they be cultivated or
primitive? . . . Was the new territory they
settled garden or desert? Caucasian, Christian,
Yankee, Southerner, Westerner—Texans found
themselves to be all of these. (20)

The ambivalence of being drawn at the same time toward such opposing forces as civilization/wilderness,
rural/urban, individual/community, past/present, ag-
gression/passivity, and numerous others is central to
the southwestern legend, and it grows in intensity in
the contemporary Southwest as the schism between old
and new tears more strongly at the human heart.

These feelings of uncertainty touch upon most of
the themes that McMurtry has explored throughout his
career: the triumph and tragedy of the tangled elements
of frontier mythology—primitivism, sexism, racism, and
violence; initiation; love and sexuality in male-female
relationships; the impermanence of the past and the
uncertainty of the future; parental and generational
conflicts and the problems of aging; and a continuing
concern about the practice of writing. McMurtry's at-
traction/repulsion toward his home and all it stands
for produces in his work a series of opposing ideas, images, motifs, and structural devices. His work often

alternates between and holds in creative tension opposing ideas, many of which stem from Texas mythology.

The Frontier Myth

Several of the major elements of the Texas myth portrayed in McMurtry's work have their foundation in frontier mythology central to the larger American experience. Frontier mythology refers to a cluster of images, values, and archetypes that grew out of the confrontation between the uncivilized and the civilized world, what Frederick Jackson Turner called the "meeting point between savagery and civilization." Civilization is associated with the past and with Europe, with society—its institutions, its laws, its demands for compromise and restriction, its cultural refinement and emphasis on manners, its industrial development, and its class distinctions. The wilderness that civilization confronts offers the possibility of individual freedom, where single individuals can test themselves against nature without the demands for social responsibility and compromises inherent in being part of a community.

Texas mythology draws from frontier mythology, particularly the emphasis on Texas as a land of freedom and opportunity, where individuals can demonstrate those values that the Texian Anglo myth reveres—courage, determination, ingenuity, loyalty, and others. But Texas's frontier history and geography produce deep feelings of ambivalence. On one hand, the vastness of its area seems to negate borders; on the other, the state's location on the edge of southern and western culture and along the long Rio Grande border with Mexico reinforces an awareness of borders. As Tom Pilkington pointed out in *My Blood's Country*, Texas is a land of borders: "Men have always been fascinated by rims and borders, ends and beginnings, areas of transition where the known and the unknown merge. In the Southwest one feels something of this fascination, because one of the central, never-changing facts about the region, I believe, is that it is a borderland" (3). Both borders and the frontier suggest a line where differing cultures, attitudes, and factions meet. Early settlers who both conquered nature and felt simultaneously at one with it began the feelings of ambivalence that McMurtry confronts and dramatizes throughout his career. In a 1979 speech at Southwest Texas State University, McMurtry pointed to the uncertainty he felt from his family as he grew up:

> There was a deep ambivalence in the way they approached the figure of the cowboy as they saw him on the screen or as they read him in these romances, because, although they didn't believe the details, somehow they believed the main message, which was that the cowboy was an extraordinary man with an extraordinary

code, a true symbol of virility and character
and various other things. ("Southwest as the
Cradle" 29)

This uncertainty stemmed from the profound disparity
between the reality of cowboy life that they lived and
the romanticized one they viewed through the lens of
popular culture:

They didn't really quite ever get, I think, to
the critical point at which they began to question the message: they simply questioned the
details. I don't think most cowboys and most
critics of those movies in those days realized
at what point they had been taken in by a romanticized image, by a romanticized myth.
They knew perfectly well that cowboying was
not anything like what was being described on
the screen, and yet they rather wanted to believe that it was and most of them managed to
convince themselves. Just the sheer fact of
John Wayne being on the screen in certain
cases with the authority that he brought to the
role seemed to convince them that there was
really something accurate about it even though
most of it was trivial and inaccurate. (29–30)

Ambivalence is also central to McMurtry's epigraph

for *Lonesome Dove,* which is a quote from T. K. Whipple's *Study Out the Land*: "All America lies at the end of the wilderness road, and our past is not a dead past, but still lives in us. Our forefathers had civilization inside themselves, the wild outside. We live in the civilization they created, but within us the wilderness still lingers. What they dreamed, we live, and what they lived, we dream." This quotation sets in relief McMurtry's focus on the complex intertwining of dream and reality in the settlement of the American West. Again and again, McMurtry's novels dramatize the irony that attends western settlement as the frontiersmen and women who advanced civilization insured the loss of the wilderness landscape that beckoned them on.

McMurtry's best work acknowledges the oppositions of frontier mythology and merges the dualities. It is not simply a question of substituting another more positive value—wilderness, for example—for a negative one, civilization. Rather, McMurtry works conflicting ideas into an operating whole that can account for the variety of American life. For McMurtry, the frontier represents amalgamation. Dualities in continual opposition produce a gestalt that is larger than the two forces by themselves. For this reason dualities are central to his work as he raises such oppositions as freedom/restriction, positive/negative, good/evil, love/hate, life/death, one/many, self/mask, visible/invisible, illusion/disillusion, ideal/real, father/son, comedy/tragedy, order/chaos, past/present, sex/violence, among others in his work. This struggle produced the ambivalent American experience. Metaphorically, the frontier, the boundary between civilization and savagery, synthesizes such opposing forces.

Three other important elements of the southwestern frontier myth were identified by Larry Goodwyn in a 1971 essay titled "The Frontier Myth and Southwestern Literature." Goodwyn first concluded that the "frontier legend is pastoral" with a strong emphasis on primitivism. Second, "the legend is inherently masculine: women are not so much without 'courage' as missing altogether; cowgirls did not ride up the Chisholm Trail." And third, Goodwyn found that the frontier myth "is primitively racialist: it provided no mystique of triumph for Mexicans, Negroes, or Indians" (161).

Much of the ambivalence in McMurtry's work stems from these older elements. The primitivism of the legend, with its emphasis on the positive values that living close to the land breeds, certainly contributes much to these feelings of uncertainty. Bookish people like him spend much of their time inside libraries or sitting in front of typewriters like the Olivetti McMurtry uses—or infernal word processing machines that others use as they contemplate the expanse of space that defines the state. And they know that the majority of Texans—over eighty-two percent—live in urban areas. They also realize that many of Texas's remaining natural areas along rivers and coastlines are threatened by some of the foulest polluters, who are free to exercise the liberty that a "guvment"-hating state allows. Many of McMurtry's novels probe the problematic relationship between Southwesterners and the natural landscape in varying ways.

Several of McMurtry's novels also confront the sexism of the old frontier myth by using women as the main characters. Relationships between men and women provide the central focus for another group of novels. Two-and-a-half decades ago, in *In a Narrow Grave*, McMurtry called for Texas writers to shift from the harsh physical landscape of the Southwest to "emotional experience," which he said in Texans "remains largely unexplored," mapping the territory for "the dramas, poems and novels" of future Texas writers. McMurtry went on to say that an "ideal place to start, it seems to me, is with the relations of the sexes, a subject from which the eyes of Texas have remained too long averted" (54). Throughout his work McMurtry has kept his eyes focused on male-female relationships in both the livelong days and the passing nights.

Although confronting racism has not been central to McMurtry's fiction, he often creates important minority characters. From Halmea in *Horseman, Pass By* to Deets in *Lonesome Dove*, McMurtry has used positive African American characters who resist stereotyping. And his Indian characters, especially in his recent novels *Buffalo Girls* and *Streets of Laredo*, counter popular myth. Although his own Hispanic characters are problematic, in *In a Narrow Grave* McMurtry attacked the racism against Mexicans that was part of the history of Texas Rangers.

To these elements of Texas mythology—ambivalence, primitivism, racism, and sexism—another ambiguous element continues from the frontier past: violence. In an *Atlantic* essay in 1975, McMurtry excoriated Texas, noting that the frontier emphasis on violence was one of the few vestiges of the old world still hanging on: "If frontier life has left any cultural residue at all, it is a residue of a most unfortunate sort— i.e., that tendency to romanticize violence which is evident on the front page of almost every Texas newspaper almost every day" ("The Texas Moon" 31). Richard Slotkin examined the implications of the myth of violence in *Regeneration through Violence: The Mythology of the American Frontier, 1600–1860*, in which he identified the archetypal pattern—the American hunter who journeys out into the wilderness, meets the Indian in a violent confrontation, and regenerates himself and his people. Contemporary Texas demonstrates the sad reality of this dubious legacy, and several of McMurtry's works examine violence in varying ways: from the Texas propensity to promote violence in hunting, bar fights, casual confrontations, and random savagery. In several recent novels such as *Anything for Billy* and *Streets of Laredo*, southwestern violence is a pervasive theme.

Initiation

Another recurring ambivalent theme in McMurtry's work concerns initiation. Several observers have commented on McMurtry's emphasis on the theme of initiation, especially in his early works, where Lonnie Bannon, Molly Wood, Sonny, Patsy Carpenter, and Danny Deck all seem to undergo initiatory experiences. But as Tom Pilkington points out, another view of these youthful characters suggests that they, like several other American fictional characters, are not full initiates. They become like Ihab Hassan's radically innocent figure. Hassan asserts that "at bottom all innocence amounts to a denial of death," (325) and defines the basic aspect of the post-World War II American hero as radical innocence:

> Radical, first, because it is inherent in his character, and goes to the root or foundation of it. But radical too, because it is extreme, impulsive, anarchic, troubled with vision. The new hero brings the brilliant extremities of the American conscience and imagination to bear on the equable tenor of our present culture. . . . His innocence, therefore, does not merely revert to those simplicities which, rightly or

wrongly, have been identified with vision in America. His innocence, rather is a property of the Mythic American Self, perhaps of every anarchic Self. It is the innocence of a Self that refused to accept the immitigable rule of reality, including death, an aboriginal Self the radical imperatives of whose freedom cannot be stifled. (6–7)

Normally the young hero in the traditional *Bildungsroman* eventually becomes the initiate, an acceptable and accepting member of society. However, R. W. B. Lewis points out that in America "the valid rite of initiation for the individual in the new world is not an initiation into society, but, given the character of society, an initiation away from it: something I wish it were legitimate to call 'denitiation'" (115). Hassan agrees: "The Hero, who once figured as Initiate, ends as Rebel or Victim. The change in his condition implies destruction—and presages rebirth" (9).

Indeed, innocence often becomes the victim in McMurtry's novels, where a repeated motif is the death of innocence: the retarded Billy in *The Last Picture Show*; Wynkyn in *Somebody's Darling*; Sean, Janey, and Joe in *Lonesome Dove*; Jacy's child in *Texasville*; the mute offspring of Will Isinglass, a twelve-year-old Apache boy, and Billy Bone himself in *Anything for Billy*; and T. R. in *Some Can Whistle*. The deaths of these innocents highlight McMurtry's attack on the world into which they are introduced. One of the ultimate tests of a society's worth concerns its treatment of innocents who are incapable of caring for themselves. Again and again, and increasingly in his later novels, McMurtry's world view produces a vision of a world that destroys the innocent. These youthful characters do not achieve a "denitiation" either; they reach no awareness about being outside the society. Initiation, then, like many other McMurtry themes, appears in various guises.

The Modern World

The impulse to turn away from entry into society may result from the type of modern world that McMurtry presents. His vision of the world facing his potential initiates indicates still another element that leads to McMurtry's contradictory attitudes toward the old Southwest, which may stem from his growing dissatisfaction with the modern world. Throughout his work McMurtry has attacked aspects of the frontier such as the primitivism, racism, sexism, anti-intellectualism, and violence that he has found vexing and disturbing. On the other hand, he has also become increasingly critical of the world that replaced the old one. McMurtry's contemporary novels over the past thirty years present the twentieth century as atomistic, alienating, materialistic, violent, decadent, corrupt, and driven by a consumer economy that fosters classism and mass production of objects and entertainment, much unlike the world when the McMurtrys came to the plains during the golden days of cowboying. The old order, based on the ranching system with clear goals and methods of behavior and societal expectations, was crumbling because of overgrazing, drought, the closing of cattle trails, and quarantine laws; and the new one, based first on large-scale farming with irrigation systems and refrigerated railroad cars, was taking its place. The large farms and then the large oil companies introduced a corporate economy with a value system based on business, capitalism, and exchange of labor. In his books set in the nineteenth century—*Lonesome Dove*, *Anything for Billy*, *Buffalo Girls*, and *Streets of Laredo*— McMurtry points to the beginnings of this newer world as the bankers and railroad executives begin to manipulate the forces of production on the frontier. These themes return with vigor in the later sequels such as *Some Can Whistle* and *The Evening Star*, where McMurtry sketches a contemporary world beset with problems that confront such characters as the aging Danny Deck and Aurora Greenway.

The Pursuit of Happiness

Another ambivalent theme concerns the irony of human desire for pleasure as contrasted with the reality of sadness, illness, loss, and despair. While McMurtry often explores initiation for youthful figures, he has also consistently examined aging and death. Homer Bannon in *Horseman, Pass By* is the first aging character in McMurtry's canon, but with his sequels McMurtry returns again and again to aging characters such as Aurora Greenway, Danny Deck, and Woodrow Call. If his youthful characters do not achieve initiation into full awareness, his aging ones do not find satisfaction either. In *Leaving Cheyenne*, Gid tells his father that he intends to "enjoy [his] life." His father replies:

> "Why, any damn fool can enjoy himself. What makes you think life's supposed to be enjoyed anyhow?"
> "Well," I said, "if you ain't supposed to enjoy it, what are you supposed to do with it?"
> "Fight it. Fight the hell out of it." (27)

Indeed, the characters who are most alive in McMurtry's contemporary novels are those like Aurora Greenway, Rosie Dunlup, Danny Deck's daughter T. R., and Godwin Lloyd Jons, who continue to attempt to live their hopes and dreams despite recognizing that living is a battle and no one gets out alive. There are transcendent moments produced by art, laughter, nature, and human interaction that relieve the despair. These moments in McMurtry's novels are fleeting to be sure, but they provide these characters with the

strength to continue the struggle and to maintain the
fragile habit of hope necessary for survival.

Writing and Art

One final ambivalent element in McMurtry's work
that may be among the most significant because it is
the most pervasive concerns his sometimes contradictory attitudes toward the value of writing. At times the
uncertainty grows from the value the frontier world
placed on producing tangible products rather than
ephemeral mental constructions, and it perhaps resulted from his painful choice to follow writing rather
than cowboying as a career. He told an interviewer: "I
was raised on a ranch, and I was raised with cowboys
and [was raised] essentially to be a cowboy . . . but I
didn't" ("Novelist" 2). At other times McMurtry is conflicted by the isolation that writing demands. He
emphasized this point in an interview for *Humanities*
in 1988 as he contemplated the writer-narrator in *Anything for Billy*:

> There's always a theme that wanders
> through my books, and wanders through the
> books of many other writers, . . . what does
> writing about life really do to your capacity to
> live out your relationship to life? Is writing such
> a peculiar thing that makes it more and more

difficult for you to go on, to live satisfactorily? Does it eventually completely separate you, so that if you write perfectly satisfactorily, you live perfectly unsatisfactorily? Is there a mixture of the two? Does it gradually divorce you from real experience and lead you more and more into imagined experience only? Do you eventually reach the point where you are only comfortable in imagined experience, rather than in lived experience?

I rather think that is the case. If you really give yourself deeply enough to any art, it will completely absorb you. They say art is a jealous taskmaster—it really is. It doesn't want you to go in the direction of the family and relationships and social work; it wants you to stay with it. And the more you stay with it, the more likely it will leave you. . . .

It wants you to be devoted to it; and it doesn't care whether you have a nice marriage and children or if you're kind to your mother.

Faulkner said that he would neglect his grandmother in a minute if he could write something as great as "Ode on a Grecian Urn." (*Humanities* 6)

Self-Reflexivity, Intertextuality, Heteroglossia
As McMurtry examines his ambivalence about writ-

ing, his works demonstrate a significant self-reflexivity, especially by using writers and artists as major characters. The most important of these is Danny Deck, the most representative McMurtry alter ego, appearing as the main character in two novels and as a minor character in several others. Lonnie Bannon has apparently written the story he relates in *Horseman, Pass By*; Ben Sippy is a dime novelist in *Anything for Billy*; even Calamity Jane in *Buffalo Girls* becomes a writer, explaining herself in letters supposedly written for her daughter. In some ways, Aurora Greenway is another alter ego; even though she is not a writer, she is clearly artistic, and before the end of her life, she attempts a memory project that is Proustian in outline if not in execution.

This self-reflexivity is reinforced by what Julia Kristeva calls "intertextuality" and Mikhail Bakhtin labels "heteroglossia," in which books are made up of other books and speak to other books. Direct and indirect allusions are central to many of McMurtry's novels, but in the sequels, the books begin to speak directly to one another, with later books recounting earlier scenes and filling out the lives of characters who appear in earlier works. These references put McMurtry in dialogue with himself and suggest Bakhtin's concept of discourse as a social process. Language contains the implications of previous users and anticipates response. In *The Dialogic Imagination* Bakhtin writes:

> The linguistic significance of a given utterance
> is understood against the background of lan-
> guage, while its actual meaning is understood
> against the background of other concrete ut-
> terances on the same theme, a background
> made up of contradictory opinions, points of
> view and value judgments—that is, precisely
> that background that, as we see, complicates
> the path of any word toward its object. (281)

Tzvetan Todorov in *Mikhail Bakhtin: The Dialogical
Principle* explains that Bakhtin applied the concept to
all discourse:

> The most important feature of the utterance,
> or at least the most neglected, is its *dialogism*,
> that is, its intertextual dimension. . . . Inten-
> tional or not, all discourse is in dialogue with
> prior discourses on the same subject, as well
> as with discourses yet to come, whose reactions
> it foresees and anticipates. A single voice can
> make itself heard only by blending into the
> complex choir of other voices already in place.
> This is true not only of literature but of all dis-
> course. . . . (x)

McMurtry's novels enter into a dialogue with previous history, films, and fiction about the West, including McMurtry's own novels. As Bakhtin makes clear, later utterances alter the meaning of previous ones. McMurtry's ongoing sequelizing of his work is emblematic of the concept of language and works in dialogue.

Displacement

Among other important themes is displacement, which Raymond L. Neinstein says in *The Ghost Country* "is the central concern of the first five novels of Larry McMurtry. In four of these novels, the protagonist is either breaking away from a place, or has already done so, only to find himself rootless and lost." Neinstein continues:

> It is a country of the heart, then, a ghost country, that McMurtry celebrates and the loss of which he mourns in his novels, a country of love and of blood-ties. When those ties break down, when the love is gone, when the inheritance or inheritability of that country is somehow thwarted and its traditions are no longer viable, then the poignancy of the country's neglected beauty, that beauty, that tradition, that center, becomes the subject of McMurtry's powerful and nostalgic novels. (ii)

Structure

McMurtry has often stated that he is not a writer who concentrates on structure, saying he is more aware of texture, arriving at structure intuitively, "if I arrive at it at all." Still, repeated structural devices hold his works together. Typically, McMurtry divides his novels into sections and numbered chapters following a chronological order, usually with titles for the sections. The sections may indicate a new narrator, as in *Leaving Cheyenne* and *Somebody's Darling*, or they may indicate time and space changes. Within this general organization, McMurtry uses other structural devices. Several novels take as the starting point an event that signals a major change for the main characters—the death of a heifer, the return of a friend, a phone call from a long-lost daughter, the meeting of a notorious killer. From *Horseman, Pass By* to *Streets of Laredo* McMurtry has depended upon the journey to provide structure for his novels. Traveling is a natural act in a state that covers 266,807 square miles. It is 801 miles from the north in the Panhandle to Brownsville in the south and 773 miles from the easternmost bend in the Sabine River to the westernmost point of the Rio Grande near El Paso. With all this territory, journeying continues to be a necessary reality for the region. And many of McMurtry's titles reflect the fundamental importance of journeying. Much of his work reflects the continuing importance of journeying in Texas both literally and metaphorically. Many of his novels are structured by journeys, with searching used as a metaphor for the existential reality of contemporary life. From Saul on the road to Damascus, Oedipus on the way to Thebes, to Odysseus headed home and Huck on the river, the journey's power as archetype gains added heft in a state where expanse beckons and hinders. Much of this traveling, as Janis Stout notes, leads nowhere. But for many of these characters, such as Lonnie Bannon and Cadillac Jack McGriff, escape is a major concern. For others, such as Woodrow Call and Danny Deck, both escape and return are important patterns.

Another continuing structural device in McMurtry's work grows out of paired or triangulated characters whose personal conflicts, compromises, and agreements often symbolize larger issues. In *Horseman, Pass By*, for example, the three Bannons—Homer, Hud, and Lonnie—represent three generations and three distinctly different approaches to the changing rural Southwest. In *Leaving Cheyenne* the three men who vie for Molly Taylor's affection—Gid, the established rancher; Johnny, the footloose cowboy; and Eddie, the oilman—represent differing approaches to the landscape. And in *Lonesome Dove*, the three Rangers—Woodrow Call, Augustus McCrae, and Jake Spoon—suggest aspects of the archetypal Texas Ranger. As Ernestine Sewell points out, the three former Rang-

ers may form a composite that embodies the cowboy
god, a mythic figure that McMurtry witnessed passing
from the old Southwest.

In *The Last Picture Show* McMurtry uses the death
of a significant character to provide the structure. This
novel examines life in a small town as the older values
embodied by rural life disappeared. Sam the Lion represents the older, passing era—a character who could
love, feel sympathy and compassion, one who would
react with anger against injustice, such as banishing
Sonny from the pool hall for being involved in the sexual
initiation of the retarded boy. When Sam dies midway
through the novel, his death provides the climactic loss
of center which is the subject of the novel.

Style

Although McMurtry tends more often toward realism, he has consciously mixed styles throughout his
career. And he has remarked that he believes that an
accomplished artist ought to be able to make leaps easily: "One of the marks of a great artist is the ease with
which he moves back and forth between scenes of vastly
different scale; from the cosmic to the local, as it were;
or from gods to swineherds, the death camp to the mat-
tress factory. The confident artist makes these moves
so casually that they seem like acts of grace" (*Film Flam*
47). His own shifts occur from novel to novel (the real-

ism of *Leaving Cheyenne* gives way to the broad satire of *The Last Picture Show* and the comedy of manners in *Cadillac Jack*, which points later to a mixture of realism and postmodern self-consciousness in *Anything for Billy*), and within novels. *Terms of Endearment*, for example, moves from the sculptured lawns of Aurora Greenway's Houston River Oaks area to the beer-guzzling honkytonk where Royce Dunlup hangs out. In two later novels, McMurtry adds a futuristic tinge as he fast forwards into the twenty-first century in the conclusions of *Some Can Whistle* and *The Evening Star*.

Symbol and Image

For the most part McMurtry's images grow naturally out of the subject matter. In his first novel, *Horseman, Pass By*, the images are more obvious than in many of the later ones. The buzzards, dead heifer and diseased cattle, and the old longhorns that Homer must kill are all rather transparently symbolic. In fact, McMurtry uses animal imagery throughout his work. Horses and horsemen appear prominently, from Lonnie Bannon's horse, Stranger, to Uncle Laredo's dead and buried horse, El Caballo, in *All My Friends Are Going to Be Strangers*; to Call's Hell Bitch in *Lonesome Dove*; to Ben Sippy's mule Rosy in *Anything for Billy*. In *The Last Picture Show* humans are often compared to various animals. Rats, snakes, and pigs are also symbolic in *All My Friends Are Going to Be Strangers*, *Lonesome Dove*, and *Streets of Laredo*, where a gigantic rat becomes a menace. In *Anything for Billy* McMurtry uses "cattaloes," offspring of cattle and buffalo, for symbolic effect. In his novels set in the twentieth century, automobiles take on symbolic stature, particularly the Cadillacs driven by Hud Bannon, Aurora Greenway, and Cadillac Jack McGriff, as well as Abilene's Mercury and Vernon Dalhart's Lincoln; and the pickups driven by the rural characters in *Horseman, Pass By*, *Leaving Cheyenne*, *The Last Picture Show*, and *Moving On*. In *The Evening Star* the Goodyear Blimp, a holdover from a previous period, becomes symbolic of Aurora Greenway, who thinks of herself as a throwback. Another important mechanical image is the answering machine, symbolic of the lack of human communication in *Some Can Whistle*.

Another important repeated image in McMurtry's work concerns diminished physical skills, often symbolized by lost body parts. One such repeated figure is an old man who has lost his voice box, based no doubt on McMurtry's favorite uncle, Johnny McMurtry, who lost his voice box to cancer late in life. And in *Streets of Laredo*, many of the characters, especially Captain Woodrow Call, lose body parts. In *The Evening Star* the aging Aurora Greenway loses her ability to speak after a stroke.

Throughout his work McMurtry has been keenly aware of the power of the conflict between the reality of his rural past and the myth of the cowboy associated with it, and in his writing he has attempted to create art that can achieve the purpose he commented on in *Film Flam*:

> I have, I suspect, come to want of it [art] more or less what Matthew Arnold wanted: that is, that it perform a function once the trust of religion, that of reconciling us to our experience, whether social, domestic, or tragic. I want an art that—through style, through wit, through vision, or through heart—redeems the experience it presents; the last thing I want is an art that idly documents discontents and as idly adds them to my own. (44)

In his novels, nonfiction, and screenplays McMurtry documents and dramatizes discontented, displaced characters searching for something to provide their lives with stability and purpose, especially since the elements that provided direction in the past have disappeared. They long for ways to combine love and work into a satisfying and enduring whole. Although their lives are ultimately fraught with difficulty, pain, and uncertainty, McMurtry's art demonstrates how these characters take pleasure in moments of creativity, love, or humor. These moments reconcile the characters to their experience, and McMurtry's art, in turn, reconciles us to ours.

3

Leaving Thalia
The Rural Trilogy and *In a Narrow Grave*

McMurtry's early novels both dramatize and represent the uncertainty that is central to his work. For many years while critics praised them highly, McMurtry disparaged them as juvenile, sentimental, over-edited, or poorly realized. And yet, as Tom Pilkington noted in *Taking Stock*, they marked a radical change in Texas letters: "Despite their nostalgia and sentimentality, despite the fact that their creator would apparently disown them if he could, they continue, as we near the end of the twentieth century and confront a world far removed even from the one sketched in the novels, to speak to readers in a strong and passionate voice" (125).

These early novels take as their central theme the end of the frontier way of life and extend the reality into mythic levels, bringing the conclusions of modernists such as T. S. Eliot, F. Scott Fitzgerald, and Ernest Hemingway to bear on the sere landscape of West Texas. The Thalia novels examine a world in which the ideal and the real clash, a world bereft of the comforting values of an earlier time. They present these significant clashes and confrontations through believable characters who speak a recognizable language, and they deal with people who, for the most part, laugh and make love, who feel pain and alienation. As Thomas Landess notes, they are concerned with the "effect of the passing years on the hopes and dreams of the young" (Landess 14). They weave together the two main strands of McMurtry's attitudes toward his blood's country, what Dave Hickey calls "elegy and exorcism" (*Taking Stock* 128), with both strands often intertwined in uneasy tension. These same concerns are presented directly in McMurtry's nonfiction collection, *In a Narrow Grave*, presented in his own voice—or at least the persona he wishes to present to the public.

Horseman, Pass By (1961)

McMurtry took the title *Horseman, Pass By* from William Butler Yeats's poem, "Under Ben Bulben," which ends with the inscription on a tombstone,

Cast a cold eye
On life, on death.
Horseman, pass by!

Yeats's epitaph provides the elegiac tone that is important to the novel and suggests the comparison between Yeats's mythic horseman and the death of the cowboy god that Homer Bannon represents. Indeed, the last chapter ends with Lonnie standing in the churchyard after Homer's funeral "thinking of the horseman that had passed." Certainly, the novel pays quiet and respectful homage to the end of the rural life and the passing cowboy god McMurtry later detailed in *In a Narrow Grave.* But the novel looks both back at the old and forward to the new and makes escape and ambivalence important McMurtry themes.

Horseman, Pass By is a tightly organized, concise novel that concentrates more on a unified plot than many of McMurtry's later novels, perhaps because of the influence of editorial suggestions. Lonnie Bannon, the teenage narrator, tells the story of the death of his grandfather, Homer Bannon, shot by his stepson, Hud. The story concentrates on the days shortly before and after Homer's death with the discovery and slaughter of the diseased cattle as the major plot device. The plot follows a conventional structure of exposition (Lonnie's prologue), rising action/complication (discovery of the dead heifer), climax (slaughter of the herd/the death of Homer), falling action (Homer's funeral/Lonnie's response), and denouement (Lonnie's leaving).

In the "Prologue" Lonnie looks out on the early oats and leafing mesquites of the April plains, and he hears the zooming cars headed north to Amarillo or south to Dallas, the growling diesels moving purposely across the prairie, and especially the whistling Zephyr whose "noise cut across the dark prairie like the whistling train itself" (4). The train makes Homer "tireder and tireder" and urges him to bed early, but it excites Lonnie and sends his imagination whirling down the track toward the "airplane beacons flashing from the airport in Wichita Falls" (6). In many ways this scene is paradigmatic of the novel's movement: the old frontier order symbolized by Homer is dying out and the new one represented by Lonnie and the trains and planes to which he is attracted is arriving. Does the passing indicate a new, more powerful beginning or a degeneration, an end to something suggestively beautiful?

After the exposition of the prologue, the novel quickly introduces the complication when, as buzzards swirl above in uneasy spiral, Homer decides to have a dead heifer examined by Newt Garrett, the local veterinarian who lost his voice box to cancer and who can speak only by holding an electric buzzer against his throat. This scene sets the primary images of death, decay, and disease that pervade Lonnie's tale of partial initiation. The death of the single heifer is compounded as the state veterinarian orders the destruction of Homer's entire herd and culminates in the scene where Homer must kill the two old longhorn steers and the Hereford steer that represent the older ranching world that is now passing by. Homer explains: "I been keeping 'em to remind me how times was" (52).

Critics often conclude that *Horseman, Pass By* dramatizes the psychic indirection caused by the loss of nature and the healing values taught by a beneficent nature. E. Pauline Degenfelder in "McMurtry and the Movies: *Hud* and *The Last Picture Show*," notes that the title suggests an "elegy for the desecration of the land, the temporality of an older order, and the death of the patriarchical figure who is its embodiment" (81). Janis P. Stout in "Journeying as a Metaphor for Cultural Loss in the Novels of Larry McMurtry," finds that in *Horseman, Pass By* and several other novels McMurtry uses journeying as a "metaphor for modern life itself, which is seen as being impoverished by the demise of the old traditions and the lack of new structures of meaning and allegiance" (38). According to this view, the Prologue demonstrates that the Edenic frontier of the old cowboy has been fatally corrupted by the machine's entry into the garden. (My reference, of course, is to Leo Marx's *The Machine in the Garden.* Marx points out that in the nineteenth century the train was the archetypal image of the machine's entry into the American garden, noting the ambivalence Americans felt toward that presence: some saw it as the ultimate corruption; others felt that the machine simply provided another way for man to work his art upon the wilderness. McMurtry's Prologue allows both attitudes; the April and Lilac references may suggest "The Wasteland" or springtime.)

But another view of the novel, especially in light of some of McMurtry's comments in *In a Narrow Grave* and his body of work, reveals that in many ways *Horseman, Pass By* demonstrates the enervation of the romanticized myth of the frontier, a saddened nostalgia for a past way of life, and an embrace of the modern world that replaces the old. In fact, much of *Horseman, Pass By* indicates a good-riddance attitude that appears more directly in McMurtry's essays and later novels and dramatizes McMurtry's "contradiction of attractions" and ambivalence "as deep as the bone" (141) toward Texas and the past. While McMurtry employs an elegiac tone in describing Homer's death, he also uses Homer to strike out at the frontier emphasis on the goodness of nature and open country. He also attacks the anti-intellectual, anti-woman, anti-minority, pro-violence attitudes that were part of the old value system. In both the novel and the essays McMurtry counters the pastoralism, sexism, racism, and violence that is the consequence of much of the southwestern legend.

Old Homer Bannon, as representative of the frontier values, believes in the myth of a beneficent nature. Lonnie recalls that "he told me that nature would always work her own cures, if people would be patient enough, and give her time" (3). The land, to Homer, is sacred; he will not think of allowing oil wells on his ranch: "I guess I'm a queer, contrary old bastard, but there'll be no holes punched in this land while I'm here" (105–106). This strong, primitivist belief leads him to attack the materialism that drilling for oil would indicate:

> "What good's oil to me," he said. "What can I do with it? With a bunch a fuckin' oil wells. I can't ride out ever day an' prowl amongst 'em, like I can my cattle. I can't breed 'em or tend 'em or rope 'em or chase 'em or nothin'. I can't feel a smidgen a pride in 'em, cause they ain't none a my doin'. Money, yes. Piss on that kinda money." (106)

Lonnie recognizes the power of Homer's primitivism, so much so that he dreams of riding across a beautiful open country with his grandfather:

> I dreamed that Granddad and I were out together, riding in the early morning. The sun was just up, and the breeze cool on us as we

> rode across the high country. . . . There below us was Texas, green and brown and graying in the sun, spread wide under the clear spread of sky like the opening scene in a big western movie. There were rolling hills in the north, and cattle grazing here and there, and strings of horses under the shade trees. . . . Finally . . . we rode together into the valley toward some old ranch I couldn't see, the Llano Estacado or the old Matador. . . . (70)

Although Lonnie may dream of an Edenic world, the reality of his world does not support this romantic vision. Instead, the novel attacks many of the primitivist attitudes McMurtry later criticizes in his *In a Narrow Grave* essay entitled "Southwestern Literature?"

In it, McMurtry evaluates the similar primitivist attitudes that existed for the Big Three of Texas letters, J. Frank Dobie, Roy Bedichek, and Walter Prescott Webb. For them, McMurtry notes, "Nature was the Real. Knowledge of it made a full man, and accord with it was the first essential of the Good Life" (36). For his generation, however, McMurtry says that he doubts if "we could scrape up enough nature-lore between us to organize a decent picnic" (36). He then makes his charge against the frontier emphasis on nature more explicit:

> I spent more than twenty years in the country
> and I came away from it far from convinced
> that the country is a good place to form char-
> acter, acquire fullness, or lead the Good Life. I
> have had fine moments of rapport with nature,
> but I have seen the time, also, when I would
> have traded a lot of sunsets for a few good
> books. Sentimentalists are still fond of saying
> that nature is the best teacher—I have known
> many Texans who felt that way, and most of
> them live and die in woeful ignorance. When I
> lived in the country I have noticed no abun-
> dance of full men. (36)

The primitivist emphasis on nature as a teacher
resulted in a militant anti-intellectualism, which
McMurtry believes is one of the major weaknesses of
the frontier myth. If the only valuable learning comes
from a life of action in the natural world, then any other
education lacks worth. McMurtry notes that even Dobie
and Bedichek "displayed a marked ambivalence toward
the intellect" (43), and he laments that he grew up in a
"bookless town—in a bookless part of the state" (33).

In *Horseman, Pass By* Homer's primitivism out-
weighs any emphasis on education. Disparaging "college
fellers," he would not approve of Hud's desire to go to
college. Hud tells Homer,

You thought I oughta drive that goddamn
feed wagon for you, instead of goin' to college.
Yeah. You held on tight then, but you sure let
me go in a hurry when the draft board started
lookin' for somebody to go do the fightin'. But
hell, you were Wild Horse Homer Bannon in
them days, an' anything you did was right. I
even thought you was right myself, the most
of the time. Why, I used to think you was a
regular god. I don't no more. (78)

Homer, therefore, is in part responsible for creating the
embittered Hud who mockingly says: "You're the boss,
you must be the one who knows if anybody does. I just
work from the shoulders down, myself" (77).

As Hud's stepson status implies, he is a debased
version of Homer. Homer's world had been sustained
by the cowboy mythos, but he cannot cope with a
changing world, one with a frontier diminished by
highways and railroad tracks. Nor can he help prepare
the young to live full lives in a world dominated by cities
and cars. By denying support for Hud's education,
perhaps influenced by the anti-intellectualism of that
changing world, Homer had closed to Hud one way of
preparing for that changing world. By turning Hud
against him, Homer contributes to his own downfall as
well, just as he hastens it by buying the diseased
Mexican cattle that contaminate his herd.

Hud reveals in additional ways that he is a product of Homer Bannon's world, especially that world's
emphasis on violence. In an *Atlantic* essay titled "The
Texas Moon, and Elsewhere," McMurtry excoriated
Texas, noting that the frontier emphasis on violence
was one of the few vestiges of the old world still hanging on: "If frontier life has left any cultural residue at
all, it is a residue of a most unfortunate sort—i.e., that
tendency to romanticize violence which is evident on
the front page of almost every Texas newspaper almost
every day" (31). In *In a Narrow Grave* McMurtry comments on the way that Hud is influenced by the violence
of the fading myth:

> Hud, a twentieth-century Westerner, is a gun-
> fighter who lacks both guns and opponents.
> The land itself is the same—just as powerful
> and just as imprisoning—but the social con-
> text has changed so radically that Hud's im-
> pulse to violence is turned inward, on himself
> and his family. He is wild in a well-established
> tradition of Western wildness that involves
> drinking, fighting, fast and reckless riding and/
> or driving, and, of course, seducing. (24–25)

Not only does Hud's violent wildness manifest itself in seduction, but with Halmea, the black cook,
seduction becomes rape. He can rape her with impu-

nity because she is a *black* woman. The innocent Lonnie
tells her that the "law can take care of Hud," but she
replies, "No law gonna hear about dis', you see dey
don't. Tell de law, dey have it my fault befo' you turn
aroun'. I seen dat kinda law befo" (116–17). In "Take
My Saddle from the Wall," also in *In a Narrow Grave*,
McMurtry notes that violence toward minorities was
often part of the cowboy's world:

> The Cowboy's working life is spent in one sort
> of violent activity or another; an ability to ab-
> sorb violence and hardship is part of the
> proving of any cowboy, and it is only to be ex-
> pected that the violence will extend itself
> occasionally from animals to humans, and par-
> ticularly to those humans that class would have
> one regard as animals. (168)

While Lonnie watches Hud raping Halmea, he sees Hud
bring "his hand over her shoulder and hit her with the
heel of it, hard in the face, like he might hit a mare. . . .
'Wild bitch, ain't you?' Hud said, grinning again" (113).

Hud's rape of Halmea causes Lonnie to be aware of
his deep feelings of ambivalence. On one hand, by acting on his desire for Halmea, Hud does exactly what
Lonnie has dreamed: "What bothered me was I had
wanted to do pretty much the same thing to Halmea. I
didn't want to do it mean, like Hud did everything, but

I wanted to do it to her. . . . Watching him screw Halmea, I should have killed him, but I didn't. I stood back and I waited. Wanted to watch" (117–18).

While Hud's treatment of Halmea may have been mainly the product of racism, his attitude toward women may have been affected by their exclusion from the cowboy mythos. McMurtry discusses women in the Southwest more fully in a *Texas Monthly* article, "Unfinished Women," in which he points out that "Texas women were . . . firmly captive of a very limited and narrow masculine concept of womanhood, not to mention manhood" (164). He also notes that Texas men believed that "women were fatally tainted with silliness and a taste for the superfluous. . ." (166). In "Take My Saddle from the Wall" McMurtry says that cowboys had a "commitment to a heroic concept of life that simply takes little account of women" (148). Hud certainly has not learned how to treat women well from Homer. Women to Homer are just to be humored as he does Hud's mother, sending her to Temple to get a few fake stitches to quiet her hypochondria (66). The scene which best exemplifies their separation has them listening to separate programs on separate radios, "The two programs blaring . . . against each other" (85). These anti-women attitudes, along with other anti-minority, anti-intellectual, pro-violence ones of the frontier myth, have helped shape Hud.

If Hud is one product of the frontier myth, Jesse,

the former rodeo rider, is another. Jesse has followed
the rodeo circuit in search of an Edenic ideal: "I went
all over this cow country, looking for the exact right
place an' the exact right people, so once I got stopped I
wouldn't have to be movin' agin, like my old man always done" (148). But Jesse has never found the "exact
right place"; rather he has been worn out and crippled
by the pursuit. In *In a Narrow Grave*, McMurtry evaluates the rodeo as an alternative to the past:

> The cowboy's temperament has not changed
> much since the nineteenth century; it is his
> world that has changed, and the change has
> been a steady shrinkage. There are no more
> trail herds, no more wide open cattle towns,
> no longer that vast stretch of unfenced land
> between Laredo and Calgary. If the modern
> cowboy is footloose, there is only the rodeo cir-
> cuit, for most a very unsatisfactory life. (26)

What kind of world, then, is open for Lonnie, the
new generation, to enter? Lonnie is vaguely aware that
something is wrong with his world, but from Marlet,
the in-town kid who longs for the cowboy life, Lonnie
learns how to embody that hazy feeling in an image: he
thinks about strangling. After talking to Marlet in town,
Lonnie goes out into the dark that night and tries to
realize himself through violence, in a scene that sug-

gests Richard Slotkin's thesis in *Regeneration through Violence*. Lonnie takes the .22, walks past a cottonmouth, and begins shooting turtles and frogs in the tank. Indeed the snake is in the garden, reinforced by other snake images throughout the novel. Lonnie's attempt to assert his sense of self by dominating nature, however, does not free him from his feelings of alienation. Instead, like Marlet, the strange boy from town, Lonnie feels that he too is strangling: "Suddenly the high weeds and the darkness made me feel like Marlet, like I was strangling. 'Oh me,' I said. 'I wasted all those frogs'" (86).

After Lonnie recognizes that mindless violence against nature contributes to his feeling of strangulation, he then tries to become part of the world of wild and reckless riding. He saddles Granddad's significantly named horse Stranger and goes for a ride along Idiot Ridge. But just when he senses that he and Stranger may have reached an ecstatic peak as they race across the range, a fence, image of the diminished frontier, appears suddenly in front of them, and Lonnie takes an extremely hard fall when Stranger pulls up quickly.

While wild and violent activity is unattainable for Lonnie in this dry, dusty, diminished frontier, he does find new pastures: the world of the imagination opened by reading *From Here to Eternity*. McMurtry too had found the world of literature an alternative to the old wide-open spaces:

In their youth . . . my uncles sat on the
barn and watched the last trail herds moving
north—I sat on the self-same barn and saw
only a few oil-field pickups and a couple of dairy
trucks go by. That life died, and I am lucky to
have found so satisfying a replacement as *Don
Quixote* offered. And yet, that first life has not
quite died in me—not quite. I missed it only
by the width of a generation and, as I was
growing up, heard the whistle of its departure.
Not long after I entered the pastures of the
empty page I realized that the place where all
my stories start is the heart faced suddenly
with the loss of its country, its customary and
legendary range. (*In a Narrow Grave* 139–40)

So when Lonnie climbs into that cattle truck for a
ride to Wichita Falls as the novel ends, he will not light
out for the circuit that Jesse followed. Instead, he will
head for the cities that have now filled the wide-open
spaces of the old frontier. There he can pursue the books
now open to him. There he will become the writer of his
own story. There he will escape the stifling, strangling
world of the diminished frontier. In this light,
McMurtry's title is both a lament and a command.

For a first novel by a young writer, *Horseman, Pass
By* received a number of favorable reviews. Charles

Poore, reviewing for *The New York Times* "Books of the Times" (June 10, 1961), asserted that McMurtry was "already well up among the most promising first novelists who have appeared this year." Poore continued: "What's more, his promise is the kind that lasts. . . . The material he has at his command as a descendant of Texan generations is usable in all kinds of new ways." And Poore looked forward to McMurtry's future work: "There is a gnarled pastoral side to Texas life that has not yet been shown fully to the world. It lies in Mr. McMurtry's province. He should not pass it by— remembering that the best of our southwestern writers is still."

McMurtry's own response was negative, as it often has been once he has finished a book. Because it was a first novel by an untested writer, he had to submit to more editorial influence than has been required since. He told interviewer Patrick Bennett:

> The first book was really the only one in which I had a lot of editorial trouble. . . . In the original version of the book, I had the cattle killed right away, and the book was about the disintegration of the ranching family as a result of the loss of their herd or their work. The editor felt that to kill the herd right away destroyed a certain element of suspense in the narrative which he wanted to keep. After a certain

amount of argument, a young writer is particularly vulnerable to an intelligent editor. You
tend to think, Well, he knows better than I
know. Eventually I gave in. Also, I really
wanted to get the book published. Also, by that
time I had revised it so many times that I had
kind of stopped caring about it one way or the
other. So I did as he suggested. (25)

Even though he agreed to the changes, he continues to
maintain that "it was a mistake":

Not that it matters much; the book would not
have been a great book if I had kept it my way,
and it's not altogether the worse for having
done it his way. However, I did think it made
the end unrealistic: the collapse of the old man
is too abrupt. The movie unfortunately kept
the same structure, and again the collapse is
too abrupt. That's the only problem I had with
the way it was finally structured: just overnight
the old man, who was a terrifically strong, vig-
orous old man, is dying. There was not time,
doing it that way, to develop a natural pattern
of deterioration. After that book I've never had
any problem, never had any substantial editorial difficulty with anyone. None at all with

most books. So little that one hardly knows if
the editors are even reading. (25–26)

Some McMurtry critics assert that if McMurtry had
more editorial suggestions, he would be a much better
writer. Critics often complain that McMurtry's books
are too long, unfocused, with too much emphasis on sex
or violence. But since the editorial interference with
the first novel, McMurtry has avoided the editor's pen.

His second novel, however, received a good many
suggestions, not from editors but from his classmates
during his Stegner fellowship at Stanford. Kesey recalls that McMurtry workshopped the sections in
classes, beginning with the last section and working
backward, reminiscent of D. H. Lawrence's comment
in *Studies in Classic American Literature* about the
reverse chronology of J. Fenimore Cooper's
Leatherstocking tales: "[T]hey go backwards, from old
age to golden youth. That is the true myth of America.
She starts old, old, wrinkled and writhing in an old skin.
And there is a gradual sloughing of the old skin, to-
wards a new youth" (54).

Leaving Cheyenne (1962)

McMurtry's ambivalence about the possibility of
fulfillment in southwestern rural life is more subtly

presented in *Leaving Cheyenne*, the second novel. There, Molly tries to choose between two recognizable southwestern figures: Johnny, the unfettered, forever-free cowboy, and Gid the aspiring, settled rancher. The two impulses cannot be reconciled, nor can Molly choose. Rather, she marries a third, Eddie White, a brutal oilfield worker. Throughout the novel, she tries loving both Johnny and Gid as the three age and their world, the blood's country, passes on.

Another more symbolically ambivalent element concerns Gid's and Johnny's pursuit of Molly. McMurtry has often commented on the irony of pursuing a constantly fleeting frontier area that beckons seductively as it diminishes before the eyes, the central image of the beautiful coda to F. Scott Fitzgerald's *The Great Gatsby*.

McMurtry emphasizes this figurative thinking through his epigraph to *Leaving Cheyenne*. Like many other McMurtry novels, it takes its title from a cowboy song, "Goodbye Old Paint":

> My foot's in the stirrup,
> My pony won't stand
> Goodbye, old partner,
> I'm leaving Cheyenne.

McMurtry then adds a gloss that compounds the elegiac nostalgia: "The Cheyenne of this book is that

part of the cowboy's day's circle which is earliest and
best: his blood's country and his heart's pastureland."
The land, circles, and Cheyenne take on symbolic significance in a novel that begins on election day and
circles back in memory to the same point in the final
scene.

The title for the first section, "The Blood's Country,"
is taken from Judith Wright's *South of My Days*. This
part is narrated by Gideon Fry as he tells his version
of the story of an over forty-year relationship with
Molly Taylor. In the second part, "Ruin Hath Taught
Me," from Shakespeare's Sonnet 64, Molly tells her
story about her love for both Gid and Johnny McCloud.
Johnny narrates Part Three, "Go Turn My Horses Free,"
from a song by Teddy Blue in one of McMurtry's favorite cowboy books, *We Pointed Them North*.

Gid's section, the longest of the three, covers the
early years of the relationship, beginning on election
day when he is twenty-one. By having Gid meet Molly
at the voting station, McMurtry emphasizes the theme
of responsibility, since twenty-one was then the legal
age of adult accountability. Gid's feeling of obligation
becomes an important motif, reinforced by the saddle
Gid gives Johnny for taking him to the hospital to recover from a social disease. Gid's powerful concerns for
being responsible correspond to his equally strong con-
science and the guilt he feels about his desire for Molly.
In this light, Gid, Johnny, and Molly suggest Freud's

tripartite division of human psychology, with Gid representing the superego; the wild and free cowboy Johnny corresponding to the id; and the ever present Molly as the Ego being forced to mediate between the two.

The book, of course, is not an allegory, and these suggestions are not stretched throughout the novel. Still, the novel often points to psychological themes. For example, Gid tells how his father Adam commits suicide rather than suffer further from his illness. And he explains how in his conventional morality, Gid impulsively marries Mabel Peters, a poor, submissive girl who becomes a demanding shrew after their marriage.

Psychological effects are also important in Molly's section. The years she narrates cover World War II when she loses both of her sons. Joe, Johnny's son, dies in an air raid over Germany. Jimmy, fathered by Gid, becomes a bitter religious fanatic and later a homosexual before his death, reinforcing McMurtry's emphasis on the psychic effects of the absent and unacknowledged father. But the novel is not limited to a psychological theme. Dave Hickey found a historical counterpoint in a review of McMurtry's work, placing special emphasis on the effect of World War II on Texas: "So Texas emerged from that war with a host of honored dead, a host of men with dead professions (ex-soldiers, ex-ranchers, ex-farmers, ex-oilmen, ex-railroadmen), and a host of men whose professions had gone sour" (*Taking Stock* 129). If Molly symbolically represents the land, then her losses suggest the wrenching effect of the war on the land.

In Part Three, Johnny's section, the theme shifts to aging and loss, with a strong emphasis on mechanical images. One of the main scenes here involves the three principal characters' poor driving, as Gid rolls his Chevy over while backing up, Johnny gets his pickup stuck in a bar ditch, and Molly barely pulls it out with her old Ford. Finally, another important technological advancement receives emphasis when Gid dies while trying to repair the sucker rod on the windmill. These images reinforce the theme of the negative impact modern advancements have had on the old world.

Although McMurtry has often repudiated *Leaving Cheyenne*, he told Peavy how he was drawn to the compelling human drama concerning the nature of love examined in the novel:

> In my work there are certainly patterns of isolation and attempts at connecting. . . . The most successful connections are in *Leaving Cheyenne*, which is also the book set most completely in the country. I was then and still am most interested in situations in which a person loves or is loved by more than one person. One man loves two women, one woman loves two men, etc. Such situations seem to me extremely rich for the novelist, rich in textural possibilities.

I'm a great deal more sensitive to texture than
I am to structure. I think, humanly it's a very
interesting question, how many people one can
love. (Peavy 32)

And he has also explained his attraction to writing
in voices that require him to project imaginatively rather
than simply to draw from his own experience, especially
in Molly's section, the first time he uses a female narrator:

I am not interested in writing about those
things which I know perfectly well; I am interested in trying to cast my imagination into
areas where I myself can't go. I love to write
about women. I like particularly to write about
middle-aged and old women. I've never been a
middle-aged or old woman—probably never
will be—but I certainly enjoy the imaginative
effort of trying to penetrate how it would be;
and so [it was] in my second novel, *Leaving
Cheyenne*, which is about a very long relationship. . . . ("Southwest as Cradle" 34)

By imagining life he cannot live, McMurtry fulfills the
injunction about writing which Ken Kesey attributes
to McMurtry: "The job of the writer is to make up shit"
(Busby interview).

While he is attracted to areas where he cannot go, much of *Leaving Cheyenne* also looks back to McMurtry family history and forward to *Lonesome Dove*. The strong relationship between Gid and Johnny is based in part upon McMurtry's father and his Uncle Johnny, whom he discusses and some of whose stories he tells in *In a Narrow Grave*. McMurtry tells of a present his Uncle Johnny gave his father after Uncle Johnny had caught a social disease:

> Where he got it one can easily imagine: some grim clapboard house on the plains, with the wind moaning. Model A's parked in the grassless yard, and the girls no prettier than Belle Starr. His condition became quite serious, and had my father not gone with him to a hospital and attended him during a prolonged critical period he might well have died.
>
> Instead, he recovered, and in gratitude gave my father a present. Times were hard and Uncle Johnny poor but the present was a pair of spurs with my father's brand mounted on them in gold—extraordinary spurs for this plain country. (169)

McMurtry goes on to comment on Uncle Johnny's response to the pantheistic god he felt controlled the universe:

Uncle Johnny took on himself the cloth of penance—the sort of penance appropriate to the faith he held. For all McMurtrys and perhaps all cowboys are essentially pantheists: to them the Almighty is the name of drought, the Good Lord the name of rain and grass. Nature is the only deity they really recognize and nature's order the only order they hold truly sacred. (169)

In *Leaving Cheyenne*, the gift is transformed into a magnificent saddle, which Gid gives to his friend Johnny for accompanying him to a hospital in Kansas where he gets treated for a social disease. These family references, of course, are interesting, but the novel is satisfying in its own right as it captures the spirit of the open country that the frontier held even as it began to disappear in the early years of the twentieth century. *Leaving Cheyenne* anticipates *Lonesome Dove* by pairing differing cowboy figures (the hard-working, responsible Gid prefigures Woodrow Call, and the easy-going Johnny is a forerunner to Augustus McCrae). Both Johnny and Gid father sons by Molly, and neither ever fully acknowledges his son, just as Call will not accept paternity for Newt.

McMurtry has dismissed *Leaving Cheyenne* as an adolescent male fantasy, since beautiful, alluring Molly is always ready for a quick roll in the hay without re-

quiring any of the guys to accept responsibility for anything, calling it "a kind of 'Jules and Jim' novel about a
lifetime relationship between two men and one woman."
He continues:

> This is a popular favorite with my readers,
> *Leaving Cheyenne*, and I suspect that it's a
> popular favorite because it incorporates a popu-
> lar fantasy. I think that it's very appealing to
> believe that such relationships can endure and,
> of course, occasionally they do, but I think that
> they are fairly rare, rarer than I would have
> thought when I was a twenty-two or twenty-
> three-year-old when I set out to write that book.
> And I myself now look back on it as another
> sentimentalized treatment of conditions and
> life in Texas in the 20s and 30s. ("Southwest
> as Cradle" 34–35)

Despite his own disclaimers, the early reviews were
generally positive. Marshall Sprague asserted that
"Larry McMurtry's narrative moves at an easy lope and
it occurred to me that if Chaucer were a Texan writing
today, and only twenty-seven years old, this is how he
would have written and this is how he would have felt."
Sprague identified what other admirers of the novel
often praise, McMurtry's ability to create a sense of place
through dialogue and detail as the characters avoid

"stinging lizards," catch coyotes, and butcher hogs. The regional dialect and country expressions also provide much of the humor. For example, when Gid's father discusses the nature of love with him, he tells him that "a woman's love is like the morning dew, it's just as apt to settle on a horse turd as it is on a rose" (107).

Lon Tinkle in *The Dallas Morning News* ("Of Fate and Doom in Ranch Country") pointed out the similarity between McMurtry's first two novels:

> "Leaving Cheyenne" is almost a repeat of the first novel. There is the same "father image," nobly but harshly upright, unaware of the crippling limitations of his simplified wisdom; there is the same "brotherly" rivalry, and love-hate relationship between the two principal male characters; there is the same all purpose woman: cook, slave, mother-substitute, Maya of desires, Eternal Eve whose generosity of love and body is fatally indiscriminate. (24)

Further, Tinkle noted that despite "his great gifts, McMurtry here, it seems to us, deploys his imaginative vision without discipline and willfully. Thus, he has created effects but not people." Tinkle was especially bothered by the scene in which Molly's drunken father forces her to disrobe so her brother Richard can learn the facts of life by examining her anatomy. Tinkle found the scene "a near cartoon strip of Erskine Caldwell's *Tobacco Road* . . . neither humanly plausible nor dramatically meaningful."

But many readers are still taken by it. A. C. Greene lists it among the fifty best Texas books. Like *Horseman, Pass By*, *Leaving Cheyenne* looks to rural Texas in the early twentieth century. Its elegiac tone is stronger than the previous novel, but it also dramatizes a world of failed expectations, taking the desire for and denial of a fully reciprocated relationship as symbolic of the pursuit of a primitivist ideal. Unrequited love, impermanence, initiation, aging and loss, generational conflict—these are all important themes that return as well in the next novel, but the nostalgic tone slips to a secondary role.

The Last Picture Show (1966)

The Last Picture Show, McMurtry's third novel, was published in 1966, and its tone of satire and parody suggests the new direction that McMurtry was about to take toward his blood's country. McMurtry later said that it was "dashed off . . . in a fit of pique at my hometown" (*Film Flam* 18). But he also noted that it included his usual ambivalence: "The novel was a mixture of modes and motives. A certain amount of affection struggled in it, and a certain amount of genuine ha-

tred. Affection lost, and the predominant tone of the
novel is rather harshly satiric" (121). With a heavy dose
of sarcasm, McMurtry dedicates *The Last Picture Show*
"lovingly to my hometown," and its almost cartoon figures indicate the depth of his growing resentment of
the redneck world in which he grew up. Some of the
characters' names—the gas truck owner named Fred
Fartley, and Sonny's girlfriend with the boring breasts,
Charlene Duggs—reduce them to cardboard thinness.
And it is in *Picture Show* that McMurtry develops what
has now become a widely-held stereotype of rural Texas
boys: that they spend an inordinate amount of time examining the sexual attractions of sheep and heifers.

Like the other Thalia novels, it dramatizes the twi-
light period when the last vestiges of the frontier were
slipping away from the small Panhandle town in the
1950s. It also illustrates the growing anti-Texan attitude that was beginning to sweep Texas intellectuals
in the mid-1960s as they watched LBJ bare his scar
and drive the country deeper and deeper into Vietnam.
McMurtry directly questions the western primitivistic
myth that living with nature in the open country creates full human beings.

Unlike the first two novels told by a first person
narrator, *The Last Picture Show* uses an omniscient
narrator. Since this novel is primarily satire, it requires
an overriding consciousness to comment on the foibles
of those it skewers. The story is told primarily from

Sonny Crawford's point of view as he approaches high school graduation while playing on Thalia's losing football team, working at Sam the Lion's pool hall, sharing the pickup with Duane Moore, and engaging in the usual high school pranks. The narrator's tone is at once bored and scathing, taking a position above the silliness of the small-town boors and hypocrites that he has set out to expose. The narrator's comments about bestiality in small-town Texas (a section McMurtry liked so much that he repeated it in *In a Narrow Grave*), provide a good example of the condescending tone:

> The prospect of copulation with a blind heifer excited the younger boys almost to frenzy, but Duane and Sonny, being seniors, gave only tacit approval. They regarded such goings-on without distaste, but were no longer as rabid about animals as they had been. Sensible youths, growing up in Thalia, soon learned to make do with what there was, and in the course of their adolescence both boys had frequently had recourse to bovine outlets. At that they were considered overfastidious by the farm youth of the area, who thought only dandies restricted themselves to cows and heifers. The farm kids did it with cows, mares, sheep, dogs, and whatever else they could catch. There were reports that a boy from Scotland did it

with domesticated geese, but no one had ever
actually witnessed it. It was common knowledge that the reason boys from the dairy
farming communities were so reluctant to come
out for football was because it put them home
too late for the milking and caused them to
miss regular connection with their milk cows.
(84, *In a Narrow Grave* 66)

The novel's relentless emphasis on sex—from this
discussion of bestiality to Billy's sexual initiation with
a local whore, to Jacy's varied couplings with Duane,
Sonny, Abilene, and Bobby Sheen, the worldly, rich boy
from Wichita Falls who is known for his nude swimming parties—produced a great deal of the early
comments about the book. Elroy Bode, reviewing in *The
Texas Observer*, tired of the theme, stating that "*artisti-
cally* the book is less effective than it could be because
the sexual urge, the sexual entanglement, the sexual
act and apparatus are dealt with so relentlessly; so con-
tinuously, that the reader almost gets to the point of
not believing that the events are really happening" (17).

But Lon Tinkle, anticipating this objection, de-
fended McMurtry in *The Dallas Morning News* :

Many readers will find several scenes most
unseemly, but they are legitimately detailed
by the author to reinforce his vision, or a view,

that in Thalia there are no adequate values to
defeat herd vulgarity and ignorance. Life does
go on, pathetically at a limp.

Thus, McMurtry's work stands in the van-
guard of the new critical spirit animating Texas
fiction, as exposure of personalities limited by
a peculiar provincial environment. (2G)

Similarly, W. T. Jack, in *The New York Times Book
Review*, noted that "McMurtry takes his characters on
a trip from onanism to prostitution, with a stop at every
station in between," and responded: "Offensive?
Miraculously, no. McMurtry is an alchemist who
converts the basest materials to gold. The sexual
encounters are sad, funny, touching, sometimes
horrifying, but always honest, always human" (69).

The novel's structure, as befits its satire, is loose
and episodic, but McMurtry uses varying structural
devices to provide organization. At one level, as Kenneth
Davis has noted, the novel focuses on Sonny Crawford's
growing awareness and is thus a novel of initiation
arising from the deaths of Sam the Lion and Billy. Since
the real subject of the novel is the town itself rather
than just Sonny, other elements are important,
particularly the loss of significant values. In this light,
the major structural device is Sam the Lion's death as
the novel leads up to and away from the loss of the
character whose dignity and values provide a center.

Sam the Lion, owner of the pool hall and picture show, is the most admirable character, and his past experience mirrors Texas history. Rancher, oilfield worker, and automobile dealer, Sam, who lost his own sons, takes responsibility for the retarded boy Billy, as well as the essentially fatherless Sonny and Duane.

Primarily, *The Last Picture Show* concentrates on character more than plot. Almost all of the characters, even the undeveloped, stock ones, allow the satirist to extend his purpose in various ways. Thinner characters take the most derisive shots, such as Thalia's football coach, Herman Popper. The coach, who also teaches high school civics, is portrayed as a stupid, incompetent teacher; a cuckolded husband; and ultimately a latent homosexual who masks his own sexual inadequacy with an overly macho facade. He also uses—in Joseph McCarthy fashion—an unfounded assertion of homosexuality to ruin the career of the one good teacher at Thalia High, John Cecil, the English teacher. Similarly flat characters are the town minister, Brother Blanton, and his mousy, troubled son, Joe Bob, who provide the vehicle for McMurtry to mock the hypocrisy of restrictive and narrow religious fundamentalism through a subplot in which Joe Bob kidnaps a young girl to avoid having to preach at a revival.

Abilene, the pool hustler/oilfield worker who is Lois Farrow's lover and who seduces Jacy on a pool table, represents, like the amoral Hud, the ruthless generation of Texans who inherited frontier values but no open landscape on which to exercise those values. Abilene exudes self-confidence with women, at the pool table, and driving his souped-up Mercury. Selfishly pragmatic, Abilene is a survivor and is presented by the omniscient narrator with begrudging admiration.

Billy is another primarily symbolic character. In a novel exposing how rural Texas has been twisted by anti-intellectualism and hypocrisy and how ignorance thwarts innocence, Billy becomes the ultimate representative of perennial innocence. Under Sam the Lion's protection, Billy reaches a level he can maintain, but without Sam, Billy becomes vulnerable. In an irony comparable to Jack Burns's being run over by a truck carrying toilets in Edward Abbey's *The Brave Cowboy*, Billy is killed by a cattle truck as he routinely sweeps the street in front of the pool hall.

The women characters also vary from essentially flat characters to more fully developed ones. Several, such as Sonny's girlfriend, Charlene Duggs, and Penny, the hypocritical daytime waitress at the cafe, are flimsy. Although Jacy Farrow receives significant emphasis, she never rises above an almost mindless selfishness, concerned only with being the center of attention. But Genevieve, the night waitress, provides one of the few positive female figures. She, like Halmea from *Horseman, Pass By*, offers the boys both motherly advice and sexual fantasies.

Lois Farrow, Jacy's mother, becomes more complex and ambivalent than most of the other characters. On the one hand, McMurtry portrays her negatively as one of the most bored of the new rich in Thalia, diverting herself with alcohol, sexual dallyings with Abilene and a seduction of Sonny, and with orchestrating her daughter's social climbing. On the other, when we learn that Lois was Sam the Lion's lover in those long-ago swimming trysts at the horse tank, she becomes another example of thwarted possibility, especially when Sam says, "Being crazy about a woman like her is always the thing to do" (124). Sam and Lois's nude swimming contrasts with the vapid gatherings in Bobby Sheen's pool in Wichita Falls. And her advice to Jacy that "life is very monotonous" suggests that she is more tragic than reprehensible.

The most fully developed female character is Ruth Popper, the coach's wife, who in the course of her affair with Sonny blossoms into a full human being. Her growing sexuality, demonstrated by her becoming orgasmic, not only with Sonny but—to her shock—with the lumbering coach as well, is the first indication of her development. But her reaction to Sonny's adolescent decision to drop her in favor of Jacy, enables Ruth to become a fully-developed character who suffers and grows. When Sonny comes to her at the end of the novel—bereft of Duane, Jacy, and Billy—Ruth first attacks him for abandoning her and Billy. But the novel ends with her decision to forgive him, saying "Honey, never you mind" (220).

The novel's images reflect its themes and are reminiscent of some of the other Thalia novels: both purposeless traveling and the closing picture show, similar to Homer Bannon's longhorns and Molly Taylor's sons, are images of impermanence and loss; and McMurtry again uses lost body parts and lost abilities. When Sonny takes Ruth to the doctor about a tumor in her breast that must be removed, he sits next to a man who had "his voicebox taken out and a little screen where it ought to be" (45). And Sonny loses most of his sight in one eye after he and Duane fight.

Ruth's changing character indicates that the book moves beyond simply being a satirical attack on small-town life. Raymond Neinstein in *The Ghost Country* summarizes the overall impact of the book:

> It is about the disappearance of the land as a force of stability and tradition in people's lives, and the consequences of that disappearance. It is about the disappearance of the rituals of inheritance; about the transformation of the cowboy into a pool-playing stud with a fast car; about the transformation of outdoor space, with all its erotic energies, into interior space, mechanical, limited, and rootless; about the transformation of the west into images of it-

self, western movies and country and western songs. It is about the problem of how to write a novel about Texas without writing about cowboys and ranchers and the land. It is an attempt to deal with a place's loss of its only coherent tradition without directly addressing itself, in terms of its subject matter, to that question, but rather presenting it dramatically through pairs of images. Consider Sam the Lion's memory of swimming naked with Lois Farrow twenty years before at a lake, and the teenage naked swimming orgies that go on in the basement of a twenty-room mansion in Wichita Falls. (24)

In *The Last Picture Show* McMurtry's ambivalence about Texas swings emphatically toward the negative side of the ledger. The small-mindedness, boredom, pettiness, and hypocrisy of small-town life almost blot out the positive memories of Sam the Lion. In McMurtry's next book, he steps out from behind the novelist's mask and presents his attitudes toward Texas in his own persona.

In a Narrow Grave: Essays on Texas (1968)

Throughout his career McMurtry has consistently written nonfiction articles for various publications, from student essays on the Beat Generation in 1960 to an analysis of the Branch Davidian disaster in Waco, Texas in 1993. The fictional satire of *The Last Picture Show* was followed by a sometimes bitter, goodbye-to-all-that attitude in his first collection of essays, *In a Narrow Grave*, published by Bill Wittliff's Encino Press in 1968 during Lyndon Johnson's presidency, when being Texan was not chic among intellectuals. The book is usually described as primarily a collection of essays written for other publications. But an examination of the typescript, now in the Southwestern Writers Collection at Southwest Texas State University, reveals that McMurtry saw it as a unified collection. Indeed, the initial title "The Cowboy's Lament: An Essay on Texas," presented it as a single essay with a distinct purpose. In fact, several of the chapter titles were changed from the typescript. "Eros in Archer County" was originally "Salty Dogs—or Eros in Archer County," and "A Handful of Roses" was called "City Lights and City Limits" in typescript.

In a Narrow Grave struck at many things southwestern, such as small towns where "many Texans . . . live and die in woeful ignorance," and at the Big Three, the sacred old bulls of Texas literature, J. Frank Dobie, Roy Bedichek, and Walter Prescott Webb, immortalized in a sculpture along Barton Creek in Austin in 1994. The collection moved him from being simply an important young novelist to *enfant terrible*, angry young man, young Turk, and wise commentator on all things Texan.

But the persona McMurtry adopts in *In a Narrow Grave* is not simply embittered and hateful toward his home state; he is also melancholy, sadly aware of the strengths and weaknesses of the country in which he had then lived for over thirty-two years. And it is the voice of this ambivalent McMurtry which is most interesting to hear a quarter of a century later.

These essays cover a variety of subjects, from the making of *Hud* and western films to a car trip across Texas, an old Fiddler's reunion, Texas cities, the Astrodome, sexual mores and fears of Texans, the Big Three of Texas letters, and to the McMurtry family. Some of these essays are dated, such as the discussion of the Astrodome, now that many cities throughout America have domed stadia. Others, such as "The Old Soldier's Joy" about a trip to the Old Fiddler's reunion in Athens, is maddeningly condescending. But even the weakest contain important and provocative statements.

Several of the essays are meaningful not only for what they reveal about the novelist, but they also reach into the significant depths of southwestern life. The most consequential essays are the introductory "The God Abandons Texas," one on Texas writers, "Southwestern Literature?", and "Take My Saddle from the Wall," which remains a stunning achievement and as moving a non-fiction piece as any of the novels. As he has often done, McMurtry looked to cowboy songs for a suggestive title for the collection. In this case, it comes from "The Dying Cowboy," used as an epigraph:

> By my father's grave there let me be,
> And bury me not on the lone prairie.
>
> "Oh, bury me no—" And his voice failed there.
> But we took no heed of his dying prayer;
> In a narrow grave just six by three
> We buried him there on the lone prairie. . . .

Since it both laments the passing cowboy and points to the narrow restrictiveness that McMurtry faced as a regional Texas novelist, the title reveals as much about McMurtry's ambivalence as does the content.

In "The God Abandons Texas," McMurtry establishes the image of the passing cowboy god as the most significant southwestern archetype of the twentieth century and arguably the most important image in America, and he points to the transition from the country world of the cowboy to the city as the most important moment for writers of his generation:

> The state is at that stage of metamorphosis when it is fertile with conflict, when rural and soil traditions are competing most desperately with urban traditions—competing for the

allegiance of the young. The city will win, of
course, but its victory won't be cheap—the
country traditions were very strong. As the
cowboys gradually leave the range and learn
to accommodate themselves to the suburbs,
defeats that are tragic in quality must occur
and may be recorded. (xx–xi)

And he notes that it is this "movement, from country to
subdivision, homeplace to metropolis, that gives life in
present-day Texas its passion. Or if not its passion, its
strong, peculiar mixture of passions, part spurious and
part genuine, part ridiculous and part tragic." He emphasizes that the "transition that is taking place is very
difficult, and the situations it creates are very intense.
Living here consciously uses a great deal of one's blood;
it involves one at once in a birth, a death, and a bitter
love affair" (xiii). These conflicted feelings, of course,
are at the heart of McMurtry's life and work.

The essay "Southwestern Literature?" is also
significant because it examines the issues that are
important to southwestern literature and because it
suggests how McMurtry suffered from what Harold
Bloom calls "the anxiety of influence." Bloom examines
the relationship between writers and concludes that
younger writers with strong predecessors feel "anxiety,"
dread, or guilt about the power of the older writer's
influence. To counter these feelings, young writers must

reject the older writer's influence through what Bloom calls "poetic misprision," a deliberate misreading of the older writer "to clear the imaginative space for himself" (5). Although Bloom applies his theory to poetry, its implication for prose is equally clear:

> Poetic Influence—when it involves two strong, authentic poets—always proceeds by a misreading of the prior poet, an act of creative correction that is actually and necessarily a misinterpretation, the history of fruitful poetic influence, which is to say the main tradition of western poetry since the Renaissance, is a history of anxiety and self-saving caricature, of distortion, of perverse, willful revisionism without which modern poetry as such could not exist. (30)

Just such a misreading seems to be involved in McMurtry's attack on the older generation of Texas writers. When McMurtry imputes to them a sentimental, romantic, and inadequate vision of the Southwest's violent, racist, and sexually active history, he identifies the areas into which he will travel. According to Bloom, young poets or fiction writers misread their most significant influences to open territory for their own work. While McMurtry applies the hard-minded intellectual criticism he says is often missing in analyses of Texas literature, his discussion in several ways demonstrates his misreadings or misrepresentations.

One important misrepresentation concerns McMurtry's comments about nature. As he "makes his space" by pointing out the contrast between his generation of writers and the strong forbears, he uses their differing attitudes toward nature, noting that for Dobie, Bedichek, and Webb, nature was "the real" (36); they "hued" to it and made a "fetish" of it. McMurtry then asserts that for his generation of writers and "for the generations that follow," he doubts that they "could scrape up enough nature-lore . . . to organize a decent picnic" (36). In reality, of course, nature has been and continues to be a fundamental aspect of McMurtry's work, and the generation of Texas writers at work at the end of the century places as much, if not more, emphasis on nature as the Big Three did. Texas writers such as John Graves, Stephen Harrigan, Rick Bass, Sarah Bird, Robert Flynn, Rolando Hinojosa, Clay Reynolds, Cormac McCarthy, Walt McDonald, Naomi Nye, and Lawrence Wright join other southwestern writers such as Edward Abbey, Gary Paul Nabhan, Rudolfo Anaya, John Nichols, Frederick Turner, Terry Tempest Williams, and numerous others who value nature. McMurtry confuses an appreciation of nature with sentimentalizing the past, what he disparagingly calls practicing "symbolic frontiersmanship" (43).

As a result, McMurtry overstates the weaknesses

of the Big Three, especially in his attack on Webb. McMurtry focuses his attack on Webb's 1935 book *The Texas Rangers*, a fat and easy target. But McMurtry almost ignores both *The Great Plains* and *The Great Frontier*, Webb's most important contributions to western historiography. In fact, as Howard Lamar in "Regionalism and the Broad Methodological Problem" notes, a recent survey of American historians pointed to *The Great Plains* as the most influential book to shape their concept of the West.

Twenty-two years after his initial attack, in a 1990 review of books by "New Western historians," McMurtry acknowledged Webb's importance: "Webb, the dryland farmer turned historian, seems to me still the thinker who made the most fruitful use of Turner's frontier thesis. He was one of the first to expand it, to look at European conquest as a whole in terms the possibilities and the limitations of frontiers. . ." (35). Indeed, even new western historians that McMurtry labels proponents of "Failure Studies," such as Patricia Limerick, owe a great deal to Webb. As Leticia Gárza-Falcon-Sánchez makes clear in a soon-to-be-published dissertation, "The Chicano/a Literary Response to the Rhetoric of Dominance," *The Great Plains* is certainly open to criticism. But by focusing on Webb's hero worship of the Rangers, McMurtry distorts the record.

His attack on Dobie is also interesting, not only because he took on the then most venerated figure on the Texas scene, but because of how he attacks Dobie for traits his own work demonstrates—ambivalence, symbolic frontiersmanship, and distrusting the imagination. Dobie illustrated, McMurtry concludes, first an "ambivalence toward literary activity," second an "ambivalence about the intellectual life" by consistently praising the value of nature as a teacher, and finally "a strong uncertainty about the imagination" (45) that led him to merely embroider previous tales rather than create new ones from whole cloth. In his own work, of course, McMurtry has practiced what he disparagingly calls "symbolic frontiersmanship," looking back at frontier times, not only in his first three novels but throughout his career. And much of his work is not merely the product of an unfettered imagination. Rather, he has reconfigured stories and tales about family members, Archer City inhabitants, and legendary Texans such as Old Man Goodnight and Teddy Blue, and repackaged them in his fiction.

"Take My Saddle from the Wall: A Valediction" is all the more interesting in this light because McMurtry reveals many of the family anecdotes that have become part of his fictional landscape, such as the spilled molasses story and the story of Uncle Johnny's spurs, both of which he fictionalized in *Leaving Cheyenne*. He uses the McMurtry family history to examine the central elements of cowboy life that have often been central to his fiction: the myth of the cowboy; the cowboy's contempt for the farmer; the difference between ranching and cowboying; the role of nature; the cowboy's mixed attitudes toward women who were at once romanticized and ignored; and the cowboy's value system that prized violence, strength, hard work, and humor but devalued tolerance and mercy.

The most significant aspect of the essay concerns its emphasis on ambivalence. There McMurtry states directly that his treatment of Texas is inconsistent, "a contradiction of attraction" that produces ambivalence "as deep as the bone." He notes how, in writing this concluding essay with its focus on his family, he has infused into his attack on Texas his own deep feelings about his family:

> I realize that in closing with the McMurtrys I may only succeed in twisting a final, awkward knot into this uneven braid, for they bespeak the region—indeed, are eloquent of it—and I am quite as often split in my feelings about them as I am in my feelings about Texas. They pertain, of course, both to the Old Texas and the New, but I choose them here particularly because of another pertinence. All of them gave such religious allegiance as they had to give to that god I mentioned in my introduction: the god whose principal myth was the myth of the Cowboy,

the ground of whose divinity was the Range.
They were many things, the McMurtrys, but
to themselves they were cowboys first and last,
and the rituals of that faith they strictly kept.
(142)

Even though he has attacked much of the legacy of
cowboy life in the book, it is clear that he still has a
strong, sentimental attachment to what cowboys
represented:

Now the god has departed, thousands of
old cowboys in his train. Among them went
most of the McMurtrys, and in a few more years
the tail-end of the train will pass from sight.
All of them lived to see the ideals of the faith
degenerate, the rituals fall from use, the principal myth become corrupt. In my youth, when
they were old men, I often heard them yearn
aloud for the days when the rituals had all their
power, when they themselves had enacted the
pure, the original myth, and I know that they
found it bitter to leave the land to which they
were always faithful to the strange and god-
less heirs that they had bred. I write of them
here not to pay them homage, for the kind of
homage I could pay they would neither want
nor understand; but as a gesture of recogni-

tion, a wave such as riders sometimes give one another as they start down opposite sides of a hill. The kind of recognition I would hope to achieve is a kind that kinsmen are so frequently only able to make in time of parting. (142–43)

With *In a Narrow Grave* McMurtry tipped his hat toward Old Texas, bade it a symbolic farewell, and signaled a major change for both himself and Texas literature. No longer would Texas writers be able to lope along writing nostalgic country-and-western literature uncritically rounding up the old themes. McMurtry presented himself as a literate, critical, and sophisticated reader and writer, setting the model for later writers to follow. It also indicated that he was ready to turn away from rural Texas, and his next group of novels moves to McMurtry's favorite city, Houston.

4

The Houston Trilogy

McMurtry's next three novels mark his transition from examining the effect of change on the frontier values of small towns to considering the difficult adaptation of the new urban West to the loss of those frontier values. In a review of *Streets of Laredo*, Don Graham calls the Houston trilogy "the end of the 'Old Texas,' and the beginning of a 'New (e)rotic Texas,'" (*Austin Chronicle* 22). McMurtry himself summarized the thematic changes:

> Obviously in the first three there's the large social action that I observed as I grew up, which was the move off the land toward the cities and the gradual disintegration of the rural way

of life in this part of Texas, and the small-town
way of life too. The first three books attacked
that theme from a country and small-town
perspective, and the next three attacked it from
the perspective of people who have left the
country and found themselves in the city, a sort
of transitional generation. I think that *Horseman, Leaving Cheyenne*, and *The Last Picture
Show* have a common concern. The next three
do too—*Moving On, All My Friends*, and *Terms
of Endearment*. (Bennett interview 27)

Despite McMurtry's avowed belief that he and other
Texas writers should mine urban territory, these three
novels do not abandon the rural Southwest. In fact,
McMurtry continues to demonstrate his contradiction
of attractions for both the Old and New Texas, since
each of the Houston novels contains elements of the
Old: *Moving On* shifts between its urban plot that concentrates on the marriage of Patsy and Jim Carpenter
and the rodeo world of Sonny Shanks; *All My Friends
Are Going to Be Strangers* moves from Danny Deck's
Houston to his Uncle L's Hacienda of the Bitter Waters; and *Terms of Endearment* introduces the rural
through Vernon Dalhart, who embodies some of the old
ways.

Still, Houston is the setting, and the main characters are urban. While the general critical reaction to

these three novels has been mixed, the Houston trilogy demonstrates McMurtry's seriousness as a writer because he stretched his subject matter and style and attempted to put into practice the carefully examined conclusions that he had articulated in his nonfiction. These novels are also connected by their varying emphases on literary and artistic performances as a satisfactory replacement for the physical products of the rural, cowboy world.

Moving On (1970)

Moving On is the first of the novels about an interrelated group of characters, and, although some readers find the title appropriate, it marked one of the rare times that McMurtry did not select his own title, nor did he begin the novel with a title in mind. He told Bennett that he is "very superstitious about titles. Until I get the title, I don't know what kind of book I am going to write" and then commented on the title for the first Houston novel:

> Every single one of my books except *Moving On* has been written for the title. *Moving On* was the only title I didn't choose; that book kept squirming out from under my titles. I wanted to call it *Patsy Carpenter*, and there was ample precedent for naming it after the central char-

acter. But the publisher didn't like it, and they moved publication up to spring, and somebody suggested *Moving On*. (22)

The novel concentrates on Patsy Carpenter, the slim, dark-haired twenty-five-year-old wife of Jim Carpenter, a wealthy, drifting young Dallasite. As the novel opens, Jim dabbles with being a photographer of rodeos, then becomes a graduate student in English at Rice, later works on movies first in Texas and then in Hollywood, and finally works for IBM in California. The novel revolves around three types of characters and settings: rural, rodeo types; urban sophisticates; and Hollywood characters who use the world of illusion to bridge the two worlds by leaving L.A. for rural settings and the rodeo as subjects of films. The major rodeo characters are Sonny Shanks, world champion cowboy, a seducer of women in his white hearse with sets of longhorns painted on it; Pete Tatum, aging rodeo clown, whose first wife became involved with Sonny; Boots, Pete's young fiancée, a barrel racer; and Peewee Rankin, a teenager trying to make it in rodeo, who later drives a train in a Houston park. The major rural character not associated with rodeo is Roger Wagonner, Jim's rancher uncle who leaves the Carpenters his Panhandle ranch after he dies. Many readers believe that the best parts of the book concern the rodeo people and Wagonner, who is reminiscent of McMurtry's Uncle

Johnny and his laconic Uncle Jeff Dobbs. In fact, some of the departure scenes here are as effective as the one about Uncle Johnny in "Take my Saddle from the Wall."

Among the urban characters, the most important are Emma and Flap Horton, the Carpenters' best friends in graduate school; Hank Malory, named for Hank Williams, a Vietnam veteran who becomes Patsy's quiet lover; Bill Duffin, a lecherous Rice professor, and his enervated wife Lee. The major bridging figure is Joe Percy, an aging screen writer. Eleanor Guthrie, Sonny's wealthy, older mistress, also bridges the two worlds. In the novel's last section, McMurtry introduces California characters when Patsy goes to Stanford to check on her doper sister, Miri, and meets Stone, her hostile African-American boyfriend, and Melissa Duffin—who is coincidentally the Duffin's daughter and also at Stanford.

Although McMurtry attempts to dramatize the schism between the Old and the New, the rural and the urban Texas that he had examined in *In a Narrow Grave*, some readers have found the two parts of the novel disconnected. Kerry Ahearn, for example, while noting the similarities between the two sections, discounts connections:

> It reads like two separate but interfused novels. The problem is that they make the same effect, have the same organization, and feature

the same cast of character types. Both halves
are dominated by predatory males: Sonny
Shanks, World Champion Cowboy, and William Duffin, English professor; both predators
have a woman "accomplice" to attract Jim and
reveal the instability of the Carpenter marriage
(Eleanor Guthrie, Shanks's wealthy mistress,
and Duffin's wife Lee); the rodeo and Houston
sections each feature a sweet but eccentric
married couple, the Tatums and the Hortons,
respectively, and a true regional clown, Peewee Rankin and Dixie McCormack. (*Taking
Stock* 218)

The critical response to *Moving On* was mixed, with
four repeated complaints: the novel is too long and clut-
tered with details; its episodic structure leaves it
unfocused; it is poorly written and badly proofread; its
point of view is inconsistent. Steve Barthelme voiced
most of these objections in a *Texas Observer* review,
saying that the book was "quite simply ugly and dull
and occasionally false." Barthelme pointed to clichés,
contradictions, and awkward syntax constructions that
he thought made it ugly. In an unusual move for a writer
who often disowns novels once they are written,
McMurtry wrote a spirited, point-by-point defense of
the novel and sent it to the *Texas Observer*. McMurtry
accepted Barthelme's charges that he had not written

believable dialogue for Stone, the African-American radical, and that he had been contradictory about how the characters referred to Roger Wagonner. But he disputed the charge of formlessness, asserting: "I am indifferent to structure, but I find texture absorbing," and he struck hard against the complaint about the book's length:

> It is absurd to chide the author of a long novel for a lack of interest in economy. If economy interested me I would have written a short book. In fact I find economy a fucking bore, whether it be literary, sexual, or monetary. It bespeaks the tight-ass, and while it may be a virtue in homeowners and a word beloved of pedagogues, but it's hardly the mistress for a novelist. (23)

Unconvinced, Ahearn repeated some of the same charges in a later article, saying that "McMurtry's penchant for repetition infects his style at the most basic level" and then provided a list:

> a lecture by a famous lecturer,
> Jim had to teach a class for a friend who
>   taught a class,
> wash the pan of oatmeal before the oatmeal
>   stiffened,

to wipe up spit-ups,
sipped sly sips,
a huge pile of papers and magazines piled . . .
neither came or even came close to coming,
he began to drive in his memory all the drives
he had driven with Patsy (*Taking Stock* 221–22)

The charges about the novel's lack of structure highlight the structural devices that McMurtry uses: the
purposeless journey and the shifts from the rural/ro-
deo world to urban Texas and to the California world of
Hollywood and hippies. As he often does, McMurtry
breaks the novel into parts and chapters—four separate "books" ("The Beginning of the Evening," "Houston,
Houston, Houston," "Sleeping Around," "Summer's
Lease") with twenty chapters each.

Although several of the early reviewers responded
negatively to the novel, perhaps because it offered such
a change of pace, the novel has gained stature with the
passage of time. In a 1993 review of *Streets of Laredo*,
Don Graham looked back at it and concluded: "But even
though *Moving On* is interminable and tedious in many
places, it's the closest anyone in Texas has come to doing a Trollope number about the petty miseries of
graduate student life, and for some readers, like myself, it's strangely addictive" (*Austin Chronicle* 22).

Perhaps the most interesting aspect of reading
Moving On twenty-five years later concerns the novel's

subtle but vivid emphasis on its time. It captures the
importance of Vietnam to the generation of Texans affected most directly by the war. In this way, *Moving
On*, as *The Great Gatsby* did for its generation, portrays a time and a mood. Although Vietnam is not in
the foreground, it and the counterculture it spawned
hover behind the characters as the novel dramatizes
how the 1960s marked the irrevocable move in America
toward cynicism and questioning of traditional values.
For example, as Part One ends and Patsy and Jim leave
the rodeo world to return to Houston, they drive through
Mineral Wells, then the home of Fort Wolters (a major
training center for helicopter pilots going to Vietnam),
and see "a swarm of helicopters . . . buzzing over the
fields, the pastures, and the low hills like swarms of
giant dragonflies." Stopping at a filling station, they
learn from the attendant that they are passing by the
"[b]iggest trainin' center going" (194–95).

Another 1960s emphasis stems from McMurtry's
concern with sexual themes. Here he dramatizes the
sexual revolution to highlight the characters' searching and rootlessness and their attempt to find something
to replace the values of the passing rural world. Ahearn
points out that all of the "relationships in the novel are
defined sexually; every character either has or most obviously does not have a sexual problem. . . . [T]he people in
Houston, like their country counterparts, make physical

coupling a refuge, acting out their frustrations, illustrating the emptiness of their lives" (*Taking Stock* 220).

If sex does not provide enough relief from their lives, neither does literature. Because some of McMurtry's characters are graduate students in English, he can fill the book with literary references. As the novel begins, Patsy is reading *Catch-22*. The novel also mentions *One Flew Over the Cuckoo's Nest*, *Candy*, *The Magic Christian*, *After Strange Gods*, *The House of Fame*, *Love Among the Cannibals*, *The Faerie Queen*, *The Canterbury Tales*, *The Golden Bough*, *The Philosophy of Literary Form*, *Tristram Shandy*, and others. Hank Malory's name suggests Sir Thomas Malory's *Le morte D'Arthur*, a work about an adulterous relationship in sharp contrast to the Patsy-Jim-Hank triangle. The numerous literary references intertexualize the novel, indicate McMurtry's continuing interest in the contrast between the worlds of hard reality and illusion, and presage a central theme in the next novel: his growing ambivalence about the literary life.

All My Friends Are Going to Be Strangers (1970)

The actions of *All My Friends Are Going to Be Strangers* occur in the early 1960s before the time frame in *Moving On*, where Danny Deck is mentioned briefly. With Danny, the student-writer main character,

McMurtry created his most consistent alter ego. Discussing Danny, McMurtry told Peavy:

> Danny, as far as I'm concerned, is the first interesting young male I've done—if he is interesting at all. He's interesting to me. All the rest have been shadow figures—insubstantial, empty, just anonymous young males, really, not at all as vivid as the women. I think this is because I'm not interested in young men; I never have been. Insofar as I have been interested in men at all I'm interested in old men, like Sam and Roger, or eccentrics, like the screen writer and waifs, like Pee Wee, but I am really not interested in young men, and they are almost without exception my dullest and least vivid characters. If there is an exception it's Danny, he's more interesting than the young men in *The Last Picture Show* or *Horseman* or *Moving On*. (78)

By making Danny a young Texas writer with a biography similar to his own, McMurtry brings to the forefront his own ambivalence about literary and artistic production as a valuable alternative to cowboying and trail driving. In this portrait of the artist as a young "frontier genius" (53) torn in various directions, the title introduces the first of a series of oppositions around which the plot revolves: friendship/estrangement, change/stability, illusion/reality, taking/giving, leaving/ returning, writing/doing, mental/physical, rural/urban, and others. The title of Danny Deck's first novel, *The Restless Grass*, also reflects a contradictory or oxymoronic emphasis on opposing ideas, since grass is firmly grounded, seemingly incapable of restlessness.

McMurtry mentioned his own ambivalence about writing in different articles and interviews during the time. He told Si Dunn: "Being a writer sooner or later causes you to reflect on what you are doing and creates a kind of ambivalence. You get to wondering what it [writing] is doing to you, sitting in a corner with a machine, projecting your emotions [through characters on paper]" (Dunn 13). And in his *Atlantic* article McMurtry labels writing an act of exploitation: "[Novelists] exploit a given region, suck what thematic riches they can from it, and then, if they are able, move on to whatever regions promise yet more riches. I was halfway through my sixth Texas novel when I suddenly began to notice that where place was concerned, I was sucking air" (34).

A similar ambivalence about writing as exploitative is introduced subtly early in the novel. As the novel opens, Danny has driven from Houston to Austin to eat Mexican food, but he ends up at a party thrown by Godwin Lloyd-Jons, a doper-bisexual-profligate sociology professor at the University of Texas. There he falls in love with Sally, Godwin's latest young student "fuckist," and takes her away. Godwin questions the value of writing by charging that he hates Danny and all writers: "They ought to be imprisoned. They're all thieves" (11). Later when Godwin learns that Danny has sold his first novel, he says, "You sold your book. Now you have a license to steal any bloody thing you happen to want" (53). And then later Godwin tells him, "There are no writers in heaven, you know. They don't even know how to enjoy the bloody earth" (81). Still later when Jill Peel, the artist who lives with Danny in California, tells him a story about a baby bed passed from child to child, Danny decides to "steal it. . . . It seemed to [him] the perfect subject—a picaresque novel with a baby bed as hero" (142). Danny immediately begins writing the novel and titles it "The Man Who Never Learned."

Through these repeated references to writing as theft, the novel questions the authenticity of literary performance, and Danny questions the value of his work. For example, when Danny returns to Houston with Sally, he questions his own worth ("I lived in constant doubt about myself, and never expected anything I did to come out right" [30]). Then, to gain a sense of control over his circumstances, Danny, like Lonnie Bannon who goes out to shoot frogs to prove his mastery over nature, takes a .22 and goes out into the yard and shoots a squirrel:

I had a little single-shot .22—it had been the only gun I could afford all through my childhood, when hunting had been an obsession with me. . . . All the time I was writing my novel I could see the squirrels out the window and I kept wanting to go out and shoot one. Sometimes in the morning, before I started writing, I would sit with the .22 and shoot eight or ten squirrels in my imagination, always aiming at the ones on the highest branches. That morning in a moment of complete happiness, I had actually shot one. (16)

This scene emphasizes the writer's desire for connection with and control over the physical world. When it is coupled with Danny's part-time job as a termite exterminator, both details heighten McMurtry's concern for a writer's inevitable estrangement from physical contact with the external world: from nature, from friends, from tangible production.

Danny's doubt about the value of his writing increases as his estrangement increases. To emphasize the movement, the novel uses the separation/return/final departure structural pattern, suggesting the paradigm followed by mythic heroes described by such writers as Lord Raglan, Northrop Frye, and Joseph Campbell. Although in *Film Flam* McMurtry commented on Frye, Lord Raglan, and Will Wright's analysis of mythic patterns in western movies, *Sixguns and Society*, and is clearly aware of mythic structure, he has never read Campbell. Campbell offers the best summary of the basic pattern in *The Hero with a Thousand Faces*. According to Campbell, the mythological hero leaves a lowly home and sets out on an adventure. Encountering a shadowy figure who guards the next passage, the hero either defeats or joins the figure and enters the kingdom of the dark alive, or is killed and descends in death through either dismemberment or crucifixion. In the underworld, the hero encounters strange forces that may threaten or help him. Campbell continues:

> When he arrives at the nadir of the mythological round, he undergoes a supreme ordeal and gains his reward. The triumph may be represented as the hero's sexual union with the goddess-mother of the world (sacred marriage), his recognition by the father-creator (father atonement), his own divinization (apotheosis), or again—if the powers have remained unfriendly to him—his theft of the boon he came to gain (bride-theft, fire-theft); intrinsically it is an expansion of consciousness and therewith of being (illumination, transfiguration, freedom). The final work is that of the return. If the powers have blessed the hero, he now sets

forth under their protection (emissary); if not, he flees and is pursued (transformation flight, obstacle flight). At the return threshold the transcendental powers must remain behind; the hero re-emerges from the kingdom of dread (return, resurrection). The boon that he brings restores the world (elixir). (246)

The novel's eighteen-chapter structure reflects the escape-return-escape pattern. At the end of Chapter Six, Danny, Sally, and Godwin take off from Houston to leave for the West where Danny will work to extend his writing career. In chapter twelve, Danny returns to Texas, and in chapter eighteen he again escapes in an ambiguous conclusion. McMurtry makes his emphasis on myth explicit at the end of chapter twelve when Danny drives through a fog in the Salinas Valley and recalls an argument about

Odysseus' visit to the underworld, the day we had had the picnic. They had argued about the spirits that came out of the fog, and I had gone right home and read the chapter they had argued about. The spirits came out of the fog and approached the pool of blood at Odysseus' feet and he kept them back with his sword. It seemed to me that I was in such a fog. (174)

He examines the experience, wondering if it will help
his writing: "If I went and found a heifer and slaugh-
tered it and got a club to fight the spirits back with
perhaps the spirits would come. I could talk with
Granny and Old Man Goodnight and ask them if I had
their stories right." The underworld journey traditionally leads the mythic hero to return with a heightened
sense of awareness, now capable of performing a heroic
act. But Danny's is primarily an ironic journey; he is
now ready to return to Texas carrying his manuscript,
"The Man Who Never Learned."

Throughout the novel McMurtry uses a number of
related symbolic scenes, set black humor pieces that
flicker with satire, several of which stress the literary
theme. In Houston, for example, Danny attends a party
thrown by an effete professor, Razzy Hutton. Among
the guests are three lesbians who talk about D. H.
Lawrence, one of whom had once measured the penis
of Tony Luhan's brother. Danny is treated as a distinct
outsider, a clod with body odor. This scene is mirrored
at a Stanford party Danny attends in the California
section where he meets famous writers and goes to bed
with Renata Morris. While the spirit of Lawrence hov-
ers over the first party, Hemingway's ghost slips in with
the allusion to Renata, Colonel Cantwell's beautiful
lover in *Across the River and into the Trees*. Like
Hemingway, famous for lost manuscripts, Danny will
lose his manuscript as well. Also like Hemingway, who

often wrote about his life, McMurtry mines his own experiences, "sucking the life" out of his own background in this novel that doubts the literary enterprise.

Another symbolic scene during the California section occurs when Danny meets Leon O'Reilly, the producer making a movie of Danny's novel. To symbolize the cold, voracious Hollywood world, McMurtry has O'Reilly take Danny to eat at Thor's, a restaurant with ice walls. O'Reilly then takes Danny to see his twenty-two pound rat.

McMurtry brings in his own experiences at Stanford, having Danny visit Perry Lane, the notorious street where Kesey lived when he was first experimenting with LSD while writing *One Flew Over the Cuckoo's Nest*. Wryly, McMurtry has Danny search unsuccessfully for a Fort Worth writer called Teddy Blue.

The symbolic scene that dramatizes McMurtry's concern for the split between Old and New Texas occurs on his return to Texas when he visits his Uncle L (Laredo), a ninety-two-year-old camel rancher whose experiences, like Thomas Berger's Jack Crabb in *Little Big Man*, reflect the history of the American West— Laredo fought with the Seventh Cavalry, was at Wounded Knee, was a Texas Ranger, fought with Pancho Villa and Emiliano Zapata (192), and now owns the Hacienda of the Bitter Waters near Van Horn, Texas. Unlike Homer Bannon, who would allow no holes

punched in his land, Uncle L has drilled holes throughout his property in preparation for fences he will never
finish. Danny thinks "that he dug the holes because he
hated the earth and wanted to get in as many licks at it
as he could, before he died" (180).

Seeing Uncle L's buffalo herd causes Danny to recall Old Man Goodnight, thinking perhaps of the story
he wanted to ask the old man's ghost about during his
symbolic underworld journey. It is the story of reservation Indians who came to beg a buffalo from Goodnight
so that they could perform a symbolic ceremony long
after the buffalo herds had disappeared. To Danny the
story is the "true end of the west" (191). Goodnight's
authentic human story stands in stark contrast to
McMurtry's ironic tale of Uncle L, an obvious cartoon
figure who reminds Danny of Yosemite Sam, and is an
ironic parody of the wise mentor the archetypal hero
usually meets on his journey to heroic knowledge.

To reinforce the parodic treatment of the mythic
hero in this scene, McMurtry refers repeatedly to Antonio, a Mexican worker who drops his pants and yellow
chaps when Danny first sees him, flings himself on a
mound of earth, and begins "to fuck it passionately"
(182), mocking the mythic hero's marriage with Mother
Earth. Before he left California, Danny's neighbor Wu
had told him: "Texas you are wanting. A mistress, wife—
many things for you to seek." With Antonio's humping

the earth, McMurtry burlesques Texas as symbolic mistress.

As he leaves Uncle L's, Danny christens his car "El Chevy" in honor of his uncle's favorite horse, El Caballo, now buried near the bitter water. Although now an apotheosis as "driver" and riding off into the sunrise, Danny takes no transcendent knowledge, nor does he leave with any redemptive "boon" or elixir with which to transform the world upon his return. Rather, the medicine Danny secrets in El Chevy is the large medicine ball he stole from Uncle L's exercise room (189).

Still, when Danny returns to Houston, he feels as though he has undergone another important change, moving from being a "real writer" to being an "author" (224), symbolized by the autograph party he is to attend. Ironically, his experience is accompanied by baptism, first when Jenny Salomea's husband douses Jenny and Danny with water while they make love and then by the rain storm he must slop through to get to Mr. Stay's bookstore. Throughout the novel, as Danny takes on new incarnations of "writer," the change is accompanied by water imagery—the flash flood he, Sally, and Godwin are caught in as they leave Texas, and the flowing waters of the Rio Grande as the novel ends. Now fully reincarnated as author, he employs the tools available to him when Sally's parents, the Bynums, attack him at the hospital where Sally had given birth to their child. He yells sexual obscenities at them, wielding his words as weapons and achieving what soon feels like a "cheap victory" (236) in this mock battle.

Feeling hollow, Danny turns to Emma Horton, whom he had considered his real friend before he began changing from potential to real writer to author. They make love briefly, but rather than serving to ground Danny in the physical, human world, it estranges him from Emma and Flap as Danny senses how he has betrayed his friends (240).

Taking leave of Houston, Danny heads to Roma, Texas, not for any connection to an authentic past but because *Viva Zapata* was filmed there. Uncle L's fruitless waiting for an illusory memory of Zapata is a debased version of historical meaning, and Danny meets another debased version of Old Texas history in the form of two Texas Rangers, E. Paul and Luther, who throw Danny into a prickly pear because they are offended by his long hair and insufficient masculinity.

Unlike Brer Rabbit, Danny does not extricate himself from the prickly pear easily. Words fail him with the Rangers, and when he gets to Roma still carrying his manuscript, he realizes the failure of language:

> I looked at my pages under the flashlight. They looked odd. Pages. Words. Black marks on paper. They didn't have eyes, or bodies. They weren't people. I don't know why I put marks

on paper. It was a dull thing to do. There must
be livelier things to do. I remembered the river
books I had read. There must be thousands of
rivers to see. Seeing the flowing of rivers could
be more interesting than making black marks
on paper. The marks didn't have faces, and I
had forgotten the faces that had been in my
mind when I wrote them. Jill had a face. Emma
had a face. My words didn't. They didn't flow
like rivers, either. They had no little towns on
their banks, little towns full of whores, people,
goats. I didn't know what I was doing, spend-
ing so much time with paper .... What a waste
of me. (278)

Recalling how he had tried to drown Sally by shov-
ing her into a bathtub and suggesting the conflict among
Texas/love/writing, Danny drowns his manuscript in the
Rio Grande, his head filled with images of Gary Cooper
in underwater combat with a Seminole chief in *Distant
Drums*. He acknowledges the ambiguous borderland that
has become his real home: "It was always a borderland
I had lived on . . . a thin little strip between the country
of the normal and the country of the strange. Perhaps
my true country was the borderland, anyway" (285).

Perhaps he has become a better critic because while
he drowns what sounds like a silly novel about a baby
bed, he saves the stories of Granny Deck and Old Man

Goodnight and sends them to Emma and then ends his
story ambiguously standing in the river. The conclusion led many to believe that Danny had committed
suicide. But in a novel about symbolic deaths and re-
births, McMurtry has left him to be reincarnated in a
sequel, *Some Can Whistle*. Danny Deck, like other
youthful McMurtry heroes, has achieved anti-initiation,
crossing no significant threshold to become symbolic
hero; he has simply reached stasis, caught in an ambivalent contradiction of attractions.

The best discussion of *All My Friends* is in *The
Ghost Country* by Raymond Neinstein, who points out
how the novel "gradually fills up with texts, with language and language about language, until Danny finds
himself trapped in a maze of words, suffocating, lost,
cut off from what he had taken to be his place, his family, his friends, his lovers" (43). For Neinstein, the novel
emphasizes Danny's failure as a regional writer:

> This is a novel, then, about a regional novelist
> who gets caught in his own texts, finding out
> that his own words are the strangers whom he
> had taken to be his friends, the agents of the
> estrangement he feels. He finds that, finally,
> there was never anything there but language.
> Refusing to accept this condition, to live in a
> "house of fiction," a "city of words," he sees his
> texts as just that, as words, and becomes radi-

cally disconnected both from them, and from his own experience. (43)

It was at the time McMurtry's most personal novel, and it was perhaps so close to his experience that he looked to a different arena for his next novel.

Terms of Endearment (1975)

Leaving Danny Deck alone and awash in the Rio Grande, McMurtry next followed his goal of shifting style, of moving from the gods to the swineherds. After focusing on a narrator whose life and experience closely resembled his own, McMurtry moved far afield from his own voice and turned to a middle-aged New England widow transplanted to Houston as the central consciousness of his next novel. Throughout the novels in the Houston trilogy, McMurtry examines various sides of many of the dualities that have intrigued him throughout his career: rural/urban, old/new, male/female, isolation/community, art/life, marriage/divorce-separation-widowing, home/not-home, upper/lower, among others. With *Terms of Endearment*, he moves on from the isolated young male writer struggling in a symbolic borderland and immerses himself in imaginative recreation of an aging, urban society woman, examining the terms that endear one to another. The title, then, suggests that McMurtry is once again concerned with the power of language, the terms that express love. The title is also paradoxical, for terms may also mean the conditions that humans agree upon that are acceptable for continued endearment.

Emma Horton's mother, Aurora Greenway, had made a brief appearance in *Moving On*, and as he wrote in the 1989 preface to the Touchstone edition, McMurtry was drawn back to the character who had the "habit of parking her Cadillac two yards from the curb, so as to avoid scraping her tires" (6). If *All My Friends* is an American picaresque work, *Terms* is, as McMurtry acknowledges, his most European novel, written as he traveled in Europe, the first half on an Italian typewriter, the second on a Swiss. Perhaps these dislocations help explain what many critics charge to be the novel's greatest weakness, its strangely split structure, beginning with Aurora in Houston and ending with the cloyingly sentimental death of Emma Horton in Nebraska. As he continued to struggle with his own ambivalence about writing regional material, by turning to an educated woman born in New Haven and by using as models European writers, McMurtry perhaps attempted to broaden his subject matter and ease his uncertainly about writing.

Although Aurora is a departure from McMurtry's previous protagonists, she is still a character with an artistic sensibility who engages in a type of artistic endeavor. In addition to collecting fine art—a Renoir and

a Klee—Aurora is a type of artist herself, a social archi-
tect. Like Virginia Woolf's Mrs. Dalloway, Aurora
attempts to achieve social order by directing her
daughter's life and by presenting perfect dinner parties. She tells Emma, "Disgrace abounds, if I may coin
a phrase, but good dinner parties are rare" (77). Aurora
also manipulates her various suitors—Edward Johnson,
a bank executive; Alberto, a retired opera singer; General Hector Scott, a retired armored corps commander;
Trevor Waugh, a debonair yachtsman; and Vernon
Dalhart, a shy Texas oil millionaire. Her maid Rosie
Dunlup and her feckless husband Royce are also subjects of Aurora's orchestration.

   While Aurora's story recalls Virginia Woolf, Emma's
section also echoes influences beyond American soil. As
Emma awaits her death, she chances upon a phrase in
the *Iliad*, "among the dead," and thinks that she too is
about to join the world of shades: "Even counting people
she knew, there were a lot of dead to be among: her
father, for one, and a school chum who had been killed
in a car wreck, and Sam Burns, and she guessed, Danny
Deck, the friend of her youth. She supposed him dead,
though no one really knew" (401). This scene suggests
not only the *Iliad*, but it also recalls the conclusion of
James Joyce's "The Dead," in which after another artistic
dinner party, Greta Conroy remembers a young man
who had loved her, whose warm and passionate love
contrasts with her enervated husband's frail attempts.

Perhaps the lack of unity often complained about by the novel's critics sets in relief the theme of chaos, and the control toward which humans strive. Roberta Sorensen, for example, in a review in *Western American Literature*, found Emma's section out of unity with the rest of the book, like "dropping a pile of Emma's dirty laundry on Aurora's dinner table" (358). And Robert Towers in *The New York Times Book Review* said that "the ending—a real tear jerker—dangles from the rest of the novel like a broken tail" (4). Art can achieve unity, but life, as Herman Melville emphasized in *Billy Budd*, is imperfect, rough, and chaotic. Behind Aurora Greenway's desire to control life lies an intense fear resulting from her knowledge of life's ragged edges, which she reveals early in the novel:

> Suddenly, to Aurora's terror, life seemed to bolt straight from her grip. Something flung her heart violently, and she felt alone. She no longer felt merciless, she just—She didn't know, something was gone, nothing was certain, she was older, she had not been granted control, and what would happen? She had no way to see how things would end. In her terror she flung out her arms and caught her daughter. (22)

If Aurora achieves outer control, it is at the expense

of inner turmoil and periods of "strangeness," similar to Danny Deck's alienation, such as this moment of terror:

> In any case the strangeness was different from fever—it was more an off-centeredness, a feeling of distortion, as if already, years before her time, she was slipping away, losing touch, either falling behind or, perhaps worse, moving too far ahead. She had the feeling that everyone who knew her only saw her outward motions—the motions of a woman who constantly complained and wheedled affection. Her inward motions no one seemed to see. (149)

Aurora's reactions to her two paintings reveal similar concerns about balance and connections. Sometimes when she looks at her Renoir, "a small oil of two gay women in hats standing near some tulips" (79), tears come into her eyes. But the Klee, described as "a stark composition, just a few lines that angled sharply and never quite met" (81), had never appealed to her. Aurora's artistic outlook is also indicated by her epigrammatic style, which is apparent from the novel's first line when she says, "The success of a marriage inevitably depends on the woman" (11). Like a twentieth-century Dr. Johnson, Aurora offers pronouncements on the world in balanced or antithetical statements:

"The selection of a tasteful wardrobe is a duty, not a pastime." "The more things one can take lightly, the better chance one has" (68). "The best marriages are not performed in cheap restaurants" (62). "I've often thought that people who are too quick with their apologies can't have a very healthy attitude" (59). Of Alberto she says that "at his age impossible hopes are better than no hopes at all" (91) and she tells him that "perfection never comes easy" (85).

Perfection/flaw, unity/chaos, marriage/separation—these are the oppositions that underpin the novel and point to McMurtry's use of contrast as an important structural device. The contrasts among Aurora's various suitors provide much of the plot, but there are also the contrasts between Rosie's redneck world and Emma's academic one.

Once again, McMurtry uses a version of the Old Texas figure to point out the contrast to the New Urban Texas. In this case it is Vernon Dalhart, whose name is a combination of the names of two West Texas towns and that of a country singer. Vernon is an oilman who lives and works in a well-outfitted Lincoln in which he sleeps while it is parked on the twenty-fourth floor of a parking garage he owns. On the one hand, Vernon has made a smooth adaptation to the urban world, adjusting cleanly to concrete and commerce. On the other, as McMurtry has often pointed out about oilmen, they inherited the wheeler-dealer mentality from the old world, as well as some of its limiting values. Like the cowboy figure, Vernon is completely nonplussed by women, especially by a woman like Aurora, who overwhelms and bewilders him with smothering power. Also like the cowboy, Vernon is an *isolato*, a lonely figure looking out over the lights of Houston from his parodic godlike chamber on top of the parking garage.

Perhaps Vernon's attraction to Aurora highlights what Ernestine Sewell has pointed out about Aurora's symbolic role as the city:

> It is tempting to see Aurora as the embodiment of Houston, a city vested with the trappings of wealth, whatever is shiny and new and extravagant. Overall it is a verdant and lush place—all surface, some say—its people exuberant with the joy of following their dreams and sadly unmindful of human suffering until brought face to face with it. Aurora/ Houston, so desirable, opens her arms, if not her heart, to all who come to her, and she accepts their worship as her due. (*Taking Stock* 202)

Clearly Vernon's characterization allows McMurtry to return to his familiar critique of Old Texas. In a *Texas*

Monthly article titled "Unfinished Women," McMurtry commented on how Texas men like Vernon were incapable of responding fully to women:

> Mythically and actually, the Texas male has never been celebrated for his qualities of mind, or the capacity to feel and to express feeling. His preeminence has been as a doer: one who, above all, can get things done. And that he can. These males have settled a harsh land, sprinkled it with well-managed cities, and even seen generously to the endowment of cultural institutions and centers of learning. Their ability to do has been and remains substantial, but unfortunately for their women this ability has always been set well above any ability to feel and communicate. (164)

To change pace, examine class distinctions, and take a few shots at *echt* Texas, McMurtry includes the burlesque sections about Rosie and Royce Dunlup, especially the violence that McMurtry has said is the sad legacy of frontier life. Royce first drives his potato chip truck through the wall of the J-Bar Korral in a jealous stupor, and then later gets a machete in the chest when he is sleeping with his mistress Shirley.

These subplots revolve around the marriage theme,

which Kerry Ahearn finds the most important one in a novel he finds difficult to analyze:

> Those who make their way through *Terms of Endearment* and emerge puzzled as to what organizes and directs the novel might well think of marriage as the major theme and widow Aurora Greenway the aging prophetess. Like *Leaving Cheyenne*, this novel presents not a vision of life as it is lived but a fantasy antidote: men's savage and possessive love is somehow lulled by a strong woman who charms them so completely that she occupies the center, loved by all but controlled by none. (*Fifty* 287–88)

Other reviewers were perplexed by the various levels in the novel. Christopher Lehmann-Haupt in *The New York Times* noted that the book "can't seem to make up its mind what it wants to be when it grows up. It starts off a drawing-room farce" and "continues with the farcical story of how grandmother Aurora shrewdly avoids getting a 'somebody'" and then shifts to "the more realistic story of Emma and her domestic trials with her ineffectual scholar husband, Thomas (Flap) Horton." He continues: "Sometimes the novel swerves into pure slapstick comedy, as, for instance, when Aurora's housekeeper's husband runs off with a woman whose dream it is to have sexual relations with Houston's new Mecom fountain. . . . At other times it veers into pure sensibility. . . . (45)

Perhaps the inconsistencies in the novel reflect McMurtry's continuing ambivalence about writing, a concern he admitted in a preface written in 1989, a concern which had lasted almost an entire decade. When Emma died, he wrote, "the emptiness did seize me, and with it came a cool distaste for my own writing that didn't subside for ten years, not until the morning when Harmony went driving home at sunrise in *The Desert Rose*" (7). Indeed, his writing during that period, as the next chapter examines, often reflected his lack of enthusiasm.

5

Escape
The Trash Trilogy

    Although the next series of novels is often called "the Trash Trilogy," the name is only partially appropriate. Unlike some of McMurtry's work, *Somebody's Darling*, *Cadillac Jack*, and *The Desert Rose* have no interrelated quality; none of the characters, plots, or settings overlap. In fact, *Somebody's Darling* logically makes a quartet with his three previous novels, since two of its main characters appeared in earlier novels. (McMurtry, however, does not consider it part of the Houston grouping.) Nor are these three books necessarily "trash," but of all McMurtry's novels, these three have been more generally abused by critics than the others. Therefore, it makes a convenient as-

sortment to trash them, and certainly in the long look
at McMurtry's fiction, they rank low on the list of his
significant works. But the term also reflects the subject matter of the three novels: the glitzy but uncentered
worlds of Hollywood and Las Vegas and the trash and
garbage through which Cadillac Jack McGriff sifts.
While many critics excoriated these three books, all
three novels contain praiseworthy elements, and each
one received some positive reviews.

Because these three novels move far afield from
the southwestern settings of McMurtry's previous work,
they demonstrate how, in his shifting attitude about
his blood's country, he had tilted away from it. These
three novels reflect McMurtry's attitude at the time that
the "country—or western, or Cowboy—myth had finally
been worked through." Calling it "country and western
literature" in "Ever a Bridegroom," McMurtry indicates
how he had reached the conclusion that the myth of
the West was dead:

> It was clear by then that this myth had served
> its time, and lost its potency; insofar as it still
> functioned it was an inhibiting, rather than a
> creative, factor in our literary life. The death
> of the cowboy and the ending of the rural way
> of life had been lamented sufficiently, and there
> was really no more that needed to be said about
> it. ("Bridegroom" 18)

What makes these novels important is that they demonstrate how McMurtry examined some of his continuing techniques and themes while he worked out his ambivalence toward writing about the Southwest, even though writing remained difficult. Technically, the novels show McMurtry working with varying points of view, especially his fondness for using female narrators, and with different levels of realism. All three books are contemporaneous to the time he wrote them, and they are concerned with displaced characters searching for something to provide their lives with stability and purpose. They long for ways to combine love and work into a satisfying and enduring whole. Although their lives are ultimately fraught with difficulty, pain, and uncertainty, McMurtry demonstrates how these characters can still respond with creativity, love, or humor. These three novels also demonstrate continuity with the Houston trilogy by questioning the value of artistic achievement, focusing on the problematic nature of love, using opposition for thematic and structural purposes, and stressing in varying degrees the themes of loneliness and searching.

More significant, the novels are important because of their transitional nature. Taken together, they reveal a writer's dark night of the soul, for it was with *Somebody's Darling* that McMurtry lost his enthusiasm for writing, a condition that existed through *Cadillac*

Jack. With *The Desert Rose* McMurtry recovered it somewhat. These novels exemplify that Larry McMurtry could continue to write when his life and world were in flux. They also document how he attempted what he had long called on Texas novelists to do: to write about the urban—and urbane—world beyond Idiot Ridge, Wichita Falls, Fort Worth, and Houston. In these three books we find McMurtry leaving Texas for Hollywood, Washington, D.C., and Las Vegas.

Somebody's Darling (1978)

A publisher's note on the dust jacket of *Somebody's Darling* recognizes that McMurtry's "background is the Frontier" and asserts that this novel about Hollywood has simply moved the frontier "farther west than Texas." And Book I hints that *Somebody's Darling* concerns the way Hollywood replaced the West in the American imagination as the place symbolic of youthful hope and promise. Book I is narrated by Joe Percy, a sixty-three-year-old hack screenwriter and former novelist, who was a minor character in *Moving On*. As the novel opens, Percy is about to accompany his old friend Jill Peel (who was Danny Deck's lover in *All My Friends Are Going to Be Strangers*) to New York where she is about to achieve success as the first major woman director, for a film called *Womanly Ways*. She wants Joe to be there for the opening of the film which will establish her reputation.

Percy, a Hollywood veteran, knows how Hollywood has satisfied the needs of innocents who wanted to "make a life of the games of childhood" (71), but now he describes Los Angeles "with the reptilian coil of freeways rippling like golden boas" and understands that he has "lost the habit of hope" (126–27), which should be the product of fantasy. With these observations, Percy moves McMurtry's novel toward treating substantial themes, and critics have been quite positive about McMurtry's presentation of Joe's character.

Through Percy, McMurtry examines some of his previous themes such as loss, as well as many of the oppositions that have been important to his previous fiction: innocence/experience, art/beauty, perfection/flaw, hope/despair. The theme of loss appears in the form of Percy's lost love, his wife Claudia, who for twenty-five years gave purpose to his life. With her sudden death, Percy, like other McMurtry characters, finds himself cut off from his source of value. And also like earlier characters such as Danny Deck, Percy substitutes pursuing women for seeking art: "With Claudia gone, not there to be with, it seemed to me that chasing beautiful women was about the best thing left" (12). The young women are temporary distractions for Percy; nothing will allow him to regain the golden past. But Percy is enough of a realist, or cynic, that he accepts the present, recognizes his own limitations, and welcomes the young women into his bed gratefully.

Once he decided to pursue beautiful young women, for example, he declared:

> Myself, I had no standards to speak of—it would never occur to me to apply a word like standards to a happenstance like love. Even less would it occur to me to look askance at beauty. I have managed to love all sorts of beautiful women . . . .
>
> I suppose, if pressed, I might have to admit that beauty isn't everything, in women; but I admit that reluctantly, and I would still claim that there's a real sense in which—as some football coach said, in another context—it's the only thing. Having wrestled with it across many a fetid sheet, and having watched it vanish down many a driveway, I have to think that it offers at least as high a challenge as art. Of course, having little talent, I can't really claim to have felt the grip of the challenge of art, but it has been a long time since I have been totally free of the grip of womanly beauty, and even at that moment something inside me was being squeezed by the beauty of Jill Peel's eyes . . . . (12–13)

Late in the novel, Percy returns to his interest in the beauty suggested by Jill's eyes, as he considers the contrasts between beauty and art, hobby and craft. Joe, along with two Texas screenwriters, Elmo Buckle and Winfield Gohagen, accompanies Jill as they steal the masterprint of a film she had directed, which they intend to take to Texas. One of them says, "Texas is the ultimate last resort. It's always a good idea to go to Texas, if you can't think of anything else to do" (312–13). While Jill considers her role as a director, Joe admonishes her to stick to her real calling as an artist, rather than dabbling in film:

> Craft, not art. Art happens like love, but craft is loyalty, like marriage. To do it good is what's necessary, and that's all that's necessary. Maybe a few times in your life you get lucky and do it better than good, but that's irrelevant. Loyalty is what's necessary, if you want to get something good out of the union." (321)

When Joe is not contemplating large questions about beauty, he is considering such beautiful young things as Page Sibley, young wife of an aging producer. For Page, Percy says, the world falls into clear oppositions, since her favorite word is "perfect." Joe realizes, "Things were either perfect, or they were disgusting. She was not old enough to have observed that a lot of life lies somewhere in between" (50).

But Percy, like the author standing behind him, is

quite aware that the world does not fall cleanly; it is a world of ambivalence and equivocation:

> As a contract writer at Warners—one of a vanishing, bilious breed—I deal with equivocators every day, if not every hour. The studio equivocates about deals, producers equivocate about projects, directors equivocate about stories, agents equivocate about terms, unions equivocate about payoffs, actors and actresses equivocate about interpretations, cameramen equivocate about where to put the camera, writers equivocate about dialogue, and so on down the line to gofers, who probably equivocate about routes to the cigarette machines. The whole industry only moves in fits and starts, and I've never seen any reason to try and be better than my peers. (44–45)

The first part ends when Jill Peel meets Owen Oarson at a New York party celebrating her film. Owen becomes her lover and the narrator of Book II. A former football player at Texas Tech and a farm equipment salesman, Oarson sees that Jill will give him an easy ride to success as a producer. (His last name, one character notes, rhymes with "Whoreson.") In the mold of the Texas cowboy, Owen cannot articulate his feelings; his narration is also inarticulate and, many critics felt,

boring. Perhaps McMurtry tried to dramatize Hollywood enervation by allowing the manipulators to demonstrate that they are unimaginative and dislikeable.
The problem is that the book begins to show the same
characteristics.

Through Owen and through the two Texas screenwriters, McMurtry returns to his attack on Old Texas.
Owen lacks depth and understanding. Although they
are treated somewhat more sympathetically than Owen,
Elmo and Winfield are once again debased versions of
Texans. They wander through their place in Tujunga
Canyon throwing hunting knives at trees, beer cans
seemingly stuck to their hands, tan young girls trailing
at the heels of their boots. Driving their pink Cadillac,
they have inherited the legacy of Hud—a directionless
world where the only connection to the Old West comes
through the illusory world of movies.

Book III is narrated by Jill, as she continues her
affair with Owen knowing it is based purely on his selfish motives. They co-produce a western set in West
Texas, which Jill directs, but soon Owen is advancing
his career by sleeping with Sherry Solare, the star. The
circumstances deteriorate and conclude with the death
of Sherry's twelve-year-old son Wynkyn, an act that dramatizes the problematic relationship between Hollywood and innocence that Joe Percy introduced in Book
I. Hollywood, Joe had mused, attracts "people who
weren't meant to grow up and live in marriages, or work

at jobs. . . . [P]ictures had seemed to them the answer
to their need, which was to make a life of the games of
childhood" (71). Instead, Hollywood slaughters many
of these innocents, as Wynkyn's death suggests.

The last section of *Somebody's Darling* is
reminiscent of the conclusion of *All My Friends Are
Going to Be Strangers*. Where Godwin Lloyd-Jons in
the earlier novel had accused Danny of "stealing" as a
writer, Jill actually steals the print of her film and then
realizes that it is a foolish act and returns it. Godwin
appears briefly in the Austin section, saying he is not
sorry for Danny Deck and other writers, who are all
"liars" who "steal" (335). Jill remembers Danny as she
drives toward Austin in the screenwriter's Cadillac. In
her loneliness and estrangement, her trip is similar to
Danny's drive across South Texas, as she realizes that
she has "no reason in God's name to be in Austin, Texas,"
and that she has "forgotten the names and addresses"
of her "true friends, rooted friends, sane friends, stable
friends" (336).

Much of Book III recounts the strange sexual and
personal misadventures of the characters. At the end
of the novel, Jill and Joe capture a brief moment of pleasure as Jill, in a purely unselfish act, helps Joe regain
sexual vigor. Unlike Danny, who cannot return to
friends, Jill returns briefly and even renounces Hollywood for a short time. But the novel ends with Joe's

death and with Jill's uncertainty about the ties that bound them together.

The result of all this, as I asserted in a *Houston Chronicle* review, is that *Somebody's Darling* "tears promisingly out of the chute, but soon stumbles, falls, and wallows in the mire." And in his review in *Texas Monthly*, Gene Lyons concluded:

> *Somebody's Darling* turns to pulp at the end, the climax of all the bed hopping coming in the accidental shooting death of a child—a killing for which we are quite unprepared and which seems to have been cooked up out of the *Novelists' Book of Tricks* as a way of punishing the characters for their sins. It is an ending terrible without being understandable, inexplicable without being mysterious. (*Taking Stock* 277)

McMurtry has called the book an example of bad timing. He initially was drawn to Jill Peel's character after he created her in *All My Friends Are Going to Be Strangers*, but by the time he got around to writing about her, he could not sustain his interest.

McMurtry told Patrick Bennett that writing *Somebody's Darling* was "an unpleasant writing experience." Because he did not feel "really engaged; it was

forced" (30). He attributes the novel's difficulty to two
problems. First, he tried to force two impulses: one was
to write a novel about Hollywood; the second was his
desire to write again about Jill Peel. When he finally
merged the two and began writing, the "original energy had gone" (29). The second problem arose from his
unfamiliarity with California: "Because you happen to
know how people talk, you feel you know more about
Californians than you really do" (29).

In the years following the publication of *Somebody's
Darling*, only one critical article, an updated entry in
the *Dictionary of Literary Biography* by Brooks Landon,
has focused specifically on it. Landon called it a "frequently hilarious, finally sad, always engaging book."
He identifies its primary theme as loneliness (*Taking
Stock* 271). Some critics have referred briefly to the
novel. Ahearn in his *Fifty Western Writers* article finds
some value in it, noting that the "focus on a non-Texas
milieu seems to ease McMurtry away from the stereotypes, punning, and facile black humor of the previous
four novels and toward a more subtle and sensitive use
of character." He points out that it "continues the theme
of skepticism about marriage, and its preoccupation is
with loss and the inevitable victimization of sensitive
and kind human beings" (288). Jane Nelson, in her article in *A Literary History of the American West*, notes
that McMurtry has apparently disowned the novel and
finds that it lacks the power of McMurtry's best work

because "none of these Hollywood characters faces the loss of a home that forms the emotional center of his previous novels" (617).

Cadillac Jack (1982)

Standing on a street corner in Washington, D.C., Larry McMurtry found his title before he had a novel to hang it on. A man in a Cadillac pulled to a stop, and a black man on the street sang out, "Hi, Ho Cadillac Jack." Soon, he had a character and then a plot that moved away from Texas. *Cadillac Jack* is set mainly in Washington, but it provides a sympathetic treatment of a Texan for the first time in a decade of work critical of almost all things Texan. Jack McGriff is by no means completely positive, because he is a wanderer who cannot accept the permanence of love, but he is much more admirable than most of the characters in the novel. *Cadillac Jack* is a humorous trip through the detritus of contemporary America, a picaresque ramble with a man who can find something of value in the trash heaps and flea markets of American life.

McGriff, a thirty-three-year-old former bulldogger from Solino, Texas, stands 6 foot 5 inches in his yellow armadillo boots. With his brown beaver Stetson and doeskin jacket, Jack is an antique and doodad scout always on the lookout for the unusual as he travels the country in a pearl-colored Cadillac with peach velour

interior. In some ways Jack suggests McMurtry himself, for during this period McMurtry lived in Washington and roamed the area searching for books for his
rare book store, Booked Up. *Somebody's Darling* includes a brief reference to a rare book dealer, and
McMurtry toyed with making his main character a
bookman, but he decided to concentrate on the larger
world of antique collecting rather than the rarified world
of book collecting. In an article in *Western American
Literature* (an update of her earlier article, "Journeying as a Metaphor for Cultural Loss in the Novels of
Larry McMurtry"), Janis Stout points out the similarities between McMurtry and his character:

> In *Cadillac Jack*, the freewheeling hero is
> very much a projection of McMurtry himself,
> who in his capacity as rare book dealer, is
> known to wander the width of America in his
> own Cadillac, departing on marathon drives
> at a moment's notice, carrying his treasures in
> his trunk. The hero's occupation, too, is an apt
> projection of McMurtry's bits-and-pieces kind
> of novelistic virtuosity. Cadillac Jack is a "scout"
> for salable antiques, collectibles, and curiosi-
> ties of all kinds. (244)

Through the presentation of Jack McGriff,
McMurtry's ambivalence about his own writing and

isolated life again enters subtly. Previously, the gaudy, materialistic, womanizing Texan would have received the brunt of McMurtry's satire, but not in *Cadillac Jack*. In fact, McMurtry embraces much of Jack's Texas outlook, and the satire is directed outward—at the effete and the snobbish, the social climbers and bureaucrats of Washington. Still, Jack is an equivocal character, since he, like Danny Deck, is incapable of establishing long-term, full human relationships. It is also, McMurtry has written, a novel about the instability of human love, either for objects or other human beings. In fact, the novel's use of objects emphasizes McMurtry's phenomenological theme in which he demonstrates the meaning people place on objects, whether it is a dog house in *Texasville* or Billy the Kid's boots in *Cadillac Jack*.

As the novel begins, Jack has come to Washington in the middle of the urban cowboy craze to dump a load of cowboy regalia. His friend, Boog Miller, a wealthy oilman who owns Winkler County, Texas, introduces him to Cindy Sanders, a dabbler in antique dealing and full-time beauty and social climber. Because too many of the people in Washington are "shrimps," Jack provides Cindy with a tall diversion. Jack, object connoisseur, is inspired by Cindy's physical perfection.

Cindy soon introduces Jack to her Washington friends, a crew as odd as the bar gang from *Star Wars*, with names like Sir Cripps Crisp, Moorcock Malone,

Khaki Descartes, Freddy Fu, Spud Breyfogle, Oblivia Brown, Prub Bosque, and Brisling Bowker. The names indicate how McMurtry moved away from the realism of *Somebody's Darling* and into the lightly satirical comedy of manners in *Cadillac Jack*. Between bouts of love-making, Jack convinces Cindy that she should replace the bread sculpture exhibit in her shop with a boot display centered around Billy the Kid's boots, owned by a 108-year-old friend of Jack's in Fort Sumner, New Mexico.

But Jack, forever the scout, soon finds something else to attract him at an estate sale: Jean Arber, another antique dealer. In this way McMurtry returns to his familiar structural device of triangulation, as Jack finds himself torn between attractions to women who represent different values. Jean is a soon-to-be divorced young mother of two daughters whose down-to-earth family life offers a stability that Cindy's Dickensian society does not, and Jack's deflected interest reinforces McMurtry's point about the instability of human love.

While Jack's sexual forays make up a good part of the book, much of the best that is here comes from Jack's straightforward, good-humored approach to the possibility of life for one who is on the lookout. He takes his motto from Zack Jenks, a Coke bottle scout, who once told him: "Anything can be anywhere" (23). On this expedition to Washington, though, Jack also casts a critical eye. His response to the people of Washington

demonstrates the contrast between his western open-
ness and their restricted timidity. The bureaucrats, the
GS-12s, come under his scrutiny, and, in an effective
metaphor, he finds their dull similarity limiting:

> I was getting the sense that Washington was
> a very cellular place. The motif of the cell re-
> curred. All the men in trench coats and woolen
> hats, probably spent their days in cell-like of-
> fices in vast gray buildings. Then when the
> government let them out they squirmed like
> larvae into small cell-like cars and rushed
> across the river or around the Beltway to vast
> gray apartment buildings, where they inhab-
> ited cell-like apartments. (123)

A man who hears the song of the open road, Jack
finds the cell-like life disgusting. But all is not sweetness
and treasure for Jack in this book, for his faith in himself
is shaken when Jean refuses to marry him, telling him
that he lacks the ability to love, since love requires a
rootedness that the wandering scout cannot achieve:

> "What might keep you from loving me a lot is
> that you don't want to love anyone a lot, I don't
> think," she said. "It's tiresome work. Means
> holding still and being bored half the time. I
> think you'd just rather move around collecting

little loves. Affections. Little light ones that you
can put in your car for a while and then get rid
of." (386)

As the novel concludes, Jack hits the road, continues to
find unusual objects in odd places, and refuses to realize that he has substituted objects for emotion.

The initial reviews were mixed. In *Texas Monthly*
Dominique Browning praised the novel on the grounds
that its main character is a true American eccentric in
a comic novel that mines significant American themes:

Some great novels—*Moby Dick* and *The Great
Gatsby* and *All the Kings Men*—deal straight-
forwardly with major themes like power and
love. But there's another tradition of American fiction, one in which a novel can be straight-
forwardly humorous and deal with major
themes obliquely. Such novels are about an id-
iosyncratic human condition—they portray the
world view of a particular, often eccentric character writ large as another way of thinking
about what it all means. *Cadillac Jack* is in
this second tradition. Jack isn't going to preach
about what constitutes the good life or what it
means to do right by others, but it's easy to see
what his values are by watching him yearn
his way across America. "I guess I buy and sell

in hope of style—or maybe as a style of hope,
and . . . there are always others as restless as
myself, who constantly buy and sell, too, for
their own reasons." (*Taking Stock* 281)

Clay Reynolds, on the other hand, finds Jack's
directionless wandering symptomatic of his creator's
loss of roots:

The book is, to borrow a word from the jacket
blurb, "slouchy," as unanchored and disorga-
nized as McMurtry's hero. Although there are
several promises of plot development—the
clandestine sale of the Smithsonian's contents,
for example—none of them ever get anywhere.
In fact, the book is full of dead ends, sloppy
summations, and helplessly dangling loose
threads that continue to tantalize as Jack finds
himself at the novel's end alone in a Colorado
motel room reading the classified ads and wondering what in the world he might do next.
(*Taking Stock* 282)

Although Jane Nelson concludes that *Cadillac
Jack*'s "political and social intrigues . . . are . . . no more
convincing than the Hollywood scenes of *Somebody's
Darling*," she finds that "[i]n learning to accept himself
as a perpetual wanderer, Jack becomes the most satis-

fying male character McMurtry had yet created, almost
a match for his strong female characters." Nelson also
notes the interesting contrast between *Cadillac Jack*
and McMurtry's first two novels:

> Idiot Ridge and any corresponding nostalgia
> for the western landscape have disappeared
> from his novels in *Cadillac Jack*. Now the west-
> ern past is represented by a cattle rancher who
> is a drug addict; the modern West is run by a
> network of female real estate agents who are
> directed by a powerful and dynamic woman
> living in the East. In his first two novels, lonely
> women are encircled and engulfed by men who
> both love and abuse them. *Cadillac Jack* is
> peopled largely by women, many of whom use
> and then discard the lonely men in their lives.
> Because of Jack's quiet acceptance of his fate,
> *Cadillac Jack* becomes the first McMurtry
> novel in which man and woman seem almost
> equal. (618)

If McMurtry's treatment of the sexes changed,
his use of what Raymond Neinstein has called his central theme, displacement, continues to be important in
Cadillac Jack. He concludes: "Displacement is the central concern of the first five novels of Larry McMurtry.
In four of the novels, the protagonist is either breaking

away from a place, or has already done so, only to find himself rootless and lost" (i). McMurtry told Patrick Bennett that Jack Kerouac's *On the Road* was a significant influence (17), and *Cadillac Jack* provides ample evidence of Kerouac's legacy, for Jack is a rootless, searching figure who finds life on the road. Like some of McMurtry's earlier characters, Jack spends his life searching for a center, a home that will again allow lost virtues to be regained.

The Desert Rose (1983)

McMurtry was working on *Lonesome Dove* and had gotten bogged down in the details of his trail drive novel when he got a call from a Hollywood producer who wanted him to write a film script about a Las Vegas showgirl. Loaded with the names of people to contact and needing a break from the current project, he headed to Las Vegas where he met a real former showgirl who raised peacocks and gave him a new character. He sensed a connection that interested him, which he noted in the preface to the paperback edition of *The Desert Rose*: "I have always been attracted to dying crafts—cowboying is one such. It became clear that the showgirls were the cowboys of Las Vegas; there were fewer and fewer jobs and they faced bleak futures, some with grace, and some without it" (7). The story's outline came next: "Dying breeds aren't the only thing I'm at-

tracted to. I also like mother-daughter stories. Why not
a mother-daughter story in which the daughter replaces
the mother on her own stage in the show in which she's
been a star for some years?" (7). What resulted was the
character of Harmony, the mother, and Pepper, the
daughter, and a variation on the "old-matador-going-
down-vs.-the young-matador-coming-up motif, except
with a family twist" (7). In fact, the novel's strength
derives from its poignant human story: Harmony, a
thirty-eight-year-old showgirl who has long been called
the most beautiful woman in Las Vegas, is aging, and
Bonventre, her hard-hearted dance manager, has decided to hire her daughter Pepper to take the lead
dancer's place and to fire Harmony. McMurtry wrote
the novel in three weeks.

Some critics found elements to appreciate. Emily
Benedek, for example, reviewing for *The New Leader*,
found an effective "contrapuntal pattern" in the careful
organization of the novel:

> The novel is carefully constructed, its six parts
> focusing alternately on Harmony and Pepper.
> Their stories run in opposite directions, with
> Harmony's luck falling as her daughter's rises.
> Their fates are inevitably the same. McMurtry
> uses the contrapuntal pattern effectively to
> emphasize the curious routes of human sym-

pathy and the quality of bonds in the lives of the dislocated. (*Taking Stock* 289)

Despite the potential, the book received some of the harshest reviews of any of McMurtry's novels. Most reacted as did Rod Davis, reviewing for *Texas Monthly*, when he took McMurtry to task for creating shallow characters and then treating them condescendingly: "McMurtry purports to make Harmony's life believable and, worse, typical by setting it amid matter-of-fact contemporary banality. . . . [B]ut he does so from a point of retreat and disengagement, and his data barely mask his contempt" (*Taking Stock* 293).

To replicate the paltriness of Harmony's imagination, McMurtry chose to tell the story first from her point of view and then later from that of her sixteen-year-old daughter. Committed to a realistic approach, McMurtry decided to have his characters speak and think authentically. The result is vapid vocabulary and anemic thought. For example, in the following passage, Harmony considers her wardrobe:

After all, wearing those costumes every night, being a feathered beauty as Bonventre used to call her, sort of changed your attitude toward clothes. After the costumes it was sort of hard to know you were there if you didn't wear clothes with a little color in them. Pepper just didn't realize that, she was so beautiful she didn't even need makeup yet. (14)

Several other reviewers responded as did D. Keith Mano in *National Review*, finding the novel "brain-sphinctering" (149), and noting that by choosing dumb characters for point-of-view, McMurtry's vocabulary is reduced. Charles L. Adams in *Western American Literature* pointed to the same weakness:

> The fundamental technical problem with the novel is this presentation through the eyes and voices of two women of limited intelligence. The use of an outside narrator might perhaps have made it an amusing fantasy, and indeed, McMurtry's almost patronizing tone does come through, but all in all, the lives of these women as told by them are anything but amusing. (167)

These comments indicate the need for good editing. Ever since his first editor forced McMurtry to change the ending of *Horseman, Pass By*, he has resented editorial interference. While McMurtry's fame may have diminished the need to listen to editorial suggestions, *The Desert Rose* demonstrates that even a good writer can benefit from editing.

To his credit, McMurtry gets many readers to care for the main characters and some of the other weird ones in this menagerie—Myrtle, an alcoholic neighbor who sits in the yard drinking, waiting for customers for her rummage sale and watching her goat Maude eat either Cheerios or the bottoms out of the chairs; Myrtle's boyfriend, Wendall, who cleans the MGM Grand pool and works at the AMOCO station; Gary, the gay customer who is a confidant of all the girls; Mel, the mysterious former fashion photographer, who is so taken by his films of Pepper in old lingerie that he decides to marry her and watch her grow up. Given the language and limited intelligence level McMurtry chose to portray, it is an accomplishment that we begin to feel anything for these characters. McMurtry is, in fact, taken with them, noting that they taught him that "optimism is a form of courage" (8). He wrote a sequel titled *The Late Child,* published just as this book was going to press, which he says is about recovery from grief.

There are other suggestive elements here. For example, Harmony is often concerned about the pet peacocks that she keeps around her house. Harmony's caring for these beautiful natural creatures suggests that she is worthy of our interest. McMurtry juxtaposes these beautiful birds with Harmony, who often wears a dance costume that makes her a "feathered beauty," but he allows the irony of the two images to remain undeveloped. In Flannery O'Connor's fiction, the universe in the pattern of a peacock's feathers became symbolic of the wonders of the invisible world, but McMurtry's world here, unlike O'Connor's, lacks a transcendent power that gives life meaning.

In the context of McMurtry's career, *The Desert Rose* is interesting because it includes a number of McMurtry themes, images, and techniques: nostalgia for a dying craft, the complex intertwining of affection and anger in mother-daughter relationships (explored earlier in *Terms of Endearment*), the process by which emotions become reified as objects of barter, varying points-of-view, and the metaphor of journeying. As the novel ends, Harmony takes the bus to Reno, where she faces her limited future with grace and dignity. Janis Stout finds the use of the journeying metaphor more satisfying here than in other McMurtry novels, saying: "*The Desert Rose* ends . . . by using departure as a fully functional metaphor." She continues:

> The act of travelling conveys Harmony's act of deciding to break out of a stale pattern. Here, far more than in the books of continual wandering, McMurtry uses the road as a powerful structural element drawing everything else together. The novel ends on a note of renewal and open possibility—which are inherent and available values of the road as image. ("Cadillac Larry" 248)

Ultimately, what is most important about *The Desert Rose* is that it marks a turning point in Larry McMurtry's career. With this book he regained the enthusiasm for writing he had lost writing *Somebody's Darling*. With his renewed energy, he returned to the trail drive novel—and to Texas as both a part-time home and the subject for his fiction. He soon finished the novel he had been tinkering with for years, *Lonesome Dove*; the Pulitzer Prize and other accolades followed.

6

Return

Lonesome Dove

With *Lonesome Dove* (1985), a novel in which the most powerful scenes concern one Texas Ranger's promise to return his friend and partner's body to Texas for burial, McMurtry circled back to Texas and the old Southwest as the subject and setting for his fiction. He seems to have been able to reconcile his contradiction of attractions about Texas and his balky approach to writing about regional material. Only two years earlier he had again attacked Texas writers for writing "an endless stream . . . of literature" that "is disgracefully insular and uninformed. Writing is nourished by reading—broad, curious, sustained reading; it flows from a profound alertness, fine-tuned by both literature and life" (quoted in Clifford and Pilkington, *Range Wars* 20). At the same time McMurtry wrote this attack, he continued to work on the trail drive novel he had mentioned in interviews for several years.

Lonesome Dove actually began as a movie treatment titled "Streets of Laredo," now held in the Southwestern Writers Collection at Southwest Texas State University. A retelling of two older films, it was to have been a vehicle for John Wayne, James Stewart, and Henry Fonda. With the success of *The Last Picture Show*, Hollywood thought that the team of McMurtry and Bogdanovich could make a film about the end of the West, and McMurtry set out to write the script about the three aging characters who set out on a last adventure. At the end, everything is over—the West and the three characters' careers. Stewart and Fonda eventually accepted the parts reluctantly, but Wayne absolutely refused, seeing it as the end of his career if he made the movie—"putting a period to the career," as McMurtry put it in a talk at Southwest Texas State University in 1986. McMurtry put the script aside and later began to think of it as a novel.

As early as 1979 he spoke of working on a trail drive novel, telling Patrick Bennett:

> I've been thinking about a novel for a couple of years now that I would really like to write, a novel about nineteenth-century Texas, particu-

larly a trail-driving novel, since it seems to me
that the trail drives were an extremely crucial
experience, odd in that the whole period of the
trail drives was so extremely brief, and yet out
of it grew such an extraordinarily potent myth.
That fascinates me a bit, and I've been vaguely
working toward a trail-driving novel. But all
I've done in the way of actual work is that every time I think of a good name, or see one, or
chance upon one anywhere, in my reading perhaps, I jot it down. Place names, things like
that. (23–24)

He had spoken about the topic in his 1978 lecture
at Southwest Texas State University, but he also
sounded a note of caution about novelists who attempt
to recreate historical time periods:

It's a powerful subject, the end of the Old West,
and because I grew up when I did and had direct contact with numbers of people who lived
through it and who were pioneers, I think I
might have just a chance to be able to deal
imaginatively with that time. It's very danger-
ous to write outside your own time, I think. I
certainly have been leery of it up until now.
But—again it's a matter of being able to cast

your imagination into places you have not really been, and sufficient contact with the people
I grew up knowing may have provided me with
the kind of key. ("Southwest as Cradle" 38)

In many ways *Lonesome Dove* is the culmination
of McMurtry's work, the book he had been pointed toward all his life. As the son and grandson of cattle people,
as one who touched the garment of the passing cowboy
god, as a voracious reader and moviegoer who knew
both the literature and movies that had exalted the frontier myth, McMurtry was uniquely prepared to retell
the story in an ambivalent novel that both laments and
dramatizes the contradictory story of those now mythic
figures—the Texas Rangers, trail drivers, Indian fight-
ers, whores, frontier women—who pushed the
civilization west, the same civilization that then doomed
the lives they had lived. It is the novel his critics had
called for him to write since he first appeared on the
literary scene in the 1960s, and the subject of the novel
is the kind he had solidly attacked for fifteen years. It
is a novel filled with memorable and believable characters and exciting adventures; developed with details
that ring with truth—Hawkens and Henrys, half-breeds
and hackamores, riatas and remudas; told with language that is supple and clear; presented with humor,
compassion, and understanding; and it is undergirded

with themes, images, allusions, and structural devices that lift it far beyond the scrub literature McMurtry had attacked.

Despite some critics' belief that McMurtry contradicted himself by first attacking and then writing a novel about the past, it should be clear that McMurtry did not simply serve up a nostalgic formula western. Rather, as he had done throughout his career, McMurtry continued his anti-mythic ways. The major characters— former Texas Rangers Augustus McCrae and Woodrow Call, along with the reprobate Jake Spoon, the scout Deets, the slow but steady Pea Eye, the longing initiate Newt, and the competent but cowlike Dish—form a composite figure that personifies the best, the worst, and the various traits of the mythic passing southwesterner and counters those McMurtry often attacked in books by writers who played at being "symbolic frontiersmen." McMurtry's heroic figures Gus and Call embody mythic traits by being physically strong, loyal, creative, diligent, self-reliant, resourceful, and courageous. McMurtry also provides them with positive traits that are *not* part of the traditional myth by making them witty, talkative, sexually aware, and part of a supportive community. Additionally, he presents them as having human weaknesses: laziness; inability to achieve sustained, reciprocal heterosexual love; unethical behavior (the cattle and horses they drive north are stolen); and foolishness for undertaking the long drive without clear reason. But for many of his readers, these flaws do not destroy the myth; instead, by humanizing them, McMurtry creates more fully realized human characters than the "country and western" formula fiction could ever achieve.

In a 1988 interview with Mervyn Rothstein, McMurtry stated emphatically that his purpose in *Lonesome Dove* and *Anything for Billy* was to dispel the myth of the cowboy. "I'm a critic of the myth of the cowboys," McMurtry said. "I don't feel that it's a myth that pertains, and since it's a part of my heritage I feel it's a legitimate task to criticize it. . . . The myth of the clean-living cowboy devoted to agrarian pursuits and the rural way of life is extremely limiting." McMurtry pointed out that by romanticizing our frontier figures, we fail to see the fullness and complexity of their humanity:

> The flaws in the structure are rarely described, are rarely pointed out. I don't think these myths do justice to the richness of human possibility. The idea that men are men and women are women and horses are best of all is not a myth that makes for the best sort of domestic life. It's very exclusionary. It is a code that for all practical purposes excludes women. It shuts almost everything out except nature and work, and I don't think that's good. (C17)

If McMurtry set out to explode the myth completely, he did not succeed, and he acknowledged to Rothstein that many who read *Lonesome Dove* did not realize his anti-mythic purpose. But McMurtry attributed their failure to understand to the power of the original myth rather than to his ambivalent presentation. He says:

> Sometimes the resistance is total. . . . Some people read *Lonesome Dove* as a reinforcement of the myth. They want to believe that these are very good men. They are clinging to an idealization, to the pastoral way of life as being essentially less corrupt than the urban way. And thinking otherwise threatens them, threatens the little comfort they've had. (C17)

Ultimately, the strength of *Lonesome Dove* is the complex way that it intertwines myth and anti-myth into an intricate whole, for it is not simply an attack on the myth, nor is it simply a formula novel serving up larger-than-life heroes without real human traits. Rather it uses most of the elements of the old—the trail drive structure, archetypal Texas Rangers, standard obstacles (river crossings, thunderstorms, sandstorms, hailstorms, wind storms, lightning storms, grasshopper storms, stampedes, Indian attacks, quicksand bogs, drought, rustlers, snakes, a bear), a captivity narrative, love stories (love acknowledged—Gus/Clara; love

denied—Call/Newt), search for the father. These elements are presented in numerous memorable scenes
that translate easily to film: the roundup of the cattle,
the old Rangers ill-treated by a bartender in the
Buckhorn in San Antonio, the ill-fated river crossing
with snakes, the kidnapping of Lorena, the return of
Lorena, the death of Deets, the wounding of Gus, the
death of Gus, Call's return of Gus's body, the death of
Blue Duck, and related subplots.

The various characters demonstrate McMurtry's
use of the conventional and unconventional. The stock
figures are there, from the cantankerous and philosophical Mexican cooks Bol and Po Campo, to the anxious
teenager Newt, to the soiled dove Lorena, to the strong
frontier woman Clara, to the hesitant deputy Roscoe,
to the dirty buffalo hunters, to numerous others along
the way.

Blue Duck, the "renegade Indian," offers an interesting case study in McMurtry's use of supporting characters. Although he works hard to turn cowboy stereotypes upside down, his Indian characters in *Lonesome
Dove* recall the usual stereotypes, especially Blue Duck,
who from his first entry, acts more as an agent to move
the novel along than as a real character. When he first
appears, he seems larger than life: "The Indian called
Blue Duck was frightening. Now that he stood close to
them his head seemed bigger than ever, and his hands
too. He held the rifle in the crook of his arm, handling it

like a toy" (382). Blue Duck's background, however, is obscure. He obviously had crossed Gus's and Call's path in the past, but his tribal affiliation is never clearly established. In fact, Gus calls him a "Comanchero":

> "One we ought to have hung ten years ago," Augustus said. "Couldn't catch him. He's a Comanchero. He's got a greasy bunch of murderers and child-stealers. He used to work the Red River country from New Mexico all the way across to Arkansas, hitting settlers. They'd butcher the grownups and take the horses and kids." (383)

Although the term "Comanchero" sounds like "Comanche," historically the "comancheros" were Spaniards who traded with the Comanches, rather than the Indians themselves; occasionally they were Pueblo or other Indian traders. By making Blue Duck a trader, McMurtry introduces his subtle attack on the modern industrial economy that signaled the downfall of the old order. Blue Duck is clearly a trader, and it is Lorena who becomes the object of barter. In his treatment of Lorena, Blue Duck displays his viciousness and lack of humanity. From the very beginning of her time in captivity, Blue Duck makes his potential sadism clear:

> "I got a treatment for women that try to run

away," he said casually. "I cut a little hole in their stomachs and pull out a gut and wrap it around a limb. Then I drag them thirty or forty feet and tie them down. That way they can watch the coyotes come and eat their guts." (419)

McMurtry continues to emphasize the power of Blue Duck's evil, but it is not a common evil like most human weaknesses. In fact, Blue Duck is not at all interested in Lorena as a woman:

Blue Duck was the only man of the bunch who seemed to take no interest in her. He had stolen her to sell, and he had sold her. It was clear that he didn't care what they did to her. When he was in camp he spent his time cleaning his gun or smoking and seldom even looked her way. Monkey John was bad, but Blue Duck still scared her more. His cold, empty eyes frightened her more than Monkey John's anger or Dog Face's craziness. (476)

Blue Duck's almost superhuman evil continues until the end. Draped in chains and handcuffed, Blue Duck still scares the deputies assigned to watch him, and he maintains his cool, sneering tone:

Blue Duck smiled. "I raped women and stole children and burned houses and shot men and run off horses and killed cattle and robbed who I pleased, all over your territory, ever since you been a law," he said. "And you never even had a good look at me until today. I don't reckon you would have killed me."

... Call knew there was truth in what Blue Duck said, and merely stood looking at the man, who was larger than he had supposed. His head was huge and his eyes cold as snake's eyes.

"I despise all you fine-haired sons of bitches," Blue Duck said. "You Rangers. I expect I'll kill a passel of you yet."

"I doubt it," Call said. "Not unless you can fly."

Blue Duck smiled a cold smile. "I can fly," he said. "An old woman taught me. And if you care to wait, you'll see me." (936–37)

Blue Duck, of course, gets the last laugh, or at least the last smile, because his prophecy almost comes true. As Call waits for Blue Duck to be escorted to his date with the hangman, he suddenly hears a scream and looks up to see Blue Duck "flying through the air in chains." As Call looks, he thinks that "the man's cold smile was fixed on him as he fell: he had managed to dive through one of the long glass windows on the third floor" taking the deputy with him. When Call walks over to examine the body, "Blue Duck was stone dead, his eyes wide open, the cruel smile still on his lips" (938).

This is a dramatic ending for the notorious Indian, one based partially on the death of the Kiowa chief Satanta, who killed himself by jumping out of a penitentiary window in 1878. Reviewers of *Lonesome Dove* found Blue Duck a convincing villain. Lee Milazzo in *The Dallas Morning News* found most of the secondary characters "no less memorably rendered" than the major characters and singled out "the sadistic, inhuman Blue Duck (who wears a necklace of human fingers)" (12C). And Bill Marvel in a later *Dallas Morning News* article commented that in *Lonesome Dove*, McMurtry "rounded up every stock figure out of western fiction and herded them into one rambling narrative," noting that Blue Duck is the "renegade Indian." But Marvel goes on to say, "Even the villain, Blue Duck, is fully realized, a psychopathic killer who has stepped right out of the headlines of yesterday's paper into horrifying life" (10C).

If Blue Duck demonstrates McMurtry's use of a traditional western character, his two main characters illustrate the balance of conventional and unconventional elements. Ernestine Sewell's argument is that the three old Rangers—Gus, Call, and Jake—comprise a Freudian tripartite figure:

> In *Lonesome Dove* the Cowboy-God is a Freud-
> ian composite of the three old Rangers: Call is
> Super-ego; Gus, Ego; and Jake, Id. Taken as
> one, the three embody the idea of Cowboy, the
> man on horseback, full of the joy of life, accept-
> ing the tragedy of life, brave, daring,
> hardworking, loyal, reliable, proud, stoic, of-
> ten ascetic, straightforward, restless,
> independent, and not without a sense of hu-
> mor. (*Taking Stock* 323)

Sewell's thesis is provocative, but it takes almost all of
the characters in the novel rolled into aggregate to make
a complete human being, and even then no fully-real-
ized, long-standing heterosexual relationship is
apparent.

It is clear, nevertheless, that McMurtry intertwines
the two main characters, telling us about Call and Gus,
that as "a team, the two of them were perfectly balanced" (180). On the surface, it appears that Call is to
represent the traditional and Gus the nontraditional,
for Call is the leader, the "Captain," who is strong-willed,
resolute, quick to act, brave, courageous, loyal. Despite
these positive traits, Call becomes the one whose values McMurtry hangs up for approbation. Call's major
weakness (to him) is that he once exhibited human
weakness through his attraction to the whore, Maggie,

a union that ultimately produced Newt. Like the thorn that infects Jake's thumb, the knowledge of his past weakness festers in Call's memory, as he thinks "what had happened with her had been unnecessary and was now uncorrectable" (391). Newt is the physical embodiment of his humanity and the agent of Call's ambivalent behavior. On the one hand, Call treats Newt with fatherly concern, constantly looking out for his welfare and reacting with uncontrolled violence when the Army scout in Ogallala quirts Newt across the face. On the other, his macho, taciturn, and, McMurtry suggests, perverted system of values, will not allow him to acknowledge his own humanity or to embrace his son and give him his name.

Gus, then, seems to represent the unconventional western hero whose positive traits counter Call's negative ones. Unlike Call, Gus is garrulous, philosophical, sexually aware, compassionate, romantic, and emotional. Gus believes in the power of language, as exhibited by both his constant talk and the Hat Creek Cattle Company sign that he labors to create and that becomes his headstone. Unlike the traditional hero who believes in nature as the best teacher, Gus holds to book-learning as important, adding the Latin motto to the sign and attributing Call's weaknesses to his lack of education ["Grown, but not what you'd call normal," Augustus said. "I put it down to lack of education." (523)] The romantic, emotional Gus, to Call's amazement, cries when he and Call stop at Clara's orchard by the Guadalupe as they begin the cattle drive. He, in fact, makes the drive because of his romantic attraction to Clara, still powerful after all these years. And it is Gus who constantly goads Call to accept and acknowledge Newt as his son.

Additionally, Gus is existentially aware of the central paradox of their lives. He understands that by their having fought to extend civilization, they have actually destroyed the uncivilized world where they felt at home. His keen vision (he can distinguish things far away better than anyone) may symbolize his ability to anticipate the future effects of their actions. On the way to San Antonio as they pass a church and a few stores, Gus remarks to Call: "The dern people are making towns everywhere. It's our fault, you know." Then he continues:

> "Does it ever occur to you that everything we done was probably a mistake? Just look at it from a nature standpoint. If you've got enough snakes around the place you won't be overrun with rats or varmints. The way I see it, the Indians and the bandits have the same job to do. Leave 'em be and you won't constantly be having to ride around these dern settlements."
>
> "You don't have to ride around with them," Call said. "What harm do they do?"

"If I'd have wanted civilization I'd have stayed in Tennessee and wrote poetry for a living," Augustus said. "Me and you done our work too well. We killed off most of the people that made this country interesting to begin with." (349)

Later he remarks to Call: "We'll be the Indians, if we last another twenty years. . . . The way this place is settling up it'll be nothing but churches and dry-goods stores before you know it. Next thing you know they'll have to round up us old rowdies and stick us on a reservation to keep us from scaring the ladies. . . . I think we spent our best years fighting on the wrong side" (357–58).

Gus, however, is not simply an unconventional hero. He, like Call, is brave, resolute, loyal, quick to act. He and Call are both Texas Rangers whose reputations still cause people to react with awe. While Gus maintains his love for Clara and nurses Lorena back to health, he never achieves a satisfying relationship with a woman. His two wives are mentioned perfunctorily. His longest-standing relationship is with Call, which causes Clara to exclaim, "I wish I knew of some way to divorce you from that man" (780), a statement that suggests a latent homosexual relationship between the two. When Call brings her Gus's letter as he takes the body back to Texas, Clara explodes:

"All you two done was ruin one another, not to mention those close to you. Another reason I didn't marry him was because I didn't want to fight you for him every day of my life. You men and your promises: they're just excuses to do what you plan to do anyway, which is leave. You think you've always done right—that's your ugly pride, Mr. Call. But you never did right and it would be a sad woman that needed anything from you. You're a vain coward, for all your fighting. I despised you then, for what you were, and I despise you now, for what you're doing." (931–32)

Like the characters, the structure of the novel also combines both traditional and nontraditional, mythic and anti-mythic elements. More than in previous novels, McMurtry uses traditional structural devices such as suspense and foreshadowing. For suspense McMurtry continues to lead the reader to wonder first about Newt's father and then, after making it clear that it is Call, when Call will accept Newt. Various characters' ends are foreshadowed, most clearly Jake's death by hanging. The capture of Lorena, of course, provides much suspense, and it is also one of the most traditional elements, for the captivity narrative is the basis of the western since its beginning with James Fenimore Cooper. McMurtry seems to allude to Cooper through a

minor character, Mr. Sedgwick, whom July Johnson
meets along the Red River: "I'm traveling through this
country looking for bugs" (332), thus recalling Cooper's
natural scientist Dr. Bat in *The Prairie*.

The trail drive novel provides a special subset of
organizational devices connected to the larger structure of the journey motif. Because of the difficulty in
negotiating barriers with a herd of cattle, crossing obstacles has traditionally been the major element of the
trail drive novel, and McMurtry uses it faithfully, high-
lighting the physical territory crossed—the rivers, from
the Nueces to the Milk; the towns; the buffalo killing
grounds; and Indian territory. Although the traditional
trail drive novel stressed the accomplishment of the
mission—the purposeful journey—in *Lonesome Dove*
McMurtry emphasizes that the end of the line is less
important than the journey itself, with each character
having a different reason for the exercise. Call wants
to further adventuring as long as possible, Gus to see
Clara in Nebraska, Newt to participate in an adult activity, Jake to avoid July Johnson, Lorena to get to San
Francisco. "Here you've brought these cattle all this way,
with all this inconvenience to me and everybody else,
and you don't have no reason in this world to be doing
it," Gus tells Call. As Janis Stout points out, "permanent restlessness," and a "fruitless geographical search"
(*Taking Stock* 67) are part of McMurtry's early novels,
but she concludes that his journey structure in *Lone-*

some Dove is unconventional, and she finds it jarring:

> With Call's decision to return to Texas, the
> reader's expectations are again shifted. It ap-
> pears that the point of the narrative was
> neither the reaching of a destination nor the
> affirmation of the road itself but something
> about returning to roots. Now, we think, we
> understand the generic affiliation of the novel.
> It appears that the Captain will at long last
> acknowledge his bastard son, entrust the new
> cattle kingdom to him, and return to his old,
> known place. But the book does not sustain
> that satisfying variant on the conventional
> form either. Call cannot bring himself to speak
> the word of acknowledgment that will pass
> authority on to his son and bring a new order
> into being. Aging and tired, the barren patri-
> arch starts back to Texas, leaving his men
> leaderless and his herd ownerless. Instead of
> reaffirming the established order (the charac-
> teristic motive force of the trail drive), moving
> from an old order to a new order (the migra-
> tion), or challenging the validity of existing
> order (the picaresque), *Lonesome Dove* has
> moved from a dissolving order to no order at
> all. ("Cadillac Larry" 248)

With readers like Stout who seek a "satisfying variant on the conventional form," McMurtry's unconventional variant seems disordered, but it is just such dissonance that he seems to have set out to create.

McMurtry's images reinforce his intertwining of themes, characters, and structural devices. In fact, the Texas Bull and Deets's pants seem to be physical embodiments of unified diversity. The Texas Bull is multicolored: "He was not exactly rainbow-colored, but his hide was mottled to an unusual extent—part brown, part red, part white, and with a touch here and there of yellow and black. He looked a sight, but he was all bull" (234). Likewise, Deets's pants are a patchwork made of quilts (61). Finally, Gus's sign is a mixture of high and low, with the comical, "We don't rent pigs" and the enigmatic Latin motto, which he doesn't understand. Several different translations are possible. Ernestine Sewell suggests this one: "The cluster of grapes—many-sided, parti-colored, diverse—through living, beget one grape" (*Taking Stock* 323). This translation suggests aggregations of diverse forces and recalls another motto, "E Pluribus Unum," from many the one. Roger Jones finds Sewell's translation

> particularly suggestive of McMurtry's ambivalence regarding language and civilization. Language and civilization do, indeed, unify, seemingly making mankind one, but beneath

comforting appearances lie various individual interpretations determined by individual needs. Augustus's Latin phrase is a perfect symbol of this, not only because Latin is associated with the origins of Western civilization, but precisely because it is sufficiently incomprehensible to allow various readings and/or misreadings. (33)

Another image that reflects McMurtry's ironic ambivalence about the passing old world is the pyramid of buffalo bones cared for by the daft Aus Frank. The bison bones are a visible lament for the loss of the old world, a critique of the consumer ethic that led the Indians to trade hides and the buffalo hunters to decimate the herds. Aus is rightly angry at the bankers ("I don't like the goddamn bank" [471]), for it is they who represent the capitalistic ethic central to the civilization Gus, Call, and the other forces of "progress" have brought to the frontier through their lifetime efforts. Gus wryly comments to Call as they think of Black Beaver, "He didn't have to go along establishing law and order and making it safe for bankers and Sunday-school teachers, like we done. . . . That's what we done, you know. Kilt the dern Indians so they wouldn't bother the bankers" (83).

McMurtry's complex mixture of old and new struck a chord in readers, for the novel won the Spur Award of the Western Writers of America, a Texas Institute of Letters Prize, and the Pulitzer Prize for fiction. There has, as usual, been some criticism. Clay Reynolds, while finding much to praise, noted these problems: vague chronology, unrelated subplots, and "a series of incredible coincidences where characters who know one another continually meet each other by accident in the utterly void expanses of the Great Plains with the casual familiarity of old acquaintances running into themselves on the crowded streets of San Antonio" (*Taking Stock* 331). F. E. Abernethy finds lapses in McMurtry's adherence to realism, noting that the memorable scene where Sean dies in a tangle of snakes is biologically inconsistent:

> [M]occasins are never in a nest. Moccasins are ovoviviparous, and the mother carries the eggs within her. As soon as the eggs (seldom more than five) are passed, the infant breaks out of the sac fully fanged, ready to strike, and very independent. Water moccasins, young or old, are not social creatures hanging about in "swarms" of twenty (Call's count) waiting for a passing cowboy or waterskier, even though Call, not known for exaggeration, says that he once rode his horse into a shallow lake that had hundreds, and the "puddles were like nests, filled with wriggling snakes." (1)

Despite this criticism, *Lonesome Dove*, with sales of 300,000 copies in hardcover, lifted McMurtry into the lofty realm of serious American novelists who make the bestseller list. It made the onetime bad boy of Texas letters the preeminent Texas writer and signaled that Larry McMurtry had come home.

7

Thalia, Houston Redux

Texasville, Some Can Whistle, and
The Evening Star

After his decision to refute
his own guidance and become a symbolic frontiersman
by writing about the old Southwest, Larry McMurtry
returned to his divided strands and began a new pattern
where his contradiction of attractions toward the old
and new were satisfied in steady rotation between the
two. Since 1987, McMurtry has published six novels,
alternating between contemporary sequels and frontier
novels, until *Streets of Laredo* in 1993 merged the two
braids with a sequel set in the late nineteenth century.

The contemporary sequels return to the characters
from previous novels and bring their lives up to date

and in some cases project them into the future. In this way McMurtry can emphasize his continuing concern for the insubstantial nature of a modern world ironically filled with material possessions and mass entertainment that provide little support. In each of these contemporary sequels McMurtry dramatizes a world in sharp contrast to the heroic world of Augustus McCrae and Woodrow Call. The universe of Duane Moore, Sonny Crawford, Jacy Farrow, Danny Deck, Godwin Lloyd-Jons, Aurora Greenway, and Rosie Dunlup is one marked by steady diminishment and loss; fragmented and destroyed families; diseased and disturbed minds; a cosmos fraught with sadness, suffering, and insignificant sex; relieved only occasionally with moments of humor and compassion. The relationship between past and present, both the mythic past and a character's personal past, becomes part of the central concern in each novel.

Texasville (1987)

When Larry McMurtry wrote *The Last Picture Show* in 1966, its biting satire about small-town Texas was winningly original. Even though McMurtry's Thalia then was peopled mainly with cartoon figures with tag names like Charlene Duggs, there was also the full-blown, believable character, Sam the Lion, the owner of the pool hall whose compassion gave the book strength. In 1987—after a decade of the nighttime soap *Dallas* filled with stick figures based on a stereotypical view of the Texas rich—it was not easy to find originality in the problems of Texas millionaires. What makes *Texasville* initially interesting is McMurtry's premise: an audience might want to know what happened in the last twenty years to those characters he created in *The Last Picture Show*. And those characters are memorable to many—from those who have been reading McMurtry all along to those who first met Sonny, Duane, and Jacy in the Peter Bogdanovich 1971 film starring Timothy Bottoms, Jeff Bridges, and Cybill Shepherd, to whom *Texasville* is dedicated. *Texasville* is also interesting because, as the first of several sequels, it indicates continuity and change in McMurtry's career.

Sonny, Duane, and Jacy are back in *Texasville*. Sonny owns the Quik-Sack drive-in store along with several rent houses, but he is losing his grip on reality. Often he finds himself staring out at the world and mentally watching an old movie. "It's like I have a VCR in my brain," he says. His old flame, Ruth Popper, who as the Coach's wife provided Sonny his first important sexual experience, now works for Duane and is an aging jogger. While Sonny was the dominant character in *The Last Picture Show*, *Texasville* concentrates on Duane. He became a millionaire during the oil boom, but the novel takes place in 1986, the year of the 150th anniversary of Texas independence, and as Thalia is

going under with the oil bust, its inhabitants demonstrate the schism of going from boom to bust is such a
short period.

Duane, for example, exhibits the excesses of the
boom: he lives in a large, expensive house, complete
with hot tub, various guest rooms, and the gadgets of
the rich. When he gets depressed, he goes out back and
shoots at the two-story, log-cabin-style dog house, which
his dog has sense enough not to use. This is Thalia's
frontier legacy, debased to a doghouse and to the silly
festival planned to celebrate the county history. Duane
serves on the local arrangements committee for the
centennial celebration for Hardtop County. One of the
plans is to build a replica of the first settlement, called
Texasville, and to give a pageant that recalls the major
historical events of the area and the state, including
Texas independence. The title, in fact, points to
McMurtry's continuing criticism of his home state,
reducing the state to village status and suggesting
McMurtry's evaluation of the contemporary stature of
his materialistic, grasping home state.

Sometimes Duane tries to console Lester Marlow,
who is now the bank president. As oil prices plunge,
Lester waits glumly for his bank to fold and his trial for
bank fraud to begin, and he contemplates suicide. At
other times Duane carries on spiritless affairs with two
women, Suzie Nolan, who is actually in love with
Duane's son, Dickie, and Janene Wells, the county clerk.

Duane is less interested in his wife, Karla, generally acknowledged as one of the most beautiful and outspoken women in the county. Karla wears t-shirts with slogans like *"YOU'RE THE REASON OUR CHILDREN ARE UGLY"*; *"I'VE GOT THE SADDLE, WHERE'S THE HORSE?"*; and *"YOU CAN'T BE FIRST, BUT YOU CAN BE NEXT."*

Duane is partially aroused from lethargy by Jacy, his high school sweetheart, who has returned to Thalia after a movie career in Europe, several marriages, and most recently, the accidental death of her child, a six-year-old son who was electrocuted on a movie set. The mature Jacy is much more interesting than she was as a materialistic teenager, and *Texasville* concentrates on her maturation. As it often is in McMurtry's work, the death of a child provides for an important human and symbolic moment and provides the impetus for characters like Jacy or Danny Deck to respond. For Jacy it is a return to Thalia, to isolation from her recent career, and to the friends of her youth. Jacy's return, the upcoming centennial celebration, and the oil bust lead Duane and the other characters to examine their memories.

When Duane first sees Jacy swimming in the lake near his fishing boat, he recalls the distance between the past and present. He remembers her as a flirt, who was vain about her looks, "studying her face or body for the slightest blemish." As he sees the marks the goggles have made on her face, he thinks about the marks that life has left on her. This scene coalesces several of the themes and images that are important to the novel: water imagery, personal history, memory, past and present. It points out the disparity between the younger, immature, narcissistic Jacy who swam naked in Bobby Sheen's pool in Wichita Falls and the older woman buffeted by life. Seeking rebirth, she swims in Lake Kickapoo; Duane lounges in his hot tub or sleeps in his gigantic waterbed. But he realizes that although he is $12 million in debt, his problems pale in comparison to Jacy's loss of her son.

While the water imagery suggests baptism and rebirth, the novel is almost mute about the methods of achieving either personal or communal regeneration, presenting only fleeting glimpses of the possibility of renewal. Jacy, by returning and attempting to reconnect with her home town, perhaps comes closer to achieving significant character development than any of them. She tries to make Duane aware of his tension and inarticulate responses to her, berating him for never starting a conversation: "I get tired of starting every [conversation] we have. You start one for a change" (408). Finally, in what approaches an epiphantic moment, Duane asks Jacy directly why she had earlier asserted that she was not ready for love. This willingness to communicate about her personal tragedy should indicate a personal breakthrough for Duane, but it is only a momentary, passing insight. He also seems to come to some heightened understanding of his role as husband and father, but these insights are also brief, leading to no recognizable changes in Duane's approach to his life.

Neither does the past provide any support for Sonny. Instead, his nostalgic return to the movies and places of his youth becomes destructive as he drives through the rooms that replaced the carport in the house built where Ruth used to live. And as the novel ends, Jacy, Duane, and Karla interrupt Sonny as he sits in the bleachers above the empty rodeo arena attempting to redeem himself by becoming Dean Martin as Dude in *Rio Bravo*, projecting the movie in memory on the sky above Thalia: "He had a chance to redeem himself, to make things up to his friends" (538). Interrupted, "Sonny felt hopeless. The movie was lost. His chance was lost. He began to cry from disappointment" (539).

How one deals with personal difficulty is a significant question in the novel, but it usually treats fundamental questions with broad humor. Most of the elements of the centennial celebration—the time capsule, the model of old Texasville, the historical reenactments, the class reunion—lead the readers if not the characters to examine the relationship between past and present and to consider aging, maturation, death, and loss. In a skit Duane and Jacy play Adam and Eve and reenact the fall of man. Jacy tempts Duane with an apple and then "Adam and Eve walked hand in hand

out of Eden, toward the bucking chutes" (407). This is
the fall from grace, *Texasville* suggests, the fall into
work and time, aging and death. What might be able
to redeem the residents of Thalia is a sense of history.
But the past's only purpose here is a materialistic one.
The past, as Sonny says, is now "just a gimmick to get
people to come here and buy souvenirs. It doesn't have
a thing to do with the real past."

"Surely in Thalia," McMurtry writes, "far removed
from big-city temptations, people ought to be living on
the old model—putting their families and neighbors
first, leading more or less orderly, more or less responsible lives." Instead, McMurtry continues, "the old
model had been shattered. The arrival of money had
cracked the mode; its departure shattered it. Irratio-
nality now flowered as prolifically as broom weeds in a
wet year" (314–15).

As he does in other novels set in contemporary
times, McMurtry suggests that these characters are
pawns of large economic forces that they are ill-
equipped to handle. Their souls are not furnished with
vision or strength enough to overcome the vicissitudes
of the marketplace. No wealth of VCRs, hot tubs, or
satellite dishes tuned to "Dr. Ruth" will help them find
a meaningful existence. This point is clear from the
opening sentence: "Duane was in the hot tub, shooting
at his new doghouse with a .44 Magnum." Once
McMurtry makes the point that these characters lead

boring lives, his narrative problem is to sustain interest for the rest of the novel.

McMurtry tries to overcome this difficulty with high-energy zaniness, indicating that humor has redemptive power. As a result, scenes read like set pieces: there's a scene where the marathon to start the pageant is disrupted by a gigantic tumbleweed stampede just as the governor's helicopter is trying to land. Then comes a gigantic egg-tossing scene where Duane and Karla's eleven-year-old twins lead the other local kids in rifling an egg truck loaded with 60,000 eggs and pelting the town. The children's energy is in marked contrast to the lethargy of the adults, suggesting perhaps that if there is any hope for Thalia, it will come through the children. But these eggs seem more symbolic of wasted possibility rather than rebirth. Unfortunately, these children of affluence, who turn to things to support them, have no adult models. Sam the Lion has been dead for over thirty years; no one in *Texasville* has his compassion or understanding. Perhaps Jacy, who recalls Keats's poetry and sings a hymn with the line "Hope is an action to keep us" at the celebration, will grow into a model. Although her power to influence others is suggested, the novel leaves this possibility muted.

Roger Jones finds Jacy a fully realized redemptive figure and reads the conclusion as a "moment of spiritual renewal" for Jacy, concluding that the novel dem-

onstrates the human loss resulting from losing contact
with nature:

> In *Texasville* and *Somebody's Darling*,
> McMurtry shows what happens to modern civi-
> lized characters who become too removed from
> nature: They either seek a healthy balance or
> become miserable and self-destruct. These are
> the works of a man deeply divided between his
> worldly success as a writer and his simple ru-
> ral heritage. And why not? After all, for all the
> potential comforting peace and security civili-
> zation may provide, especially for the culturally
> inclined and the disadvantaged, it is at best a
> deadly reductive peace which in some ways
> inevitably isolates (much as language, however
> wonderful at expressing ideas, cannot ever do
> more than hint at reality's true complexity and
> vitality). These are major concerns, and while
> McMurtry presents no easy answers for rec-
> onciliation between nature and civilization,
> between his and our country's past and present,
> his fiction does, in true Victorian fashion, find
> hope in the confrontation of such problems with
> personal courage and the possibility of mo-
> ments of transcendence shared with others.
> And if one takes . . . the endings of *Somebody's
> Darling* and *Texasville* [as an example], then

the answer, however difficult today, lies in a
constant civilized striving for accommodation
between the id-like selfish demands of nature
and the potentially over-repressive and reduc-
tive forces associated with civilization. (48–49)

Although this is an appealing interpretation, it
requires a generous reading of both Jacy's character
and Duane's response as the novel ends. The novel is
less clear about Jacy's maturation and Duane's growth
in understanding than Jones suggests. *Texasville*, then,
especially when compared to *The Last Picture Show*,
demonstrates McMurtry's continuing ambivalence
about the influence of the past and the power of writing.
The writer who stands behind the characters in
Texasville understands their weaknesses, but unlike
the author of *The Last Picture Show*, he does not
reveal much faith in the power of literature to alter
human behavior.

It is particularly interesting to compare *Texasville*
to *The Last Picture Show*. McMurtry emphasizes the
intertextuality of the sequel by recalling scenes from
the previous novel. Sonny, for example, paints a scene
for the art contest that recalls the Thalia of the 1950s
with Sam the Lion and Billy. But in several ways,
McMurtry seems to deny the points of the earlier novel.
The Last Picture Show used satire to point to a
corrective: if the Thalians were not so hypocritical about

sex, perhaps they could lead full, unrepressed lives. Two characters return ironically: John Cecil and Joe Bob Blanton. In the previous novel, both characters served to criticize the hypocrisy and repressiveness of the small town. When Coach Popper accused John Cecil of homosexuality, the charge was based on the Coach's jealousy of Cecil's treatment of a star athlete, Bobby Logan. Merely the hint of homosexuality was enough to ruin a good teacher and family man's life. The novel suggested strongly that the charge was groundless, and "John Cecil left Thalia for good, to go back to Plainview to his brother's grocery store" (*The Last Picture Show* 156), but he returns in *Texasville*: "Fired from his teaching position for alleged homosexuality, John had stubbornly refused to leave town. Instead he bought one of the town's two grocery stores, hung on and eventually prospered." However, his is not a story of triumph over injustice: "Duane would sometimes see him cruising Ohio Street, Wichita Falls's grim little two-block tenderloin. He looked very lonely at such times, peering into the bars, hoping to meet an equally lonely recruit from the nearby air base" (163). Rather than validating the earlier novel's point about the coach's projection of his own repressed homosexuality onto an innocent person, *Texasville* affirms the coach's charges about Cecil's sexuality.

Likewise, Joe Bob Blanton's return in the sequel overturns the suggestions of the previous novel. In

The Last Picture Show, Joe Bob's major crime was masturbating to pictures of Esther Williams. To keep from having to preach at a revival, he kidnapped a young girl. Joe Bob got her to take off her panties, but apparently did not touch her. The target of the satire was Joe Bob's father, Brother Blanton, an oppressive, hypocritical figure. But in *Texasville*, Joe Bob returns to the reunion from Syracuse, New York, where he is the spokesman for the "pedophilic community" and edits the newsletter *Child's Play* (396). In the previous novel, Joe Bob was the victim of a repressive community; in the sequel he is an example of the world gone awry. This is a significant change; where the earlier novel indicated that satire might have the power to change human behavior through its withering insights, the sequel undercuts those insights and presents the foibles of humanity with resignation. These characters' return in the sequel highlights an awareness of life's ironies, but, unlike the first novel, the characters serve no clear satiric purpose.

Another interpretation of the reappearance of these two characters supports themes of *Texasville*— that the past continues to impinge upon the present, sometimes in debilitating ways, and that language affects reality. Once John Cecil was labeled a "queer" and Joe Bob Blanton a child molester, they became what they had been labeled. This point overturns the stereotype that the past, the frontier myth for example, sustains the present. The past may be withering as well. The question that *Texasville* does not answer clearly concerns whether the past can be redeemed. But the same question returns in the next novel with a contemporary setting, which marks the reappearance of Danny Deck, in whose home Jacy lives upon her return to Thalia.

Some Can Whistle (1989)

In *Some Can Whistle* McMurtry returns to his most consistent alter-ego Danny Deck, the struggling writer in *All My Friends Are Going to Be Strangers*. The earlier novel concentrated on examining the problems faced by a young writer torn by the demands of living in the world and the need for solitude and isolation required for success in the writing life. In *Some Can Whistle*, a fifty-one-year-old Deck, last seen drowning his novel in the Rio Grande, returns. Now an overweight multi-millionaire who suffers from migraines, Deck lives in a large Spanish-style house near Thalia, named appropriately Los Dolores, with an aging housekeeper, Gladys, and Godwin Lloyd-Jons, his old British friend, a bisexual and former sociology and classics professor. Deck made his millions as the primary scriptwriter for a top-grossing sitcom, *Al and Sal*, that drew its laughs from the foibles of an ordinary family who "experienced the normal strains, the normal delights, the normal tragedies of American life . . ." (44). The irony is that Danny, after leaving his wife Sally and their daughter following a confrontation with his mother and father-in-law at the Houston hospital where the birth occurred, has led a solitary life devoid of any family connections: "I was a loner and a loser who had pretty much failed at everything: at the novel, at screenwriting, at marriage, and over and over again, at romance. I had never enjoyed one day of normal domestic life, and I knew perfectly well I probably never would" (44).

As he contemplates writing a novel again after all these years laboring in the field of mass television and considers the first line of his novel-in-progress, his isolation is broken by what is the first line of McMurtry's novel: "Mister Deck, are you my stinkin' Daddy?" This scene indicates the primary thematic opposition of the novel: communication-connection-community instead of silence-disconnection-isolation. Danny has become a master at avoiding personal communication. Although he sports a harem of former girlfriends, mostly aging actresses he has known over the years, they all communicate by answering machines, the apt symbol for the novel's emphasis on the modern world's disconnectedness: "Most of the time now I talked to their message machines, a new and seductive form of communication that most of us seemed to be coming to prefer" (39).

In fits and starts, with calls interrupted by jets flying overhead, Danny and his daughter T. R., whose ini-

tials stand for Tyler Rose, reconnect briefly, leading
Danny to drive to Houston to pick her up, along with
her two children, Bo and Jessie, and a menagerie of
T. R.'s co-workers from the Mr. Burger, and to break
the children's father, Muddy Box, out of jail and take
them all back with him to Thalia. Danny's muddled
life is symbolized by the massive migraines that come
upon and paralyze him suddenly. Presented variously
as a gigantic truck bearing down on the slow-moving
motorist or as a stalking Comanche tracking the un-
prepared victim, one of these migraines forces Deck and
his entourage to stop in his least-favorite city, Arlington, which he disparagingly calls the city of cul-de-sacs.
They hole up in Ye Olde Camelot Inn, staying in the
King Arthur suite and the Lancelot and Guinevere
rooms, leading Danny to think:

> I felt a little like King Arthur myself, or maybe
> Richard the Lionhearted or some triumphant
> Crusader. The trip to Houston had been my
> Crusade. I had awakened from deep slumber—
> the slumber of emotional withdrawal—and
> fought the well-armed Saracen, indifference.
> Somewhere in the sun-splashed water park
> across the teeming freeway, my family were
> probably swimming or otherwise disporting
> themselves. They were the Grail I had recov-
> ered. (185)

It is a fanciful, ironic analogy that points on the one hand to the humor of comparing such a mundane event as stopping in a cheesy motel to a crusade or a quest for the grail. On the other hand, for the modern anti-hero deadened by money, mass communication, and things, it is a large, heroic act to regain a lost sense of family and humanity. (This analogy recalls references to myth in *All My Friends Are Going to Be Strangers*, where Danny reenacted in mock-epic fashion the hero's journey as examined in Chapter Three.)

But as F. Scott Fitzgerald noted, there are no second acts in American life, and while Danny hopes to regain the past, he is only partially successful. Like Jay Gatsby, who tried to impress his lost love Daisy Fay with his array of expensive shirts, Danny Deck lavishes things on Tyler Rose. Over the years he kept sending her birthday and Christmas presents only to have them returned by Sally. At Los Dolores, Danny and T.R. open the years of presents and "[a]s the fetus recapitulates the history of the species, T. R. and I recapitulated her own history and mine, a history that had floated unborn in both our consciousnesses until that hour" (229).

These things can only partially bridge the lost past, for they cannot make up for T. R.'s lost emotional ties to a father, and she angrily tells him, "All I want to do is love you" (283). Nor can he provide her with the

taste and awareness that growing up in a lower class
life removed her from: "We were about as close to being
niggers as you could get in Tyler, considering that we
were white." When he tells her that Jill Peel (his artist/
girlfriend from before) had "impeccable taste," T. R. also
gets angry at him, acknowledging that she has been
devoid of taste. Through these references to things and
taste, McMurtry returns to his criticism of the contemporary world's classism and materialism.

Before the novel ends, it also returns to McMurtry's
concern for the violent legacies left over from the frontier
past, symbolized by the mindless Earl Dee, T. R.'s former
lover. Earl Dee breaks out of prison in Huntsville and
stalks and ultimately kills T. R. and Godwin at a Thalia
gas station. Besides the opposition between community
and solitude, the novel also points to the contrast
between civilization and nature, which is another
continuing McMurtry theme. As Roger Jones points out
in *Larry McMurtry and the Victorian Novel*, T. R. is the
natural character, largely untouched by civilization,
which is embodied by Godwin Lloyd-Jons:

> If T.R. symbolizes the fertile reality of
> nature Danny has too long ignored, his old
> British sociology-turned-classics professor,
> Godwin, symbolizes the opposite extreme of
> civilization turned in upon itself and its past.
> Given over to drugs and late night homosexual

encounters as he loiters about his former
student's empty house, Godwin embodies the
pathetic plight Danny might find himself in if
he were to continue his retreat from the world
of normal relationships; this is especially
significant since this is also the vulnerable
moment Danny's imaginative powers have
begun to flag. (74–75)

McMurtry points to this contrast between Godwin
and T. R. by referring to their initial encounter as a
"delicious Jamesian one" between "T. R., beautiful despite her terrible-taste new clothes, sailing up to the
house with Jesse on her hip, the epitome of American
youth, American good looks, American ignorance,
American energy; and Godwin Lloyd-Jons, the ultimate
Euro, drugged out, fucked out, arted out—nothing left
but brain" (191). The Henry James references, repeated
several times, suggest McMurtry's use of James's American theme, in which James contrasted such American
innocents as Daisy Miller with enervated Europeans
or Europeanized Americans such as Frederick Winterbourne. As Jones notes:

The references to James are particularly apt,
for in the novelist's earlier repeated introduc-
tions of naive and immature American heroines
to the cultivated but sterile world of European

aristocrats, ironic and dramatic echoes abound
of T. R.'s introduction to Danny's sophisticated
world, in which plans are soon made to take
her to Europe. Like Daisy Miller, T. R. is ill-
bred, outgoing, and blessed with beauty and
vitality. Yet unlike her predecessor, T. R. will
never get the dubious privilege of bumping up
against European refinement and possibly self-
destructing in response to social snobbery;
instead, she will be brutally murdered in a type
of incident all too common in modern American life. (74)

That the two characters' names recall flowers also indicates the similarity. Likewise, Winterbourne's frosty
withdrawal from life is similar to Danny Deck's. But
the image of T. R. "as a tolerant young lioness, finishing off a light snack, perhaps of antelope, while playing
with her cubs" (126) is suggestive of another James
story, "The Beast in the Jungle," in which a character
lives a life of solitude trying to avoid the terrible fate he
thinks will befall him. Ironically the fate he tries to avoid
is living a life of solitude. Danny, of course, sidesteps
this fate when T. R. breaks his wall of solitude and leads
him out into the world, forcing him to the profound self-
realization that he has missed life. By taking her
dancing and helping her fulfill a childhood fantasy, he
partially redeems himself and prepares for raising his

granddaughter Jesse to be able to live in the world.

The novel also returns to McMurtry's concern for mass entertainment. Both movies and television come under scrutiny. When T. R. asks him about Jill Peel, Danny returns to and completes the story of an important character in other novels, intertexualizing *Some Can Whistle* beyond its sequel status. Jill's story calls into question the Hollywood world, for although she had been an important director, Hollywood had used her up and forgotten her. Jill had been killed mysteriously, bludgeoned to death in her apartment, and Danny had been made the executor of her estate. Entering her apartment to dispose of the things, Danny discovers a portfolio of drawings labeled "For Danny." These sketches, titled "Let the Stranger Consider," are self-portraits, and they cause Danny, who has been a constant stranger to others, to consider how Jill had abandoned her real calling as an artist to expend her energies in the unforgiving world of movies.

Danny, of course, has devoted his time to television. After T. R.'s death, in an attempt to fill in the blankness of her earlier history, Deck journeys to East Texas to visit her grandfather, her Big Pa Lloyd Bynum, the evangelist-seducer-dope dealer who had introduced her to Earl Dee and sealed her doom. Ultimately, he writes a novel about Big Pa and entitles it *Let the Stranger Consider*, using Jill's legacy. Big Pa wants to tell Danny, noted TV writer, of his idea for a good television show, one about Texas oilmen, telling Danny that a TV series about Texas oilmen would "make a fortune." The series, of course, sounds strangely reminiscent of *Dallas*, another mass entertainment that drew from and created another major Texas myth, the myth of the ruthless oilman.

The trip to visit Big Pa is one of many journeys, as McMurtry again uses such random side-trips as the ones to the motel in Arlington and to a dance in Fort Worth. Structurally, *Some Can Whistle* also depends on the escape-and-return pattern, as it begins with the father's return to his daughter, reenacted with the trip to Houston and return to Thalia. The novel also consciously points out the contrast between the city and the plain, much as Hemingway uses the mountain and the plain as positive and negative landscapes in *A Farewell to Arms*. Danny muses that "the rules of happiness are as strict as the rules of sorrow" and then concludes that the "two states have different densities, I've come to think. The lives of happy people are dense with their own doings—crowded, active, thick—urban, I would almost say." On the other hand, the "sorrowing are nomads, on a plain with few landmarks and no boundaries; sorrow's horizons are vague and its demands few." The frontier is of the plains, and its legacy, as Alan Trachtenberg notes in comments about Frederick Jackson Turner, was the kind of rampant individualism that *Some Can Whistle* confronts:

If the frontier had provided the defining experience for Americans, how would the values learned in that experience now fare in the new world of cities—a new world brought into being as if blindly by the same forces which had proffered the apparent gift of land? Would the America fashioned on the frontier survive the caldrons of the city? Turner responded to the challenge by an act of distillation. To be sure, he argued, the story of the frontier had reached its end, but the product of that experience remains. It remains in the predominant character, the traits of selfhood, with which the frontier experience had endowed Americans, that "dominant individualism" which now must learn to cope with novel demands. The thesis projects a national character, a type of person fit for the struggles and strategies of an urban future. (15–16)

Some Can Whistle examines the frontier legacy of individualism and reveals it to be limiting and isolating. McMurtry also allows Danny Deck to achieve partial redemption. At the novel's end, McMurtry takes his characters into the future, as he also does in *The Evening Star*, recounting the deaths of Earl Dee, Muddy Box, Gladys, and others. But the conclusion points to

the contrast with the beginning of the novel where hesi-
tating phone calls reestablish communication with
T. R. Instead, Jesse "called and called, she called and
called," as she moved around the world. Jesse's voice
reminds him of the European actresses Danny had
counted among his friends, how they had all "once
whistled the brainy, sexual whistle of youth and health,
tunes that those who once could whistle too lose but
never forget" (384). Some can whistle and respond; others may listen but miss the call for communication.

The Evening Star (1992)

If Danny Deck, the writer withdrawn from life, is
McMurtry's masculine alter ego, then perhaps Aurora
Greenway is the feminine counterpart. Danny spends
his life pursuing art and entertainment and finds himself alienated from life and family; Aurora, despite her
artistic sensibility, never achieves the artistic goal she
thought that she was meant to produce. But she lives
her life as fully as she can in a world where fate, tragedy, class distinctions, aging, and the vicissitudes of
daily life beset her constantly.

With *The Evening Star* McMurtry returns to characters from *Terms of Endearment*. The title harkens to
an earlier McMurtry practice of titling books with elegiac titles that point to the sense of an ending. The
star of the evening of this novel is Aurora Greenway,

goddess of dawn and River Oaks in the earlier novel and aging seductress in the sequel. Her paramour from the earlier novel, General Hector Scott, has moved in with Aurora and her maid Rosie Dunlup. (The General was imaginatively transformed into Jack Nicholson's astronaut in the film version of the earlier novel, and in another McMurtry self-reflexive turn, Nicholson is mentioned in this novel.) Even though she is now a septuagenarian, Aurora remains the self-absorbed character she was before, and as before she continues to spend much of her time manipulating suitors and contemplating seductions. Besides the general, who in his late eighties flirts with senility and flashes Rosie and the neighbors, Aurora's most persistent suitor is a Frenchman named Pascal, whose most significant feature is a bent penis. Her major seduction occurs when she decides to direct her energies toward Jerry Bruckner, a lay psychiatrist over thirty years her junior.

When she is not fretting over her loss of sexual energies, Aurora worries about her grandchildren. Her daughter Emma, of course, died of cancer at the end of *Terms of Endearment*, but she left three offspring who are the source of trouble for Aurora. Tommy is in prison in Huntsville for killing his former girlfriend. Aurora and Rosie drive up I-45 in Aurora's aging Cadillac to visit him regularly, but he has worked to reduce his emotions to zero, and the visits enervate Aurora. The other grandson, Teddy, recovering from mental illness, is working at a local 7-11, living with Jane, a bisexual who also suffers from psychiatric problems, and caring for their young child, Bump. Aurora's granddaughter, Melanie, is pregnant, probably by her current selfish boyfriend, whom she follows to L.A., where he hopes to become an actor.

The novel spans a forty-year period, beginning in the late 1980s and jumping forward to the future as McMurtry spins out the epilogue. Like *Lonesome Dove*, *The Evening Star* is about aging and death, but as if to point out the contrast between the final acts of Gus and Call and those of Aurora and Rosie, not much of outward importance happens to anyone here. While the blue pigs follow Gus and Call to Montana; Aurora drives over to her favorite eatery, the Pig Stand, for pie. Other characters from McMurtry's stable either appear or are mentioned. Patsy Carpenter, the main character in *Moving On*, now widowed, competes with Aurora for Jerry's affection. Danny Deck's troubles with his daughter, the subject of *Some Can Whistle*, receive mention. We learn that Jill Peel, the main character of *Somebody's Darling*, died, as did Vernon Dalhart, the laconic, virginal oilman who lived in his Lincoln on the top floor of a parking garage.

By returning to the details of his earlier novels, McMurtry seems to be engaging in a similar process to Aurora's project—a Proustian undertaking to recall her past and try to recover from "a profound sense of wasted time" (560). By going through her scrapbooks and memorabilia, she is trying to recapture every moment of her life, but it is a daunting and ultimately impossible project:

> Somehow she had let her life slip by, achieving nothing. She did not suppose, in her hours of regret, that she had ever had mind enough to achieve a great work, like Monsieur Proust. Perhaps she hadn't mind enough to achieve a work of even modest scope—yet it did seem to her that she had mind enough and sufficient individuality that she ought to have achieved more. . . . She had, in the end, merely lived, partaking rather fully of the human experience, absorbing it, and yet doing nothing with it. (560)

In some ways Aurora Greenway finds herself in a position similar to Leo Tolstoy's Ivan Ilych, who tries as he faces death to redeem a meaningless life. Her memory project fails, but in the conclusion to *The Evening Star*, McMurtry suggests that through her artistic sensibility, Aurora may prevail. Projecting into the future, McMurtry traces Aurora's life into the twenty-first century. In her nineties, Aurora has a stroke and loses the power of speech, but she maintains her

love of music, and she bequeaths the love to her grandson Henry by playing Brahm's *Requiem* to the baby,
causing him to look into her eyes and recall

> the Other Place—the place where there were
> no Bigs. The sight startled Henry—it confused
> and upset him a little . . . and yet when he
> looked into the old woman's eyes and saw that
> she could see the Other Place, he felt confused,
> and not happy. Perplexed, he batted at his ear
> or rubbed his face unhappily, as he did when
> he wanted to go to sleep. Sometimes he made
> an indecisive sound—a sound part laugh and
> part cry. He wanted something, but didn't know
> what. He tried to remember the Other Place,
> but he couldn't. He didn't understand the old
> woman, but he wanted to stay with her any-
> way. (629)

Roger Jones finds in this scene a connection to
William Wordsworth's "Ode: Intimations of Immortality
from Recollections of Early Childhood," which points to
a child's connection to a transcendent world:

> Aurora's moving deathbed scene, where she
> holds Tommy's baby while both experience a
> transcendent moment listening to Brahm's
> *Requiem*, is notable in a number of ways. As

with the scene at the end of *Horseman, Pass By*, an artist's music lifts people into a spiritual realm which offers consolation from the hardships of this world. Most importantly, the scene is the first ever in McMurtry's fiction to explicitly assert, like Wordsworth, the *reality*, not just the possibility, of such a spiritual realm from which all are born and all return. (69)

Years later, when Henry listens to Brahms' *Requiem*, Aurora's powerful legacy returns:

Before he knew it, the music had taken him to another place—to an old place in his memory, to a place so old that he could not really even find a memory, or put a picture to it, or a face. He just had the emptying sense that he had once had someone or something very important: something or someone that he could not even remember, except as a loss—something or someone that he would never have again. (637)

No doubt McMurtry was drawn back to Aurora Greenway because she was a powerfully memorable character, one who allowed him to enter into the world of an urban, sophisticated, eastern woman and extend the limits of his own life experiences and the possibilities of his imagination. Her despair over the troubles of her family is a deep human concern, and her story, trivial as it is in many ways, is a human one. Still, many reviewers did not respond well to *The Evening Star*. Thomas R. Edwards in *The New York Review of Books* found "the positive thinking attached to the novel's ending ... unearned" and called the novel "a surprisingly lax book" with no "coherent point of view." He continues: "What may perhaps be represented here is an author's boredom with his own most popular creatures, in conflict with his understanding that many people want an easy, undemanding way of killing time while reading about geriatric sex, random violence, and disaster, along with black humor" (54). Mark Starr in *Newsweek* also responded negatively:

> McMurtry apparently intends *The Evening Star* as a serious reflection on aging and death, themes dealt with so successfully in *Lonesome Dove*. But his characters are so sex-obsessed, and the sex—from geriatric couplings to impotence—is handled in such frivolous fashion, that larger issues are obscured. (58)

In my initial review in *Southwestern American Literature*, I pointed to the density of the seemingly insignificant details:

If this were a family history, it would make
perfect sense, but it is a novel. The old adage
"Life is messy; art isn't" comes to mind. This is
a messy novel, which seems to try to repro-
duce the randomness of life in its 637 pages.
But other than the interest longtime McMurtry
fans might have about whatever happens to
Aurora, Rosie, and the General, it lacks any
clearly unified purpose. It's hard to sustain
interest in the seductive wiles of an overweight,
selfish grandmother in her mid-seventies. (101)

Although the novel is weighted down by details,
the randomness and lack of purpose in many people's
lives are central to the book's purpose. Throughout *The
Evening Star* McMurtry examines the forces that keep
humans from being able to provide direction to their
lives and achieve happiness. For Jerry Bruckner it is
class. Although he is drawn to women like Aurora and
Patsy, he constantly feels the burden of the class
differences between them and him. Their education and
upbringing contrast to his paltry background growing
up as the son of a Las Vegas showgirl. He is keenly
aware that his "psychiatric" training, such as it was,
consisted mainly of his standup comedy routines about
psychiatrists. He tells Patsy, "Maybe I just have a class
problem. . . . I'm just not confident with upper-class
women" (359). Aurora, on the other hand, recalling her

mother's affair with Sam the houseboy, never lets class get in the way of her life, and she makes her maid, Rosie, her dearest friend. She also encourages relationships with men as diverse as the Frenchman Pascal, the General, Hector Scott, as well as two Greek fishermen who wear undershirts, Theo and Vassily Petrakis.

For Mickey, a prison inmate who eventually stabs Tommy Horton, both race and class short-circuit his sense of direction. "In Mickey's bloodshot eyes was the hatred of the despised—the not-good-enough southern swamper, more scorned even than negroes in the small towns strung around the wetlands of the South" (572).

Classism, racism, and the weight of daily life inhibit human ability to achieve purpose. Structurally, the novel also suggests how forces keep people from direction. *The Evening Star* generally follows chronological order and is divided into five parts: Part I, "The Children and the Men," Part II, "The Decorative Woman," Part III, "Aurora's Project," Part IV, "Rosie's Problem," and Part V, "Last Love, First Loss." Within this structure McMurtry again employs recognizable devices: the random journey, as Aurora drives back and forth to Huntsville to visit Tommy and travels to California. Much of the structure draws from the powerful use of contrast: past/present, youth/age, love/death, significance/meaninglessness. As he has also done before, McMurtry uses paired characters for contrast and structure. In this case, the contrast between the upperclass Aurora and the blue collar maid Rosie Dunlup add to the novel's structure and themes.

As usual, McMurtry's images grow easily from the subject matter. Aurora's Cadillac returns from before, and along the drive from Houston to the Huntsville prison, Aurora passes the Goodyear Blimp, which is housed near I-45. Aurora finds the blimp "quite majestic" and observes:

> It was an aircraft from another era, and yet it managed to survive and flourish, to retain its dignity and power in their own degraded time. In her happy, confident moments, she felt rather like a peer of the blimp—but today was not one of her happy, confident days, and when they passed the blimp, anchored tranquilly to its guy wires, she looked at it wistfully. (242)

Certainly, Aurora Greenway survives with dignity and power as she ages. Although she never achieves complete control over the past through her memory project, she manages to influence the future through her relationship with her grandchild, leaving him an artistic legacy that, unlike Danny Deck's frontier legacy of an individualism that weakens his ability to connect, is not harmful.

These three contemporary sequels—*Texasville*,

Some Can Whistle, and *The Evening Star*—continue
McMurtry's critique of twentieth-century American
life. They return to his characters, themes, and settings
of previous novels, continuing his criticism of materialism, classism, individualism, and religious hypocrisy
and returning to an ambivalent treatment of the writing life. These three contemporary novels also present
aging characters who, although they suffer from the
problems of contemporary life, increasingly find something of value in their lives. This possibility is less
clearly realized in *Texasville*, but in both *Some Can
Whistle* and *The Evening Star*, the main characters'
projected futures reveal moments of transcendence
that validate their individual lives.

8

The Symbolic
Frontiersman
Anything for Billy, *Buffalo Girls*, and
Streets of Laredo

After his initial series of
novels about the rural Southwest, Larry McMurtry
shifted his focus to urban settings, first in Texas then
in Hollywood, Washington, D.C., and Las Vegas and
the dislocations of the (post)modern world. At the same
time he continued to urge Texas writers to eschew the
frontier and concentrate on urban settings. With the
success of *Lonesome Dove*, McMurtry seemed to reconcile himself to writing about subjects his critics had long

suggested he was suited to: the cowboy on the frontier. But since then, McMurtry has chosen to alternate between novels set in the past—*Anything for Billy*, *Buffalo Girls*, and *Streets of Laredo*, covered in this chapter—and sequels to earlier novels updated to the present, *Texasville*, *Some Can Whistle*, and *The Evening Star*, discussed in the previous chapter. The nineteenth-century novels focus on historical characters Billy the Kid, Calamity Jane, and Charles Goodnight, and each sets out to explode much of the myth of the frontier and the legendary figures who have carried the stories. These frontier novels make it clear that although McMurtry may return to the frontier as a setting, his themes remain the same and reveal the universal aspects of human fear and desire. Additionally, the first two books return to another of McMurtry's continuing themes: his ambivalence about the role of the writer. Both books display nineteenth-century novelistic conventions; *Anything for Billy* is narrated by a dime novelist and becomes something of a dime novel in the process. *Buffalo Girls* uses the epistolary format, with Calamity Jane as the primary writer. *Streets of Laredo* combines McMurtry's two recent trends, since it is both a novel set on the frontier and a sequel to an earlier novel.

Anything for Billy (1988)

McMurtry was surprised by the powerful romantic reaction to *Lonesome Dove*. While he had set out to
debunk the myth, he discovered instead that many readers filtered out the anti-mythic material and responded
only to the powerful romance of the western legends.
With *Anything for Billy* McMurtry leaves little room
for readers to find anything heroic about his imaginative recreation of Billy the Kid, who went by various
names—William Henry Bonney, Henry McCarty, Billy
McCarty, Henry Antrim, William Antrim, Billy Antrim.
(According to Robert Utley's recent book, *Billy the Kid:
A Short and Violent Life*, his real name was Henry
McCarty, and he was born in New York City in the late
1850s, probably 1859.) McMurtry chooses to call his
youthful killer Billy Bone, partially to indicate that this
is *his* fictional creation and partially to nod to his literary forbears, Herman Melville's Billy Budd and Ken
Kesey's Billy Bibbit. Like them, Billy Bone is an innocent, and he eventually becomes the victim of his own
legend, one that McMurtry makes clear initially had
little basis in reality. But eventually, young Billy feels
the weight of his reputation and sets out to make the
reality fit the myth. The name "Bone" is suggestive of
the bones produced by the legendary killer and when
pronounced "Bon-e" or "Bonny," it recalls the name
"Bonney." As Ben Sippy sees him, he is also a bonny

boy. In an interview shortly after the novel was published, McMurtry told Mervyn Rothstein of *The New York Times*,

> "I'm interested in how legends arise," he says. "Take Billy the Kid. Here was a man, a boy, really who had a short, commonplace life. How could he have produced a legend, and a bibliography with thousands of items in it? There's an element of sheer publicity in it. It was a time when the Old West was becoming very useful in popular fiction, for the exploits of westerners were beginning to have importance in the national imagination.
>
> "That moment [the 1870s and 80s] the West, which has been so glamorized in myth, was actually ending. The open West was gone, the cowtowns were becoming respectable, the mining towns were petering out. The ground for that body of myth was changing, becoming civilized, suburbanized. And more or less at the same moment, the popular press, as represented by the dime novel, was beginning to transform a very crude environment and an uncertain way of life into something heroic—which mostly it wasn't." (C17)

Ugly and unappealing, suffering from migraines

and myopia, frightened of lightning and shadows in the night that remind him of the "Death Dog," a poor shot and poorer horseman, and a failed cowboy, certainly Billy Bone is not an heroic figure. (Some of these traits prefigure those exhibited in Clint Eastwood's popular anti-mythic western, *Unforgiven*.) In fact, McMurtry's unremitting emphasis on Billy's shortcomings makes it difficult to understand why *anyone* likes him at all. Still, the narrator, Ben Sippy, says, "Though now, when I think of Billy Bone giggling at one of his own little sallies, I soon grow blind with tears—sentimental, I guess. But there was a time when I would have done anything for Billy" (4).

Although the novel's ostensible focus is on the title character, this is also another novel that examines the writer and the writing process with an ambivalence similar to that in *All My Friends Are Going to Be Strangers*. Ben is a dime novelist from Philadelphia who escapes the marriage, family, and tedious life on Chestnut Street to discover the West he learned of in dime novels. Ben's interest began as a reader. He became so enthralled by the world of the novels, he developed a fever, "a kind of mental malaria" (16), treated only by more reading. When his suppliers could not produce enough hits to satisfy his habit, Sippy had to begin writing his own. His initials B. S., his street name "Chestnut," and his name reflect the insipid work he begins to produce.

By using a writer involved in a significant historical event, McMurtry is able to examine several themes
that have interested him over the years. Of primary
importance is the frontier myth, along with the forces
that have created and sustained it over the years, the
dime-novels and movies. But he also takes on the question of subjective history. In an interview in *Humanities*, McMurtry explained that using a bad writer who
gets involved with an outlaw, "enabled [him] to just play
with several kinds of interesting things, particularly,
how different history is for the people who have lived a
particular portion of it than for historians who come
along and study it." It also allows him to examine the
irony of success: "Ironically he's the world's most successful dime novelist. When he's living in the East, he
knows nothing real about the West. He goes to the West;
he gets involved with the most famous outlaw that's
ever been; he goes back home expecting to be even more
successful, and he is a complete failure" (5).

While McMurtry seems to have come to terms with
his ambivalence about the frontier West by taking such
a hard anti-mythic approach, overturning the legends
at every turn, he transforms his own ambivalence into
Sippy's wavering response to Billy Bone. Sippy clearly
realizes that Billy is a cold killer. He watches him kill
Elmer Fay, a good and decent man who should not have
died, and he also witnesses his cold-blooded murder of
Jody Fay, who comes into Skunkwater Flats under a

flag of truce, and, finally, he sees Billy's senseless killing of an unarmed Apache boy. Sippy has absolutely no
reason to continue to be attracted to Billy, and yet his
attraction to him perseveres in the face of everything
that counters it. Riding his mule Rosie, not Rosinante,
Sippy becomes the Quixotic romanticizer in this attack
on the falsity of romantic legends and recalls
McMurtry's powerful attraction to the book that inspired
him as a young man growing up amid powerful myths:
Don Quixote.

McMurtry, perhaps acknowledging the misreadings
of *Lonesome Dove*, takes a swipe at readers who misin-
terpret an author's intentions through the character of
Sister Blandina, a nun who is a friend of Billy's. When
she learns that Sippy is an author, she tells him that
he is her favorite author and that his half-dimer *Wed-
ded but Not Won* is her favorite book. But she then takes
him to task for his portrayal of the wife: "I don't believe
you were at all fair to the wife. Why, all she sought was
a little kind attention, and perhaps a loving word now
and then. If she'd got her due, she soon would have
been won." Sippy cannot believe her response: "Kind
attention. Loving words. Got her due? 'Why, the woman
had her due!' I exclaimed, amazed that any reader would
think she hadn't" (199).

As Clay Reynolds points out in the introduction to
Taking Stock, in one of the best discussions to date on
Anything for Billy, McMurtry both uses and changes

popular historical accounts of Billy the Kid so that, on the one hand, he can connect to the historical period that produced the outlaw myth and, on the other, so that he can present *his* version of history.

> Hence, Stinking Springs, the site of a famous shoot-out between William Bonney and a feuding faction, becomes Skunkwater Flats, where Billy Bone and a collection of loosely aligned gunfighters are beset by cowboys hired to ride them down and kill them. Charles Bowdrie, the first man killed in that foray, becomes Barbecue Campbell; Pat Garrett becomes Tully Roebuck; John Chisum, rancher and Territorial power mogul, becomes Will Isinglass, an intelligent and farsighted man but a creature impervious to evil and capable of almost superhuman frontier feats—and, significantly, the villain of the piece.

Reynolds notes that McMurtry alters other aspects of the historical accounts:

> The famous escape from the Lincoln County Jail where Billy kills Bell—renamed Snookie Brown—is present, but McMurtry neatly avoids the sensational shooting down of

Olinger and the derisive breaking up of the weapon before an hour's cavort through the building. Instead, Billy Bone falls under his horse and makes his getaway ignominiously across the saddle of his sometime lover and Isinglass's outlaw illegitimate daughter, Katie Garza. Additionally, McMurtry avoids the complications of the Lincoln County War, which becomes the Whiskey Glass War, a simpler conflict centering on Isinglass's attempt to run buffalo hunters and gunfighters off his three million acres. (*Taking Stock* 19–20)

Just as he merges history and fiction with Billy the Kid's story, and just as he merges conventional and unconventional elements in *Lonesome Dove*, McMurtry also blends traditional and untraditional western characters in *Anything for Billy*. Included are many recognizable figures: the outlaw (Billy), the taciturn cowboy (Joe Lovelady), the wealthy, grasping rancher (Will Isinglass), the effete easterner (Ben Sippy), the beautiful girl (Katie Garza), the sheriff (Tully Roebuck), the sharpshooting gunfighter (Hill Coe), the half-breed Indian (Bloody Feathers), the fortune teller (La Tulipe), the bartender (Des Montaignes), and the supporting characters—the buffalo hunters, gunfighters, Texans, drunks and hangers-on. (Des Montaignes's name, by the way, seems to be a fun poke at two figures who helped produce the philosophical climate that produced the frontier myth: Montaigne and Descartes.)

Along the way McMurtry introduces his untraditional characters and attacks not only the supposedly heroic figures who make up the legend but also some of the major elements of southwestern legend identified by Larry Goodwyn: primitivism, racism, and sexism. The entire novel undermines the notion of primitivism, which is the belief that living close to nature breeds full men and women. Over and over again Sippy remarks that although the natural landscape is beautiful, the human one is violent and deadly:

> The prairie was sunlit and fair; the meadowlarks were singing and the hawks circling high. The beauty of the country was unsurpassed, with antelope frolicking near and the grass so endless.
>
> Yet, within a day, I had seen three men meet their deaths. I was beginning to have to reckon with the fact that I was riding around in a place where it was rather hard to last. (139)

Shortly after that Sippy again notes how the beautiful landscape is muted by the human sadness caused by the deaths: "I liked to watch the flare of colors over the mountains to the east as the sun rose—the fresh air and the clear light brought a brief exemption from the sadness I was struggling with" (167). While the West produces an aesthetic attraction, the reality behind the appearance of the West, Sippy remarks shortly after his arrival, is that it is filled with bugs.

Ultimately McMurtry uses genetics and an untraditional character to attack the primitivistic myth of the power of the western landscape to produce full living creatures. Lady Cecily Snow's father, Lord Snow, was a friend and follower of Charles Darwin, and he introduced Isinglass to genetic principles. Lord Snow had failed badly in his attempt to breed buffalo and cattle, producing a "museum of failures" (266). The cattalo, Lady Cecily tells Sippy, "represent rather a downward step on the ladder of evolution" (283). Isinglass had then attempted to produce superior offspring by Lady Snow, only to create the mute boys Billy eventually kills. And Lady Cecily, cold and single-minded, provides one of two untraditional female characters in this western.

McMurtry points to the racism inherent in the older world by making Katie Garza aware of the powerful racism directed against Mexicans in Texas during the golden days of cowboying. Despite the fact that she is a dead shot and the daughter of one of the most powerful figures in New Mexico, she is aware of the prejudice practiced against Mexicans in Texas, learning it, she

says, from her father: "He said I'd get no help from the
law, so I'd better learn to shoot. He said the law would
be my enemy, and I already see he's right." When Billy
asks, "Why would the law be your enemy?", she replies,
"Because I'm brown . . . and that's Texas, across the
river" (169). Another untraditional character who undermines the inherent racism of the frontier myth is
Mesty-Woolah, the seven-foot African, called the
"nigger" by Lady Cecily, who is Isinglass's villainous
counterpart. Wielding his long sword and riding his
camel, Mesty-Woolah strikes fear in the hearts of Billy's
countrymen and counters the traditional characters
McMurtry imports from the formula western.

Katie Garza's mere presence as the beautiful heroic figure in the novel along with Lady Cecily as the
conspiring villain, counters the fact that women were
often missing from the traditional tales. Almost nothing about Katie's character is traditional, other than
the fact that she falls in love with Billy and provides
the love interest in the story. A dead shot, she
singlehandedly causes Hill Coe to fall from grace as a
gunfighter by challenging him to a shooting match,
which he loses. An accomplished horsewoman, she rides
to Mexico and entices Billy to join her by stripping off
her clothes and riding across the Rio Grande despite
La Tulipe's prediction that Billy would die if he crossed
it. Ultimately, McMurtry turns the frontier myth upside down when Katie becomes the one who actually

kills Billy. Although Clay Reynolds thinks that McMurtry still makes the western myth a masculine one, both Katie Garza's and Lady Cecily Snow's actions challenge his interpretation. Reynolds states:

> In *Anything for Billy* the women—even La Tulipe, the seer who recalls such philosophically oriented characters from Halmea to Ruth Popper to Aurora's maid—are catalytic; but they are not central, for McMurtry understands and points out in a way he hasn't since *Horseman, Pass By* that the frontier myth is, if anything, a male myth, the archetype a male archetype. The West might not be hard on horses, because they were valuable, he has written, but with women, it was a different story. . . . Women may be consorts, even conduits, for men and the actions they take; their stories may form the centerpiece of a novel, and their actions may ultimately determine a plot's outcome; but the story of the West— mythical, frontier, modern, urban—remains a man's story. Annie Oakley was a side-show attraction; Buffalo Bill was a hero. (*Taking Stock* 28)

Just as the characters merge various elements, the structure combines traditional dime novel elements with organizational methods common to other McMurtry novels. It is divided into six parts, made up of many short chapters which reflect the traditional structure of the dime novel. With Billy and Joe Lovelady, McMurtry again produces paired figures: "Call them sidekicks, *compañeros*, or what you like, I doubt they could have been separated, except by the one thing that did separate them, finally" (*Anything for Billy* 32). McMurtry also employs his random geographical journeying device with Billy and Sippy moving from New Mexico to Texas to Mexico and back with the journeys based only on Billy's whim. But the novel also uses the familiar escape-and-return pattern, as Sippy begins the story by recounting what led him to leave Philadelphia for the West and ends with his return after his adventures and his final escape from family, marriage, and writing. Like Danny Deck he bids adieu to writing and acknowledges his own complicity in the movie industry, claiming credit for having inspired "Eddie" (Edwin S.) Porter to create the first western film, *The Great Train Robbery*. Despite McMurtry's turning upside down older myths, Sippy's altered character actually reenacts the pattern of regeneration through violence described by Richard Slotkin. Sippy's powerful experiences with violence in the wilderness produce an equally powerful transformation of character.

One major question remains. Why did Larry McMurtry choose to retell the story of Billy the Kid?

There are several possible answers. Certainly one of the reasons stems from McMurtry's desire to debunk the frontier myth, and it was natural for him to select one of the two major western figures (Custer being the other). But there are other reasons. McMurtry was no doubt drawn to the conflicting aspects of Billy's character. As Robert M. Utley indicates in *Billy the Kid: A Short and Violent Life*, Billy is a powerfully suggestive character:

> Billy the Kid died as America enthusiastically plunged into the Gilded Age. The transformation of an agrarian nation into an industrial giant launched a frenzy of material acquisitiveness that corrupted national institutions with the same ethical laxity so conspicuous on the frontier.... Only in a quick reliance on violence did the frontier differ from the nation as a whole in the relentless quest for power and wealth, and then it was largely a difference of degree.
>
> The twin specters of corruption and violence remained embedded in American culture, periodically to surface separately or in tandem. Whether originating in the frontier experience or in some dark stain in the American character, they continue to find ambiguous expression in the legend of the youth who lived both. More

than a century after his death, Billy the Kid still rides boldly across America's mental landscape, symbolizing an enduring national ambivalence toward corruption and violence.

For a life that ended at twenty-one, that is a powerful and disturbing legacy. (206–207)

But as Stephen Tatum makes clear in a 1990 review-essay of Utley's book in *New Mexico Historical Review*, Billy represents more than the simple transition from agrarian to industrial economy. His life also points to the powerful changes in all aspects of American life, which the change to a corporate economy signaled.

The transformation in American life at this time was not simply that from an agrarian to an industrial nation but more precisely from a market to a corporate economy and society, which meant among other things that not only were space and time divided differently but also that the social fabric of family- and village-centered life was corroded by the market relations. In place of this damaged social fabric, simulated "authentic" families were formed through public leisure activities (concerts, parks, cafes, etc.) and through the consumption of mass-produced literature. . . .

From this perspective, the Kid's life reveals not only the "muddied ethics" of his era or our culture's ambivalent attraction to spectacles of violence. The Kid's celebrity status, both while he was alive and after his death, also reveals an "industrial" literature's response to the specific forms of alienation in American life. Indeed, at every point of the Kid's short and violent life—his family's migration westward; the mining and military economies; the arrival of Tunstall on the scene; the media status; even the availability of firearms—we can detect the imprint of the larger cultural and economic context engendered by the mechanism of expanding capital. (89–90)

Despite McMurtry's attack on the western myth, some readers were still not sure of his intention. Suzanne Winckler, reviewing for *Texas Monthly*, was undecided about the book's purpose:

McMurtry tries to make a case that our affections for certain people are irrational, but Billy has so little to recommend him (he's not even handsome) that it is hard to buy that thesis, and it is a considerable relief when he bites the dust. . . .

Sippy's rambling soliloquies make *Any-*

thing for Billy a little perplexing. What is
McMurtry up to? Is he pulling our leg, or is he
telling us about the pitfalls inherent in romanticizing the Old West? (148)

If readers missed the point in *Anything for Billy*,
McMurtry tried to make it again in his next novel about
a nineteenth-century character.

Buffalo Girls (1990)

Although *Buffalo Girls* uses such legendary characters as Calamity Jane, Buffalo Bill Cody, Teddy Blue,
Texas Jack Omohundro, Sitting Bull, and Annie Oakley,
the novel presents them not as larger-than-life heroes
but reveals them to be suffering from loneliness, dislo-
cation, lack of community, sexual frustration, and fear
of loss and death. They long for love or fame, but they
set out on journeys that lead not to fulfillment but only
to further searching and loss.

Buffalo Girls dramatizes both McMurtry's lament
for the loss of the frontier and his attack on the nostalgia associated with the loss. But it also emphasizes that
the frontier is a metaphor for a continuing human condition. Loss, of course, permeates human consciousness
and remains a continuing subject for literature—loss
of Eden, Rome, Utopia, the trail drive, the cowboy god,
Gatsby's Daisy, Benjy's field, Rabbit Angstrom's youth,

and the last picture show. Cast out of the womb,
McMurtry's characters search for a center, a home that
offers unity and permanency, only to find a tomb. Such
is the stuff of life, and the activity, whether in Dead-
wood in the 1890s, Thalia in the 1950s, or Washington
in the 1970s, is fraught with sadness and humor. The
title suggests a double vision; on the one hand, it recalls the song of the Buffalo Gals, beckoning them to
"come out tonight and dance by the light of the moon."
On the other, like the buffalo, which the novel tells us
again and again have almost completely disappeared,
these Buffalo Girls and the life they represent are about
to become extinct.

By merging historical and fictional characters like
Sitting Bull and No Ears, *Buffalo Girls* is a companion
piece to *Anything for Billy*, a novel that used the rough
historical and legendary outlines of Billy the Kid's life.
While McMurtry chose to alter the historical characters' names in the earlier novel, in *Buffalo Girls* he re-
tains them, as well as the real Calamity Jane's life as
the frame. McMurtry seems to have adopted the story
that Martha Jane Cannary's nickname came from her
proclivity to be drawn to disasters, as McMurtry's Calamity recalls with great sadness the youthful innocents
who died when she nursed them during a smallpox
epidemic.

Much of the novel, particularly in the first and last
parts, uses the epistolary form. As Calamity Jane writes

to her daughter Jane and proclaims in the first letter, "I *am* the Wild West, Janey, no show about it, I was one of the people that kept it wild. . . ." (14). With the letters, Jane functions as Ben Sippy did: a first-hand reporter on the reality of the mythic West. For example, she writes that she "shed no tears for Custer when he fell" because she had seen "him quirt soldiers for the least little thing." Like Sippy she questions the historians, writing her daughter: "You will read of all this in the histories, Janey, do not let them tell you Custer was a hero, he was cold and careless, listened to no one" (96).

But the Jane that McMurtry presents is hardly the rough-and-tumble figure of legend. Rather she is a sad and lonely woman who, often in a drunken stupor instead of with a spirit of adventure, either rides her horse, Satan, throughout the West looking for her best friend Dora DuFran, an aging madam and lover of Teddy Blue, or joins Buffalo Bill's troupe on a trip to England. Before it is all over, she questions her sexuality, acknowledges her loneliness, and, in a nod to *Who's Afraid of Virginia Woolf*, confesses her own mythmaking.

Along the way she runs into a number of McMurtry's fictional creations who hark back to earlier McMurtry works. Her two closest friends are Bartle Bone and Jim Ragg, aging mountain men, one garrulous and the other taciturn, who are reminiscent of Gus and Call from *Lonesome Dove*. With Bartle and Jim, as well as the other characters who make up Jane's friends—No Ears, Dora, and Potato Creek Johnny—McMurtry portrays a West that does not celebrate individuality, but one that intensifies the need for friendship. With the names, McMurtry both alludes to Yeats's line about the "foul rag and bone shop of the heart"—the reality that is the basis for all good art—and has some fun with the Bartles and James of wine-cooler ads. With Bartle Bone, McMurtry connects the fictional worlds of *Anything for Billy* and *Buffalo Girls* through both characters' last names. At one point, Buffalo Bill asks Bartle if he is ready to "outshine your young cousin in New Mexico" (107), but Bartle denies kinship.

Jim Ragg offers another view of the end-of-the-West theme, because his world is fixed on beaver trapping. Realizing that the beaver are going the way of the buffalo, Ragg becomes despondent, buoyed only by discovering a beaver colony in a London zoo. In a final irony, Jim Ragg—the American mountain man, long an icon of ultimate freedom on the frontier—dies by the hand of a Chicago anarchist who mistakes Jim for the Emperor of Austria.

These characters straddle a fine line between reality and parody: on one page is a send-up revealing the falsity of western myth and legend, and on another is a sentimental rendering of real human emotion at the loss of the frontier or the death of a friend. The ambivalence gives many readers difficulty as they respond

positively to one part of *Buffalo Girls* and negatively to
the other. For some the satire satisfies and the sentimentality is cloying; for others, it is the other way
around. To its credit, *Buffalo Girls* balances the two
impulses well.

A good example of a figure who merges parody, realism, and myth is the Indian, No Ears. In *Lonesome
Dove*, McMurtry's Indians conform to traditional stereotypes—from the few wandering and pathetic ones
who come to beg beeves from the trail drivers to the
villainous and thoroughly evil Blue Duck—kidnapper
and cold-blooded killer. But *Buffalo Girls* and *Streets of
Laredo* present a generally moderate view of Indians.
Although Sitting Bull in *Buffalo Girls* is cantankerous
and lecherous, squeezing white women when they come
for his autograph, with No Ears from the same novel
and, to a lesser extent, Famous Shoes from *Streets of
Laredo*, McMurtry creates full and sympathetic Indian
characters who grapple with both personal difficulties
and the reality of the large events at the end of the
frontier. Both become positive affirmations of Indian
culture within McMurtry's typically elegiac view of the
passing West. These differing views of Indians may reflect McMurtry's desire for balance, or they may indicate the deep ambivalence that McMurtry has expressed
about Texas and the West throughout his career.

McMurtry uses the Indian No Ears to serve as the
wise observer, as the "chorus" to comment on the usu-

ally foolish actions of men and women. An aging scout,
No Ears had been at the Little Big Horn. When he was
ten, he had lost his ears after being captured by French
traders who "shot all the Indians and cut their ears
off." As a consequence, he developed a keen sense of
smell. "He could smell buffalo and he could smell rain.
He could sniff a woman's belly and tell if she were fertile, and he could smell babies in the womb within a
few days of their conception. Above all, he could smell
death" (26).

McMurtry uses No Ears to reflect on the foibles of
whites. No Ears thinks that "there might be a link between the fact that white people had weak eyes and
the fact that they had little attachment to their true
names." He realizes that he "had puzzled over white
people's lack of insight for a good many years without
reaching a firm conclusion about it. His suspicion was
that white people simply had no serious interest in
truth. What they managed to see was usually enough
truth for them, even if it was only half of what was
there to see" (47).

No Ears experiences the world with the fullness of
human capacity for wonder. When, on a trip to England
with Buffalo Bill's Wild West Show, he sees a whale, No
Ears is led to contemplate large questions:

It seemed to No Ears that the great fish he
had just seen might be as old as the world it-

self; it might have been only a minnow when the world began. If the whale was indeed the oldest fish, all the fish in the ocean or in the world might be his children. It was thought by some old people he had talked to on his trip with the Blackfoot that the first beasts were both male and female and each could make its own young. Perhaps the great whale fish he had just seen was the grandfather of all the fish in the world. (153–54)

Later, after No Ears tries to wear wax ears from the Wax Museum, he realizes "he had been foolish to take pride in the ears from England. Because of his great desire to acquire ears before he died, he had made the worst mistake of all; he had allowed himself to be deceived by the look of things. In fact, the objects he had taken such pride in had not been ears at all; they had merely been wax. . . " (292).

Suzanne Winckler's *Texas Monthly* review points out the importance of No Ears, noting that he is the character "who seems most in touch with the nuances of this world and with the implications of its loss." She continues:

The sweetest, funniest, most instructive, and most beautifully written passages in *Buffalo Girls* spin around No Ears: when he crouches behind a sage bush to hide from the whooping cranes, which he fears are about to fly off with his spirit; when aboard a ship sailing for England with Cody's Wild West troupe, he compares the ocean to the plains; when he first sees a whale; when he encounters the musk-ox, flamingo, hippopotamus, and ostrich in the London zoo; when he considers the loss of his ears; when he crawls off to die.

. . . No Ears embodies *Buffalo Girls's* full lament. While the loss or conversion of a landscape—in this case the nineteenth-century West—is sad enough, outliving a familiar, confiding landscape is sadder still. Rebuffed by his kin, No Ears realizes that "if you lived beyond your time it was hard to find people with the proper sensibility, people who could evaluate important facts when they were discovered." (70)

Buffalo Girls returns to another theme important in *Anything for Billy*: the power of the western myths and the methods of presenting them. The previous frontier novel concentrated on the dime novels and ended with references to the beginning of western movies. In *Buffalo Girls* dime novels also appear through references to the character Ned Buntline who promises to write Calamity's stories, but the primary vehicle that

extends the western myth is Buffalo Bill's Wild West
Show. Where McMurtry's attack on dime novels in the
earlier novel was intense, Buffalo Bill is treated more
moderately, never directly attacked for his false presentation of the western experience. In fact, although
Jane acknowledges that Cody made his reputation as
an Indian fighter out of killing only one Indian, Yellow
Hair, she praises him, saying Bill was "never unkind to
me, I wish him well" (336). And again and again characters acknowledge his vision for recognizing the reality of the end of the West and the powerful need for the
western myth as a form of entertainment. *Buffalo Girls*
acknowledges the human need for the hopes and dreams
that help people to maintain purpose in life. Dora
Dufran's Hotel Hope is symbolic of her desire for an
ideal relationship with Teddy Blue, one that she can
never achieve. Similarly, Buffalo Bill's Wild West Show
symbolizes the power of human dreams, like the dream
of the West, to provide purpose.

Ultimately, then, *Buffalo Girls* returns to the powerful ambivalence that McMurtry has felt about the
western myth. On the one hand, throughout the novel,
McMurtry punctures the legends of western heroes like
Buffalo Bill, Calamity Jane, General Custer, mountain
men, and Sitting Bull, but he recognizes clearly the
power of dreams and the necessity of hope. Calamity
Jane herself becomes a symbol of the doubleness the
novel acknowledges about reality and illusion, truth and

untruth. As the novel winds down and all the characters die around her—Dora by childbirth, Ogden by lightning, No Ears by natural causes, her dog Cody by wolves—Jane kills off her fictional daughter, whom she had made up when she began to write a diary: "I started to write 'Dear Diary' and I wrote 'Darling Jane' instead. I wanted you so much I made you up" (343). She acknowledges her physical doubleness, writing that she "was born odd" with a large word used by doctors in England to refer to her condition, which Bartle Bone confirms to be "hermaphrodite" at novel's end. Male/female, reality/illusion, truth/fiction, these oppositions are intertwined in Jane. As a writer, she creates fiction, but fiction satisfies the powerful human need for hope: "I guess you rose out of my hopes, Janey. . . . But we don't have the say about our hopes, Janey—truth, if that's what it is, can't stop us from hoping" (344).

McMurtry's reference to an upcoming exposition in Chicago where Buffalo Bill hopes to take his troupe indicates his awareness of Frederick Jackson Turner's famous presentation in 1893, "The Significance of the Frontier in American History," at a meeting of the American Historical Association as part of the famous World's Columbian Exposition. Turner's speech is widely identified as the beginning of American recognition of the end of the frontier and the power of the frontier myth. Turner established the end of the physical frontier and ushered in the era when the imaginative fron-

tier flourished. Alan Trachtenberg in *The Incorporation of America* points out:

> Thus we can see that in the contours of its
> argument as well as in the sinews of its sen-
> tences, the Turner thesis belongs to the new
> world made palpable and vivid in Chicago in
> 1893; it is of a piece with White City. Like the
> Columbian Exposition, the Turner thesis por-
> trayed an America at a critical juncture. Both
> affirmed drastic change since the days when
> it might have been possible to imagine the na-
> tion as a society of freeholders. Both embraced
> the change—the rise of cities, industrial capi-
> talism, corporate forms of business and social
> activities—and yet they attempted to preserve
> older values and traditional outlooks. (15)

A journey to the Exposition is but one repeat of
familiar patterns, as *Buffalo Girls* also uses triangulated characters and the escape-and-return pattern.
Both Jane and Dora engage in random journeys: Calamity wanders around the West and Dora impulsively
moves from whorehouse to hotel. The novel concentrates
on a double set of triangulated characters, moving and
merging the stories of Bartle Bone, Jim Ragg, and Calamity Jane with the story of Dora Dufran, Teddy Blue,
and Ogden Prideaux, with secondary characters like

No Ears and Buffalo Bill orbiting around the primary stories, which are connected through the paired relationship between Jane and Dora. Finally, the novel uses the large escape-and-return pattern as the first part of the novel sets up the beginning of Bill's Wild West Show, then takes its performers to England, and finally returns them to America and the West.

At the Popular Culture Association meeting in San Antonio in 1991, in a session entitled "The Western: Is there Anything More to Say?" critic Jack Nachbar bashed *Dances with Wolves* as rehashed, new-age *Little Big Man* and suggested that western movies have said all that could be said and should be laid to rest. Holding up a copy of *Buffalo Girls*, he indicated that McMurtry had the right idea by killing off the heroes of western legend. But McMurtry did not drive a stake in the heart of western myth and legend. Instead, he highlighted the ironic continuing resurrection of interest in its dying throes. The end of the American frontier represents humanity's universal loss and hope for recovery, proven again in his next novel set at the end of the nineteenth century.

Streets of Laredo (1993)

When *Streets of Laredo* appeared in August 1993, the "long-awaited sequel" to *Lonesome Dove* popped out of the chute, hit the bestseller list, and marked a sig-

nificant point in Larry McMurtry's long and productive career—the first time McMurtry had written a sequel to a novel set in the nineteenth century. In it Captain Call returns and sets out to hunt down a notorious
killer and bandit named Joey Garza by gathering a band
that includes Pea Eye (who—hard to believe—is married to Lorena). Don Graham, in *The Austin Chronicle*,
found that reading "the new novel is sort of like looking
through old annuals of *Lonesome Dove* High" (20) and
wryly noted that it gives us Call and Lorena redux but
"not Blue dux" (22). Indeed, many of the old characters
return, but the vision and tone in the sequel are quite
different from the original.

McMurtry appends three epigraphs, including lines
from the title song about the sadness of the death of
a comrade who had "done wrong," lines from
Chateaubriand about America's solitude and wildness,
and a biblical passage from Ruth 1:16: "Intreate mee
not to leave thee, or to returne from following after thee."
The ambiguous references here are suggestive of both
Call and Joey Garza, who had both done wrong, and of
Maria, Pea Eye, and Lorena, all of whom are involved
in leavings and followings. The pull of loyalty, in fact, is
one of the central themes of this novel written by a writer
whose career has wavered between leaving and returning to the home he hates and loves. Over and over again,
characters point to the demands of loyalty. Early in the

novel, when Pea Eye decides not to go with the Captain, Call contemplates loyalty:

> It seemed to him the highest principle, loyalty. He had never been exactly sure what men meant when they spoke of their honor, though it had been a popular word during the time of the War. He *was* sure, though, what he meant when he spoke of loyalty. A man didn't desert his comrades, his troops, his leader. If he did he was, in Call's book, worthless. . . .
>
> Pea was not a man who could be said to be without loyalty. But he had *changed* loyalties, and what did that say? The whole point of loyalty was not to change: stick with those who stuck with you. (44–45)

For a writer whose career has been marked by divided loyalty about his profession and his home country, this novel makes wavering allegiances central both to theme and structure. Again, random journeying provides much of the structure, as Call and Brookshire leave Amarillo by train to search for Joey Garza in Texas and Mexico. But as Call travels south, Joey leaves for Crowtown in the Texas Panhandle. These two contrapuntal journeys produce others. When Maria learns that Call is trailing Joey, she leaves for Crowtown to warn

Joey. Although Pea Eye first refuses to join Call on this adventure, his guilt soon leads him to join his captain. Then, when Lorena learns from Goodnight of the return of Mox Mox, known as the Manburner when he had threatened her as a member of Blue Duck's gang, she leaves to find Pea Eye. Thus, the novel is structured around the journeys of loyalty of Maria and Lorena, as they seek son and husband, both evoking the biblical allusion from Ruth used as an epigraph.

These counterpointing journeys produce opposite results, for Maria cannot find and protect her son Joey. Instead, in an ironic reversal of the Hispanic *la llorana* myth about the wailing woman searching for her children whom she had murdered by the river, Maria dies near the river by her own son's hand. Lorena, however, finds and saves not only her wounded husband but also Captain Call. Through her persistent will, Lorena, like Hester Prynne, redeems her past and becomes an angel of mercy.

In one way Blue Duck does "redux" because Joey Garza is almost as sadistic as Blue Duck. He smiles as he kills, and he learned his passion for violence from the Apache, to whom he was sold by a stepfather at age six. His mother Maria is herself part Apache. But if Joey reincarnates the sadism of Blue Duck, one secondary character partially reenacts the patience and wisdom of No Ears, the sympathetic Indian character from *Buffalo Girls*, and that is Famous Shoes, a noted

Kickapoo tracker and also a famous walker. Once Famous Shoes decided to walk to the north, to what he called the edge of the earth, to find the source of the ducks and geese that flew south for the winter. As the fall approached and as he moved onto the Great Plains, Famous Shoes began to fear the coming winter and in despair turned back south. At first he thought the birds' calls mocked him for being unable to find the edge of the earth, but sitting beside eagle, he learned to accept his place in the universe: "But once back in the Sierra Madre, watching the great eagles that lived near his home, Famous Shoes gradually lost his bitterness. In the presence of the great eagles, he became ashamed of himself. . . . Their dignity made him feel that he had been silly, to expect the ducks and geese, or any birds, to take an interest in his movements" (200).

Although Famous Shoes, like No Ears, possesses acute natural skills ("No one in the West could see farther, or more clearly, than the old Kickapoo" [194]), McMurtry tends to blur his individuality by verging on making Famous Shoes a noble savage. As Noel Perrin points out in *The New York Times Book Review*, soon Famous Shoes moves toward caricature and mock epic when McMurtry moves Famous Shoes's exploits from the sublime to the ridiculous:

> Famous Shoes here is something out of a comedy routine. The old Indian can glance at a

> bunch of horse tracks and announce that there
> are eight men with two extra horses. Impres-
> sive. But when he adds that three are "Mexi-
> cans who spur their horses too much," one is a
> Cherokee, and so on, the book topples into ab-
> surdity. Or into the western tall tale, anyway.
> (9)

McMurtry adds to this comic irony by making the
Indian a materialistic character and thereby returning
to his subtle attack on capitalistic economy introduced
in *Lonesome Dove*. Famous Shoes is keenly aware of
money, basing his actions on the highest bid rather than
on ethics. When he helps Pea Eye identify where
Brookshire's shotgun lies, he does so because Pea Eye
gives him a gold piece.

This characterization of Famous Shoes shifts the
emphasis in *Streets of Laredo* from character to theme.
The novel, like *Buffalo Girls*, is an end-of-the-West
novel, but it connects with McMurtry's other novels with
contemporary settings, *The Evening Sun* and *Some Can
Whistle*, which concern the larger themes of aging and
loss. In fact, No Ears's lack of ears suggests McMurtry's
use of the loss of body parts as a metaphor for human
loss that is dramatically presented in *Streets of Laredo*.
Captain Call, unlike Augustus McCrae, decides to allow his leg to be amputated. And the agent of his am-
putation is Lorena, who has been transformed from

whore in *Lonesome Dove* to wife and schoolmarm—archetypal images of civilization—in *Streets of Laredo*. Images of diminished bodies and spirits permeate *Laredo*: after Call allows Lorena to take his leg, a doctor has to remove one of Call's arms; Pea Eye loses toes; Joey Garza cuts off the hands and feet of one of his mother's husbands; Billy Williams shoots an ear off an abusive Texas sheriff; Maria's daughter Theresa has no sight, her son Rafael no mind; the easterner Brookshire from the beginning fears that he will blow away in the Texas wind; Old Man Goodnight speaks of leaking. While these Anglo southwesterners are diminished by events, Famous Shoes gains. His last act is to ask for and get Joey's telescope as a reward for helping Pea Eye shoot Garza.

Famous Shoes has survived the psychopathic killer partially by singing his death song without fear as Garza approaches him, and he ironically survives to return to his home country along the Sierra Madre and to seek the company of his beloved eagles. In this way McMurtry uses an Indian character to provide ironic contrast to the Anglo conquerors. While the Anglos who survive are reduced, Famous Shoes survives intact, and he overcomes adversity partially by adopting the materialistic economy they represent.

This reference to materialism is one of many in the novel. One of the more disagreeable characters, who appears only briefly, is Brookshire's boss Colonel Terry, the president of the railroad, presented as arrogant, hypocritical, insensitive, and a womanizer. As the book begins, Call and Goodnight discuss Terry and the wealth that he represents, and it is apparent that both westerners disparage the rich. Call rejects the engraved Colt pistol Terry sent him and thinks: "[H]e had never met a governor or a president of a railroad or a senator or a rich man that he liked or felt comfortable with" (15). Likewise Goodnight tells Call, "I don't number too many rich fools among my friends . . ." (16). Colonel Terry is another diminished character; when he comes looking for Brookshire late in the novel, Call notices that Terry had lost an arm.

Such losses reinforce the novel's dark and grim tone, unrelieved by the humor and sexuality of McMurtry's earlier works. Perhaps this desolate vision was the result of McMurtry's brush with mortality when he had a heart bypass operation in 1992. Whatever the reason, this sequel's tone is quite different from *Lonesome Dove*. Bleak and violent, *Streets of Laredo* is a clenched-teeth novel. Again and again, characters refer to a profound sense of ending, such as when Call thinks about the changes he has witnessed and the old men who had been part of the "adventure":

> But all of them, and those like them who had fallen—Gus McCrae and old Kit Carson, the Bent brothers, Shanghai Pierce and Captain

Marcy—had been part of the adventure. . . .

Now, the settling had happened. Ben Lily
and Goodnight and Roy Bean and, he supposed,
himself—for he, too, had become one of the old
ones of the West—were just echoes of what had
been. When Lily fell, and Goodnight, and Bean
and himself, there wouldn't even be echoes, just
memories. (336)

Ben Lily, whose legend was recorded by Dobie, is
another ironic image, suggestive of one of the old ones
whose singular adventure ended the great adventure,
for his goal, as McMurtry presents him, is to kill all
the lions and bears in the West: "The old man walked
the West endlessly, killing bears and cougars as he went
. . . . His aim was to kill all the lions and bears between
the Gulf Coast and Canada" (183).

McMurtry seems equally set on killing off most of
the characters who inhabited his earlier novel. Characters such as Newt and Clara Allen are recalled and
killed off perfunctorily. Newt dies ironically when the
Hell Bitch, Call's gift to his unacknowledged son,
crushes the boy's heart, suggesting that Call is responsible for his son's literally broken heart. McMurtry even
creates fictional deaths for some historical characters,
having Judge Roy Bean die by the hand of Joey Garza
rather than following the course of recorded Texas history. Perhaps McMurtry realized that characters can

live several lives, as has Captain Call in McMurtry's two novels and in two television miniseries where Call was portrayed first by Tommy Lee Jones and then by Jon Voight.

Just as the novel moves with irrevocable purpose and lacks the humor and sexuality of other McMurtry novels, the conclusion also provides a different direction for McMurtry's fiction. The marriage of Pea Eye and Lorena, while an apparently incongruous match between a gangly, slow-witted former Ranger and a beautiful former whore, proves to be the most powerful and sustained marriage in all of McMurtry's fiction. Pea Eye's divided loyalty between the Captain and Lorena is clearly resolved when Pea Eye realizes that he should never have left his family:

> Pea Eye wanted badly to tell them all how sorry he was that he had left them. He wanted them to know how much he regretted putting Captain Call first, and not them. It had been a terrible wrong. He wanted them to know that never again would he put any duty before his duty to them, to Lorena and his children. (475)

Through his desire to see his wife and children again, Pea Eye summons the strength and courage to run to Brookshire's eight-gauge shotgun lying in the river bed and shoot Joey Garza before he can get his rifle.

The novel ends with McMurtry's usual return pattern, as Lorena, Pea Eye, Call, and Maria's children return to Pea Eye's home along the Quitaque. It is one of the most settled images in McMurtry's fiction, as the pregnant Lorena expands her family to include Call and Theresa and Rafael. In the final scene, Lorena, distraught after learning of the death of Clara, sends Pea Eye away to sleep in the horse barn. But she relents, comes to the barn, and summons her husband, who "followed his wife back to their house" (589). Marriage, family, stability, and home—these are the forces that will face the newly arriving century.

The critical reaction to *Streets of Laredo* has been quite mixed. Malcolm Jones in *Newsweek* responded positively, finding it "one of his most affectingly melancholy books. Its heroes are frail, and their ideals are often compromised" (52). Jones noted that the novel continues McMurtry's emphasis on ambivalence, because it is "a story about divided loyalties, and about the trouble visited upon those with one foot planted in civilization and the other in the wilderness" (52). Don Graham also pointed to the novel's emphasis on conflicting attractions, especially the "the struggle between the claims of heart and home versus those of nomadic derring-do and violence. Hence, for a woman to stand by her man, she sometimes has to take to the trail herself" (20).

On the other hand, Robert Draper in *Texas Monthly*

faulted the novel for geographical and thematic pur-
poselessness: "A lack of articulated purpose permeates
the entire book" (42). Draper concludes that "violence
is the only primal element the book has to offer. . . .
Lacking the passion and humor of *Lonesome Dove,
Streets of Laredo* delivers solely through brute force"
(42). Draper did praise the dialogue between Call and
Goodnight, saying it "captures wonderfully the spartan
language that westerners speak" (43).

Graham also commended the characterization of
Old Man Goodnight. But Graham took McMurtry to
task for rewriting history, pointing out that the real
Roy Bean died in 1903 from lung and heart complications:

> In terms of McMurtry's career, *Streets of
> Laredo* seems to summarize several recent ten-
> dencies. One, as noted before here, is the self-
> reflexive reinvention of previous characters
> and themes. Another is the location of his vi-
> sion in the late nineteenth century, the very
> terrain of romance and myth that McMurtry
> spent much of his earlier career ironizing and
> avoiding. (20, 22)

One of the major points that McMurtry emphasizes
in these nineteenth-century novels, according to Roger
Jones, focuses on the conflict between civilization and

wilderness, with *Streets of Laredo* dramatizing the loss of Gus's mediating influence:

> The importance of Gus as a positive balance between the wild, potentially dangerous impulses of nature and the restrictive forces of civilization is underscored by the world of harsh alternatives in McMurtry's sequel to *Lonesome Dove, Streets of Laredo*. In this richly dark novel, aging Call is reduced to tracking robbers for railroad barons under barbaric conditions while Lorena, now a proper schoolteacher married to Pea Eye, becomes an aggressive embodiment of the smothering feminine power of civilization and language. . . . The novel concludes on an ambiguous note as gentle Pea Eye symbolically says goodbye to Call and the world of frontier men (represented by Call) and enters, with fear and trepidation, the civilized but confining world of women (represented by Lorena). (81–82)

Thus, *Streets of Laredo* both returns to and departs from a number of McMurtry's concerns.

Through much of McMurtry's literary career, as I have tried to demonstrate, his work is also marked by a fundamental ambivalence about the legacies of the old world. With this novel McMurtry makes divided loyalty a significant theme. But it is also unlike other McMurtry works, since it resolves the question of divided loyalty and ends with a strong emphasis on the power of love and family to provide stability. In this novel, the searching characters come home.

9

McMurtry and the Movies
Film Flam

McMurtry's work has often enjoyed excellent treatment in film and on television. It is not just luck that accounts for the happy results of filming McMurtry. Because he is a writer who develops memorable characters through realistic dialogue and visual scenes, it makes sense that among the American writers who are his contemporaries, such as Thomas Pynchon, Joseph Heller, John Updike, or John Barth, he has had great success. Only McMurtry's old friend Ken Kesey has seen at least one work treated as well by Hollywood. With his first novel, McMurtry encountered the film world; since that time three other novels have been made into movies, a fifth made into a hugely successful television miniseries, a production of *The Evening Star* with Jack Nicholson and Shirley MacLaine reprising their roles is underway, and a miniseries of *Streets of Laredo* and *Buffalo Girls* are scheduled for 1995.

Still, McMurtry has had a mixed relationship with movies. On one hand, he has enjoyed successful film and television adaptations of his work such as Martin Ritt's *Hud* (1963), Peter Bogdanovich's memorable *The Last Picture Show* (1971), James Brooks's Academy-Award-winning *Terms of Endearment* (1983), and the acclaimed *Lonesome Dove* (1989) television miniseries. On the other were Sidney Lumet's awful *Lovin' Molly* (1974), based on *Leaving Cheyenne*, and Bogdanovich's largely forgettable *Texasville* (1990). In both *In a Narrow Grave* and his second book of nonfiction, *Film Flam* (1987), which collects his essays about movies, McMurtry distances himself from movies. But he has worked on them steadily over the years. In 1994 he estimated that he had written thirty-three screen- or teleplays, and he was still working on other projects. In addition to writing the screenplay for a contemporary western for TNT called *Montana* (1990), adapting a Horton Foote novel, *Memphis*, as a vehicle for Cybill Shepherd; and writing the screenplay for *Falling from*

Grace (1992)—John Mellencamp's first starring role—McMurtry has written and consulted on any number of projects that were scrapped or placed on hold. More recently, he wrote the teleplay for the planned miniseries based on *Streets of Laredo*.

Not only does McMurtry write in such a way that his works lend themselves to film, but he is the product of a generation that grew up on movies and moved into maturity as film itself began to be seen as a significant art form rather than mere entertainment. Movies have therefore shaped his imagination, and the more he began to work with the industry, the more his fiction began to reflect his knowledge of it and the actors and directors with whom he became friends.

Hud (1963)

The first filmed novel, *Horseman, Pass By*, was transformed into *Hud* for the movies. As is true in the best of the films based on a McMurtry novel, the success of the film depended on effective casting. With Paul Newman as Hud, Melvyn Douglas as Granddad, Patricia Neal as Alma, and Brandon de Wilde as Lonnie, the strong cast helped ensure the success of the film. Newman dominates the screen, making the amoral Hud a heartthrob. On the posters a smirking Newman, dressed in boots and jeans, gazes out of those eyes that have caused four generations of moviegoers to swoon.

Making Hud the dominant character and de-emphasizing Lonnie's story was one of several significant changes from novel to film. Another major change involved the transformation of the black cook Halmea into Alma, who is white. With a white cook who flirts with both Hud and Lonnie, the potential romantic relationship makes Hud's drunken assault more ambiguous. In 1963 the racial divisions in America no doubt affected the decision, but Hud's brutal rape of Halmea in the novel removes any ambiguity about him. As Alma, Patricia Neal's compelling performance was winning, and she received the Academy Award for best supporting actress for 1963.

Melvyn Douglas's performance as Granddad was another winning one, getting him the Academy Award for Best Supporting Actor. Douglas's raspy voice and flinty acting made him seem like everyone's grandfather. His sudden deterioration after the death of his cattle is believable, and reviewers Bosley Crowther and Penelope Gilliatt (quoted in Pauline Kael, "Hud, Deep in the Divided Heart of Hollywood") singled out the slaughter of the herd and Douglas's response as the defining moment in the film, as they responded to the film's emphasis on the materialistic destruction of modern America.

Just as the novel includes an ambivalent approach to the passing of Homer Bannon, so does the screenplay, which was written by Harriet and Irving Ravetch and not by McMurtry. In one of the more perceptive essays about the film, Pauline Kael points out how this uncertainty strengthens the film:

> But the movie wouldn't necessarily be a good movie if its moral message was dramatically sustained in the story and action, and perhaps it isn't necessarily a bad movie if its moral message is not sustained in the story and action. By all formal theories, a work that is split cannot be a work of art, but leaving the validity of these principles aside, do they hold for lesser works—not works of art but works of commerce and craftsmanship, sometimes fused by artistry? . . . My answer is no, that in some films the more ambivalence that comes through, the more the film may mean to us or the more fun it may be. The process by which an idea for a movie is turned into the product that reaches us is so involved . . . that the tension in the product, or some sense of urgency still left in it, may be our only contact with the life in which the product was processed. (*Taking Stock* 368)

Much of McMurtry's work, as I have tried to demonstrate, achieves its power similarly, by dramatizing his own tension. The film reflects McMurtry's original ambivalence toward his subject matter, the strain that resulted from his editor's insistence on restructuring the novel, and the screenwriters' changes in character and tone. These dislocations should have produced a muddled film, but as Kael notes, the result is powerfully suggestive.

The Last Picture Show (1971)

While McMurtry's connection to *Hud* was minimal, with the next film based on one his novels, McMurtry became deeply involved. He co-wrote the screenplay for *The Last Picture Show*, which was again not only a happy circumstance of casting, but the entire production was first-rate. For many of the cast, it was the first important piece of work that launched their careers, especially Cybill Shepherd as Jacy, Jeff Bridges as Duane (whose last name is changed from Moore to Sanders in the film), Timothy Bottoms as Sonny, and Randy Quaid as Lester Marlow. The seasoned actors also were excellent: Ellen Burstyn as Lois Farrow, Clu Gullagher as Abilene, Eileen Brennan as Genevieve, and particularly Ben Johnson, who won the Academy Award for supporting actor, as Sam the Lion. Although Cloris Leachman had been acting for awhile when she was cast as Ruth Popper, the role was her most important early performance, and the Academy Award she won for supporting actress moved her career to a new level.

Director Peter Bogdanovich's decision to tone down the satire of the novel and attempt to present the story as a realistic portrayal of small-town Texas life was a significant decision that led him to shoot the film in black and white, to use McMurtry's own hometown as the location, to employ locals as bit players, and to attempt to make the film as gritty as the actual town in the early 1950s. To accomplish this purpose, Bogdanovich used realistic costumes, props, and music—including Hank Williams, Bob Wills, and other country singers of the time—and he emphasized dust, wind, and blowing tumbleweeds. The result was a film that captured the essential reality of growing up in a northwest Texas town, called Anarene in the film, but it was also representative of growing up longingly anywhere. (The town's name was changed from Thalia, perhaps to distinguish it from the Thalia of *Hud* or the real Thalia, Texas. "Anarene" was a small settlement in Archer County.)

In an article reprinted in *Film Flam*, McMurtry examines his experience writing the screenplay, noting that when he began it, he was "dead to the book" (21) and found the "parts that were about the two adolescent boys totally unreadable" (19). Ironically, because he had no emotional attachment and Bogdanovich did,

McMurtry could approach co-writing the script from an objective standpoint, and he realized that the book was "the kind of novel from which good movies are made—that is, a flatly written book with strong characterizations and a sense of period and place" (19). McMurtry and Bogdanovich chose to emphasize those elements and produced a film classic.

Lovin' Molly (1974)

Since the first two adaptations of McMurtry novels were so successful, it must have seemed to Hollywood that his other novels would work equally well. The next adaptation belied that. When Sidney Lumet turned *Leaving Cheyenne* into *Lovin' Molly*, he made all the wrong decisions about casting, location, costumes, and dialogue—the elements that made the first films work. With Beau Bridges as Johnny McCloud, Tony Perkins as Gideon Fry, and Blythe Danner as Molly Taylor, Lumet went for recognizable actors without any particular connection to the subject matter. The novel had a West Texas setting, but Lumet decided to film near Bastrop, Texas, known for an unusual physical landscape called the Lost Pines. With this stand of pine trees, Bastrop looks neither like the rest of central Texas nor West Texas. Added to these bad decisions were the costumes: shoes instead of boots; sweaters and bib overalls rather than jeans and denim jackets. In another essay in *Film Flam* McMurtry notes these weaknesses in the movie and also condemns the film's makeup, props, and script, especially a scene where Blythe Danner kisses a "slimy little newborn calf—an action that smacks of Bard College, baby, not Bastrop, Texas. . ." (126). The result of these bad decisions was a movie so roundly thrashed that, twenty years later, it had not been released on video.

Larry L. King wrote a scathing account of the making of the movie, asserting: "Should you find more than a modicum of true Texas in the film—excluding John Henry Faulk's bit role—why, then, I'll buy you a two-dollar play purty" (*Taking Stock* 381).

Terms of Endearment (1983)

The first two movie adaptations depended on the rural setting for their appeal, but James Brooks's *Terms of Endearment* turns to an urban setting and requires little regional connection. In fact, it is a major Hollywood movie with well-known actors in the major roles. Jennifer Jones originally bought the option for the script, hoping to get Cary Grant to play the general and Diane Keaton to play Emma. When she could not get the project financed, she sold it to Brooks, who changed the general to a younger astronaut and set out to cast well-known actors. With Shirley MacLaine as Aurora, Jack Nicholson as the astronaut, Debra

Winger as Emma, and Jeff Daniels as Flap, the drawing power of the film was secure. The slick combination of humor and melodrama captivated audiences, and the film won five Academy Awards.

For many, both the book and the film suffer from the same difficulties: the disparity between the conclusion's emphasis on Emma and the rest of the story's focus on Aurora, since most of the narrative is concerned with Aurora Greenway's love life and then ends with the weepy death of Emma. Brooks, recognizing the popular appeal of this sentimental ending, plays it up. The other significant difference between the novel and the film concerns the change in Aurora's suitors. The film reduces them mainly to Nicholson's character, an alcoholic former astronaut named Garret Breedlove, based seemingly on the general. Vernon Dalhart's role is diminished, and he is played rather spiritlessly by Danny Devito.

Texasville (1990)

Both the book and the film of *Texasville* demonstrate the intertwining of fiction and film in McMurtry's work. After Bogdanovich asked McMurtry to write the screenplay for *The Last Picture Show*, McMurtry began to realize that the book would have been more interesting if he had written about the middle-aged characters rather than the youthful ones: "In the case of

The Last Picture Show, the better book I discovered had to do with the older couples in the story" (*Film Flam* 23). During the filming of the earlier movie, McMurtry met and became friends with several of the actors, and he established what has become a long friendship with Cybill Shepherd. McMurtry wrote the novel *Texasville* about the middle-aged characters that he had considered more significant when he wrote the screenplay, and the novel merges the film and the earlier book. The dedication to Cybill Shepherd seals the relationship between the sequel's characterization of Jacy and Shepherd, and suggests that McMurtry was already planning the filming of the sequel. It may also explain why Jacy's character is presented much more positively in the second novel.

Like the first film, *Texasville* was shot on location in Archer City, but where the first had caused the McMurtry family much anguish and led to letters attacking McMurtry in the local newspaper, the town initially embraced the second film crew when it returned. Because *The Last Picture Show* had been an Academy Award winner that eventually brought the town much fame, and because the oil bust that was the subject of the second novel had weakened the economy, the locals generally welcomed the return, but later felt snubbed by many of the "stars," who took over the town and caused streets to be blocked.

For many of the actors, the first film had been a

watershed in their careers, and they returned happily. Timothy Bottoms found the sequel to be so personally significant that he decided to make a documentary about it. With George Hickenlooper as the writer-director, Bottoms produced *Picture This: The Times of Peter Bogdanovich in Archer City, Texas*, which included interviews with the actors, the townspeople, the people upon whom the original characters were based— McMurtry's mother and sister, and McMurtry himself. *Picture This* dramatizes the complex interrelationship between the lives of the stars of *The Last Picture Show* and their characters, for while they were playing characters whose personal lives disintegrated, their own lives changed as well. Shepherd and Bogdanovich began a long relationship during the first film, which Bogdanovich's wife, co-producer Polly Platt, had to witness stoically for the film to be completed. Ellen Burstyn and Cloris Leachman were in the middle of messy divorces. As McMurtry wrote the sequel, its characters reflect how the originals were affected by the actors who played them.

Bogdanovich's screenplay for the sequel remained generally faithful to the novel, maintaining most of its characters, narrative, and dialogue. Despite the original enthusiasm, however, the film was as poorly received as the novel, primarily for the same reasons. Even though Cybill Shepherd, Jeff Bridges, Timothy Bottoms, Cloris Leachman, Randy Quaid, and Eileen Brennan reprise their original roles, and Annie Potts plays Duane's wife Karla with verve, and all try their hardest to make these small moments of communication reveal large conclusions, the film ultimately seems to record an insignificant event. The actors' appearances may also have affected the film's reception, with Timothy Bottoms playing a graying and fogged-out Sonny with a Nixonian stubble. Jeff Bridges slouches so that he appears to have a middle-aged paunch and holds his chin down to create a jowly appearance, but Cybill Shepherd never looks much older than thirty. However, when she first surfaces from her swim across Lake Kickapoo, her face seems a ghostly white.

In the earlier film, Bogdanovich had played down the satirical tone, beefed up the cartoon characters, filmed in black and white, and created a gritty, realistic portrayal of small-town life. In the sequel, Bogdanovich films in color, maintains the satiric humor, casts a comic actor named Earl Poole Ball as Junior Nolan, and stretches for laughs. For example, when Old Man Balt attends the centennial meeting, he spits into a tobacco can so loudly that it almost drowns out the dialogue. But there are a few changes from the novel. Some of the characters and settings do not appear in the film. Abilene, Jim Bob Blanton, and John Cecil do not return. There is no mention of Danny Deck's adobe house; instead Jacy lives in a house, also called Los Dolores, left her by her parents. Another interesting change con-

cerns Sonny's movie fantasies. While Bogdanovich carefully included films of interest in *The Last Picture Show*,
he removes the film references in *Texasville*. When
Sonny stares blankly at the sky, the viewing audience
knows little about what is supposed to be happening in
his imagination. In the final scene, for example, with
Sonny precariously in the rodeo stands looking forlornly
at the sky, Bogdanovich chooses to leave out any references to Sonny's attempt to become Dude in *Rio Bravo*,
masking his motivation.

Most reviewers were not kind to the film. Michael
MacCambridge in the *Austin American Statesman*, for
example, concluded that "*Texasville* serves to besmirch
the pristine memory of Bogdanovich's superb *The Last
Picture Show*, even as his screenplay remains faithful
to the spirit of Larry McMurtry's novel" (55).

Lonesome Dove (1989)

When Bill Wittliff wrote the screenplay for the six-
hour television miniseries, his first goal was to try to
remain faithful to the novel, believing that "*Lonesome
Dove* is the star. If we take care of *Lonesome Dove*, it
will take care of us" (Harrigan 156). Wittliff's connection
with the material—added to his background as a
screenwriter, producer, director, book collector, and
publisher, along with his friendship with McMurtry—
made him the perfect choice to transfer the large novel

to the small screen. Wittliff, who grew up in Blanco, in Central Texas, was the publisher of *In a Narrow Grave* out of his Encino Press in 1968. Wittliff's film credits also include *The Black Stallion*, *Barbarosa*, *The Red Headed Stranger*, *The Cowboy Way*, and *Legends of the Fall*. And as the co-producer with Suzanne de Passe, Wittliff ensured that the film would achieve the real feel of Texas trail drives since the director, Simon Wincer, had little Texas or southwestern background. Wincer, an Australian, did have experience working with large groups of people and animals, in *Pharr Lap* and *The Light Horsemen*.

With a strong screenplay by a committed co-producer, a seasoned director, a $20 million budget, and a pledge to produce a television miniseries that was both faithful to the original and more like a movie epic than a TV production, the next major decision was the cast, and those decisions also proved to be fortunate. With Academy Award winners Robert Duvall (Augustus McCrea), Tommy Lee Jones (Woodrow Call), and Angelica Huston (Clara Allen), it was one of the most successful miniseries in recent years, perhaps signalling that the American public was ready to return to the American West for its popular culture, and blazing the trail for *Dances with Wolves* and *Unforgiven*. The other members of the cast were equally strong: Robert Urich (Jake Spoon), Danny Glover (Deets), Diane Lane (Lorena), Tim Scott (Pea Eye), Ricky Schroder (Newt),

and D. B. Sweeney (Dish Boggett). At the Southwestern Writers Collection at Southwest Texas State University, the miniseries memorabilia remains one of most
popular exhibits, especially when curator Dick Holland
wheels the prop representing Gus McCrea's dead body
through the library.

The performances of Duvall and Jones capture the
complex intertwining of the characters of Gus and Call,
and the two actors' methods were as different as Gus
and Call. Duvall created Gus through a careful
visualization of character and by adding to McMurtry's
loquacious and gregarious characterization a plethora
of hand gestures and visual tics, such as repeatedly
stroking his mustache while sucking his breath through
his teeth. It is a masterful performance by an
accomplished actor. On the set Duvall was withdrawn,
constantly studying his next scene: "Duvall was always
taut with concentration. Sitting on the porch between
takes, unapproachable and solitary, he muttered his
lines under his breath, jerking his head this way or
that with the ratchety, quizzical movements of a
songbird" (Harrigan 156). Tommy Lee Jones, on the
other hand, whose Texas roots reach to his hometown
of San Saba, approached acting as simple and
straightforward: "[H]is attitude toward acting appeared
as genial and uncomplicated as that of a high school
quarterback. . ." (Harrigan 156). Ironically, the two

actors' methods reverse the characteristics of the characters they played. In their separate ways, they inspired the rest of the cast to stretch their performances to high levels.

As Wittliff wanted, the screenplay and the production were extremely faithful to the original. One major change concerns the conclusion, but it is true to McMurtry's vision and probably strengthens the story. For the conclusion, Wittliff decided to have Call repeat Old Man Goodnight's famous line when asked if he were a man of vision, "Yes, a hell of a vision." It is a line McMurtry uses earlier in the novel and a line he had used as an epigraph in *In a Narrow Grave*. The ambivalence of the line captures the doubleness of the story and provides a final ironic statement to end the miniseries.

Screenplays: Montana, Memphis, and *Falling from Grace*

McMurtry has worked on various films over the years, but many of his projects have ended up in the back of a desk drawer or on the cutting room floor, and now housed in the archives at the University of Houston. With the success of *Lonesome Dove*, McMurtry had the clout to drive some of the older projects to trail's end. At the beginning of the 1990s three film projects completed production. Each of the three has a different audience and different purpose, but they all reveal some of McMurtry's continuing concerns.

He had worked on a script about Montana for eleven years before it became a television movie. *Montana* is a contemporary western that uses the conflict between older, more traditional values and modern industrial ones that will signal the end of the old. Richard Crenna plays Hoyce Guthrie, a longtime rancher facing the difficulties of ranching in the modern world. Hoyce and his son (Justin Deas) decide to sell the ranch to a coal company and give up the fight that ranching requires. Hoyce's wife Bess, played by Gena Rowlands, and her daughter (Lea Thompson) oppose their husband and son/father and brother and attempt to preserve the old ways. The television movie was praised for its photography, and Crenna received credit for his portrayal, but Rowlands was miscast, and the film lacked the large scope that audiences expected after *Lonesome Dove*. At the heart of the drama, of course, is the concern over the schism between old and new, long of interest to McMurtry.

In 1991 McMurtry wrote the screenplay for *Falling from Grace*, which marked John Mellencamp's acting and directing debut. Because Mellencamp had helped James McMurtry's recording career, McMurtry agreed to write the screenplay, which concerns a famous singer's return to his small Indiana town. Bud

Parks, played by Mellencamp, returns home with his
wife Alice (Mariel Hemingway) to celebrate his father's
eightieth birthday. Once there, Bud finds himself returning to old attractions, including his high school
sweetheart (Kay Lenz), and the hard-drinking and per-
ilous life he had led as a younger man, endangering his
life and his marriage. McMurtry uses Mellencamp's
Indiana past, but it could also be Archer City, and the
film recalls both *The Last Picture Show*'s emphasis on
the activities small-town people use to relieve boredom
and *Texasville*'s interest in a star's return to a small
town. (The connection between McMurtry and
Mellencamp was reflected again in 1994, when
Mellencamp named his first son "Hud.")

Texasville's star, of course, was Cybill Shepherd,
and in 1992 McMurtry worked on a teleplay for Shepherd. Along with Shepherd and Susan Rhinehart,
McMurtry adapted *Memphis*, another film produced for
TNT, from *September, September*, a novel by Shelby
Foote, who had gained fame as a Civil War historian
through the PBS series that examined that war. Set in
1957, the story portrays Shepherd as a former prosti-
tute and drifter named Reeny who along with three
others decides to kidnap the grandson of Memphis's rich-
est black citizen. The scheme goes awry when Reeny's
maternal instincts bond her to the child, and his welfare becomes more important to her than the ransom.
The film is primarily a vehicle for Shepherd, who re-

turns to a story about her hometown and who received strong reviews. McMurtry's name no doubt helped move the production along, and the film's realistic presentation of life in the 1950s, believable dialogue, conflict between individual and communal desires, with an undercurrent of violence reveal McMurtry's hand.

Film Flam (1987)

After writing several essays about film early in his career and after the successful adaptations of his novels, McMurtry was asked by *American Film* magazine to become a regular contributor in the early 1970s. Those essays, along with two published elsewhere and a previously unpublished one, constitute McMurtry's second essay collection: *Film Flam: Essays on Hollywood.* In the Foreword, McMurtry sets the tone that pervades the collection and explains his title:

> The industry has never been more malarial. The egos who slog through its swamps burn with fevers of self-praise, defensiveness, insecurity, and megalomania. Directors or producers who have big hits get so hot the capillaries in their brains promptly pop. . . . An industry that seems to have concluded that its best hope is to dramatize the comic-strip literature of an

> earlier and more vigorous era is one whose fe-
> vers have finally destroyed its nerve. With rare
> exceptions the pictures coming out of Holly-
> wood today are the last resorts of the gutless.
> In my opinion, a little film flam is all such an
> industry deserves. (x)

For a writer who has dramatized and then attacked nostalgia throughout his career, the position he takes toward the "good old days" of films is interesting in this introduction, but McMurtry maintains a jaundiced attitude toward the industry throughout this collection.

Because he approaches his subject with wariness, these essays never achieve the stature of the essays in *In a Narrow Grave*. His comments about the films of the 1970s, such as *All the President's Men*, *Seven Beauties*, and *Nashville*, do not wear well. All the articles written for *American Film* were written in the 1970s, and McMurtry began planning this collection at that time, mentioning it in the 1979 interview with Patrick Bennett. What is especially interesting about the collection are the numerous comments about his own work, about the films made from his novels, and observations about writing and art that provide insights into McMurtry the writer. In the final essay, "A Walk in Pasadena with Di-Annie and Mary Alice," McMurtry provides a profile of Diane Keaton's grandmother and reveals some details about his relationship with Keaton, one of the many aspects of his personal life that he has attempted to shield from public scrutiny.

McMurtry's personal comments and continuing disparagement of his own work led Bruce Bawer, in one of the more interesting reviews of *Film Flam*, to ask and attempt to answer an arresting question:

> Why does McMurtry keep running himself down? Part of it is doubtless sheer native honesty. Part is probably egocentrism: to read a few of the pieces in *Film Flam* is to realize that self-deprecation provides authors with a simple means of writing endlessly about themselves without seeming narcissistic. Part of it is that McMurtry likes the idea of shocking people, likes being viewed as a plainspoken maverick who lives and works and thinks at a considerable remove from the mendacious conformists of Hollywood. And part of it is, I think, that McMurtry, a scion of a big ranching clan, and nephew to a goodly number of macho cattle barons, is secretly embarrassed to be a *writer*, of all things. He doesn't want us to think he's interested in *art*, for God's sake. . . . (*Taking Stock* 109)

Bawer overstates McMurtry's ranching and cattle baron

heritage, but he senses the ambivalence toward writing in this collection of essays that permeates much of McMurtry's fiction.

Assessing the persona that McMurtry presents in these essays is, as Bawer suggested, an intriguing process. Rather than the angry young Texan of the first collection, the persona behind *Film Flam* is older, cosmopolitan, and somewhat world weary. He jets from New York to Los Angeles, spends time with famous people like Keaton, takes in seventeen movies in a two-and-a-half-day period in Times Square, and seems to approach the world if not cynically, at least from the position of one who does not have much faith in the power of film or art to alter human behavior. He also questions his younger self. For example, after viewing all those bad movies, he reflects on the youthful writer who thought he could lose the mythic West:

> I've always known secretly that my lies were more interesting and more pleasing and more helpful to people than any truth I knew, but it has taken years of watching thousands of people draw delight from the sheerest fantasy to rend me comfortable on that score. Years ago, in another essay, ruminating about my own fiction, I said that I had realized that the place where all my stories start is the heart faced with the loss of "its country, its custom-

ary and legendary range." That made for a catching phrase, though I can no longer remember the original sense of loss, or even, without straining, the original country. But I can hardly doubt that I did have it. I did as a boy sit on the barn my uncles sat on to watch the last trail herds go by, and from there ... I could see a long way, into some great sunsets and far back into the mythic reaches of the West, to which, try though I might, I could never not belong, nor ever fail to respond. So it was only a conceit of mine to imply that my heart had somehow lost its country, another deluding phrase, disguising nicely the genuine wellsprings of my writing—a sense of that customary and legendary range being the one thing my heart could never lose. (147–48).

Although this statement was originally buried in an article about bad movies, it was a significant declaration, for it acknowledged that McMurtry was struggling with reconciling himself to the knowledge that the mythic West was deeply part of his life. As I have demonstrated, it is just such a reconciliation that has been carried out in his novels as well.

10

The Roundup

What, finally, does this survey of Larry McMurtry's work indicate about him as a writer? Are his works significant, coherent, and lasting? Is he, instead, a mere popularizer, a hack writer churning out pages of escapist mush filled with sex and violence? Or is he somewhere in between these opposing positions? Reading McMurtry's work over the years, picking up new books as they appeared, I have tended to treat each one individually, usually as a reviewer judging whether the current work is a good read or not. By focusing on these works all together, I have realized that this fragmented approach does a disservice to the continuity of his work. As Malcolm Cowley taught the Stegner Fellows at Stanford, it is just as hard to write a bad book as it is to write a good one. While I acknowledge that McMurtry has written some less effective books over the years, it is now clear that all of his works have been produced by a writer who has consistently written out of a coherent pattern produced by grappling with his intense feelings for his home country. Even the doggedness that leads him to produce stems from his southwestern background.

McMurtry's highly praised early novels—*Horseman, Pass By*; *Leaving Cheyenne*; and *The Last Picture Show*—drew their strength from the contradictory impulses produced by grappling with the positive and negative values of the passing southwestern frontier mythos: anti-intellectualism, primitivism, sexism, racism, classism, violence, courage, endurance, straightforwardness, and honesty. These early novels depended upon the rural or small-town southwest for setting, themes, and characters. Generally McMurtry concentrated on youthful characters confronting the painful knowledge that the old southwest and its associated values were passing from the earth.

In *Horseman, Pass By* the conflict is between Hud and his stepfather, Homer Bannon, who represents the old way of life. Homer is being replaced by Hud, whose raw amorality signals a new course. Lonnie, the youthful narrator whose awareness grows from the conflict between Hud and Homer, tries to decide which—

if either—character's values to adopt. On the surface McMurtry seems to have him side with Homer and lament the passing of the old: Homer is a courageous, heroic figure in many ways. And yet, the novel reveals an implicit ambivalence toward the old that becomes explicit in McMurtry's later works. Homer's stubbornness and his insensitivity to Hud's youthful desires bring about the old man's downfall.

McMurtry's uncertainty toward the possibility of fulfillment in southwestern rural life is more subtly presented in *Leaving Cheyenne*. There, Molly tries to choose between two recognizable southwestern figures: Johnny, the unfettered, forever free cowboy, and Gid the acquisitive, settled rancher. The two impulses cannot be reconciled, nor can Molly choose. Rather, she marries a third, Eddie, a brutal oil field worker. Throughout, she tries loving both Johnny and Gid, and each of them tries unsuccessfully to possess her. As the three age, their world, the blood's country, passes on.

Thwarted initiation, loneliness, and unfulfillment are central to McMurtry's third novel, too. But *The Last Picture Show* is not a nostalgic lament; it is a biting satire about the small-mindedness of small-town southwestern life. Duane and Sonny try to combat the boredom of growing up in Thalia, Texas, through sex, sports, and movies; but living close to the earth in McMurtry's world does not create enlightened human beings. The most admirable character, Sam the Lion, owner of the pool hall and former rancher, dies long before the novel ends.

The satire gives way to a bitter, goodbye-to-all-that attitude in McMurtry's first collection of essays. Written during Lyndon Johnson's presidency when being Texan was not chic among intellectuals, *In a Narrow Grave* continues to strike out at many things southwestern such as small towns where "many Texans . . . live and die in woeful ignorance." This antagonism to the rural marks the shift to the second category of McMurtry novels: the urban novels—*Moving On, All My Friends Are Going to Be Strangers*, and *Terms of Endearment*—set in Texas.

Patsy Carpenter in *Moving On* is another searcher. Looking for love in strange places, she marries a wealthy young graduate student, falls in love with a poor one, is attracted to a rodeo clown, and eventually finds her own independence. Danny Deck in *All My Friends Are Going to Be Strangers* wanders from Texas to California and back. At the end of the novel he drowns his manuscript in the Rio Grande. And Emma in *Terms of Endearment* dies young from cancer after following her graduate-student, then college-professor husband Flap from Houston to Kearney, Nebraska. Of all the characters in these novels, only Aurora Greenway in *Terms of Endearment* appears to escape the suffering the others endure. However, her outward strength is belied by an inner turmoil that suddenly surfaces in frightening moments and leads her to attempt again to find order where she can.

McMurtry then moved beyond the Southwest and wrote urban novels set outside the region: Hollywood (*Somebody's Darling*), Las Vegas (*The Desert Rose*), and Washington, D.C. (*Cadillac Jack*). Reviewers generally found McMurtry's urban works less satisfying than his earlier novels, calling them formless, unfocused, and boring, but in retrospect critics find they reflect the struggles of the times. The characters are urban searchers looking for something of value to replace the chaos that resulted from the loss of the old world.

With *Lonesome Dove* (1985), which dramatizes one Texas Rangers' promise to return his friend and partner's body to Texas for burial, McMurtry came back to Texas and the old Southwest as the subject and setting for his fiction. The two major characters—former Texas Rangers Augustus McCrae and Woodrow Call—embody negative and positive traits of the mythic, passing southwesterner and counter those McMurtry often attacked in books by writers who played being "symbolic frontiersmen." McMurtry's heroic figures are not only physically strong, loyal, creative, and courageous, but they are witty, talkative, sexually aware, and part of a supportive community. Among the awards the novel won is the Pulitzer Prize in 1986.

Since *Lonesome Dove*, McMurtry has alternated

between novels with contemporary settings that return to characters from previous works (the Thalia crew in *Texasville*, a sequel to *The Last Picture Show*; Danny Deck in *Some Can Whistle*, a sequel to *All My Friends Are Going to Be Strangers;* and Aurora Greenway in *The Evening Star*, a sequel to *Terms of Endearment*) and novels about historical western characters (Billy the Kid in *Anything for Billy* and Calamity Jane in *Buffalo Girls)*. Both types demonstrate one of his predominant themes: the effects of the end of a way of life, a subject McMurtry continues to examine with a complex ambivalence. With *Streets of Laredo* McMurtry merged the two types by writing a sequel to an earlier novel and by using historical nineteenth-century figures Judge Roy Bean and Charles Goodnight as fictional characters.

Throughout his career McMurtry has enjoyed successful film and television adaptations of his work, beginning with *Hud*, starring Paul Newman (1963); Peter Bogdanovich's film *The Last Picture Show* (1971); and especially a *Lonesome Dove* television miniseries starring Robert Duvall and Tommy Lee Jones in 1989. McMurtry's second nonfiction book, *Film Flam*, is a collection of his essays about movies.

His new work, *Pretty Boy Floyd*, written in collaboration with Diana Ossana, follows the broad outline of Charles Arthur Floyd's rise from an obscure Sallisaw, Oklahoma, farm boy to Public Enemy #1 on J. Edgar

Hoover's most wanted list in 1934. The novel, his first collaborative effort, has some recognizable McMurtry traits: a realistic plot filled with much readable dialogue and some memorable supporting characters; a chronological organization structured by random, cross-country journeys; a concern for the events that lead an innocent young man astray; an interest in human sexuality (a theme that largely disappeared in the grim *Streets of Laredo*); a critique of the modern world's emphasis on materialism and on the power of the media. Despite these recognizable elements, it lacks connection with the deep themes about the loss of frontier values that have been central to McMurtry's best works such as *Horseman, Pass By* and *Lonesome Dove*. The fact that McMurtry has reconciled himself to writing about his home country and about the frontier he had refused to consider worthy of his efforts for many years indicates that he has resolved some of the ambivalence that characterizes much of his work. With his newest novel, perhaps he has adjusted to one aspect of his craft on which he has often commented—the isolation of the novelist. McMurtry describes collaboration as "different, an interesting kind of change" and says that he plans more collaborations.

In them he will no doubt continue to return to his southwestern past. When McMurtry concludes his first collection of essays, *In a Narrow Grave*, he recalls the last time his McMurtry uncles had gathered as a group at the Clarendon Country Club. He remembers how his seventy-five-year-old Uncle Johnny, sick and dying, had struggled into his Cadillac to take his leave, and McMurtry comments:

> He stood in the frame that had always contained him, the great circular frame of the plains, with the wind blowing the gray hair at his temples and the whole of the Llano Estacado at his back. When he smiled at the children who were near the pain left his face for a second and he gave them the look that had always been his greatest appeal—the look of a man who saw life to the last as a youth sees it, and who sees in any youth all that he himself had been. (172)

McMurtry then concludes the essay, noting that this image recalls the kind of "silence where fiction starts." Indeed, Larry McMurtry's fiction starts and ends with these powerful images of the old and new Southwest. Throughout his career he has drawn from the Texas legend in various ways. McMurtry understands as well as any Texas writer, that this mythic Texas is denied by reality. Yet it is a powerful myth that still grips the minds of supporters and attackers alike. McMurtry has shaped a body of work that explores these conflicted feelings, transmuting his ambivalence into art that reconciles his readers and himself to experience.

Works Cited

PRIMARY SOURCES

BOOKS

Horseman, Pass By. NY: Harper, 1961; *Penguin Books, 1979.
Leaving Cheyenne. NY: Harper, 1963; *Penguin Books, 1979.
The Last Picture Show. NY: Dial, 1966; *Penguin Books, 1979.
In a Narrow Grave. Austin: *Encino, 1968; Touchstone, 1989.
Moving On. NY: *Simon and Schuster, 1970; Touchstone, 1989.
All My Friends Are Going to Be Strangers. NY: *Simon and Schuster, 1972; Touchstone, 1989.
Terms of Endearment. NY: *Simon and Schuster, 1975; Touchstone, 1989.
Somebody's Darling. NY: *Simon and Schuster, 1978. Touchstone, 1989.
Cadillac Jack. NY: *Simon and Schuster, 1982; Touchstone, 1989.
The Desert Rose. NY: *Simon and Schuster, 1983; Touchstone, 1989.
Lonesome Dove. NY: Simon and Schuster, 1985; *Pocket Books, 1986.
Texasville. NY: *Simon and Schuster, 1987; Pocket Books, 1987.
Film Flam. NY: *Simon and Schuster, 1987.
Anything for Billy. NY: *Simon and Schuster, 1988; Pocket Books, 1989.
Some Can Whistle. NY: *Simon and Schuster, 1989; Pocket Books, 1990.
Buffalo Girls. NY: *Simon and Schuster, 1990; Pocket Books, 1991.
The Evening Star. NY: *Simon and Schuster, 1992 ; Pocket Books, 1993.

Streets of Laredo. NY: * Simon and Schuster, 1993; Pocket Books, 1994.

*Pretty Boy Floyd (*with Diana Ossana). NY: *Simon and Schuster, 1994.

The Late Child. NY: Simon and Schuster, 1995.

(*Page numbers in the text refer to this edition.)

UNCOLLECTED ARTICLES

"Ever a Bridegroom: Reflection of the Failure of Texas Literature." *Texas Observer* (23 Oct. 1981): 1, 8–19. Rpt. in *Range Wars: Heated Debates, Sober Reflections, and Other Assessments of Texas Writing*. Eds. Craig Clifford and Tom Pilkington. Dallas: SMU, 1989.

"From Mickey Spillane to Erica Jong." *The Washington Monthly* 7 (May 1975): 12–22.

"Growing Up Treeless." *Texas Homes* (July 1986): 54–58.

"Goat-Ropers and Groupies: A Requiem for a Rodeo." *New York* 5 (27 Nov. 1972): 58–62.

"How the West Was Won or Lost." *The New Republic* 203 (22 Oct. 1990): 32–38.

"Return to Waco." *The New Republic* 208 (7 June 1993): 16–19.

"Trending Back to Texas." *The Lone Star Review* (5 Apr 1981): 4, 15.

"The Southwest as the Cradle of the Novelist." In *The American Southwest: Cradle of Literary Art*. Ed. Robert W. Walts. San Marcos: Southwest Texas State U, 1979.

"The Texas Moon and Elsewhere." *Atlantic* 235.3 (Mar. 1975): 29–36.

"Unfinished Women." *Texas Monthly* 5.5 (May 1977): 106, 160–166.

SECONDARY WORKS

BIBLIOGRAPHIES

Huber, Dwight. "Larry McMurtry: A Selected Bibliography." *Larry McMurtry: Unredeemed Dreams*. Ed. Dorey Schmidt (Edinburg, TX: Pan American UP, 1978.

Peavy, Charles D. "A Larry McMurtry Bibliography." *Western American Literature* 8 (Fall 1968): 235–48.

Williams, Charles. "Bibliography." *Taking Stock: A Larry McMurtry Casebook*. Ed. Clay Reynolds. Dallas: SMU, 1989.

INTERVIEWS

Bennett, Patrick. "Larry McMurtry: Thalia, Houston, and Hollywood." *Talking with Texas Writers*. College Station: Texas A&M UP, 1980: 15–36.

Busby, Mark. Telephone Interview. San Marcos, Texas. (11 Apr. 1994).

Dunn, Si. "Ex–native Son McMurtry." *Texas Observer* (16 Jan. 1976): 13.

Jones, Malcolm. "The Ghost Writer at Home on the Range." *Newsweek* 122.5 (Aug. 2, 1993): 52–53.

"A Novelist of Characters and Place." *Humanities Interview* 7.2 (Summer 1989): 1–6.

Rothstein, Mervyn. "A Texan Who Likes to Deflate the Legends of the Golden West." *The New York Times* (1 Nov. 1988): C17+.

MANUSCRIPTS & ARCHIVES

The major collection of manuscripts and letters is in the Special Collection Room, University of Houston. Other manuscripts are in the Rare Book and Texana Collection, University of North Texas (especially his undergraduate papers and contributions to student magazines); Southwestern Writers Collection, Southwest Texas State University (manuscripts of *In a Narrow Grave*, and *Moving On* and the original movie treatment of "Streets of Laredo"); Special Collections, University of Texas of the Permian Basin; Humanities Research Center, University of Texas, Austin (*Horseman, Pass By* manuscript).

CRITICAL STUDIES

Abbott, E. C. (Teddy Blue) and Helena Huntington Smith. *We Pointed Them North*. 1939. Norman: U of Oklahoma P, 1954.

Abernethy, Francis E. "Strange and Unnatural History in *Lonesome Dove*." *Texas Books in Review* 8.2 (1988): 1–2.

Anderson, Patrick. "Lone Star: Washington's Best Texas Novelist Doesn't Live Here Anymore." *Washingtonian* 27 (June 1992): 27–30.

Ahearn, Kerry. "Larry McMurtry." *Fifty Western Writers: A Bio-Bibliographical Sourcebook*. Ed. Fred Erisman and Richard Etulain. Westport, CT: Greenwood P, 1982: 280–90.

———. "More D'Urban: The Texas Novels of Larry McMurtry." *Texas Quarterly* 19 (Autumn 1976): 109–29. Rpt. in *Critical Essays on the Western American Novel*. Ed. William T. Pilkington. Boston: G.K. Hall, 1980, 223–42. Rpt in Reynolds.

Baker, Christopher. "The Death of the Frontier in the Novels of Larry McMurtry." *McNeese Review* 28 (1981–82): 44–54. Rpt. in Reynolds.

Bakhtin. M. M. *The Dialogic Imagination*. Austin: U of Texas P, 1981.

Bloom, Harold. *The Anxiety of Influence*. New York: Oxford UP, 1973.

Brown, Norman D. "Larry McMurtry." *Southern Writers: A Bio-graphical Dictionary*. Eds. Robert Bain, Joseph M. Flora, and Louis D. Rubin, Jr. Baton Rouge: LSU P, 1979, 293–94.

Busby, Mark. "Damn the Saddle on the Wall: Anti-Myth in Larry McMurtry's *Horseman, Pass By*." *New Mexico Humanities Review* 3 (Summer 1980): 5–10. Rpt. in Reynolds.

———. "Journeys through Texas." *New Growth / 2: Contemporary Short Stories by Texas Writers*. San Antonio: Corona: 1993.

———. "Larry McMurtry." *Twentieth-Century Western Writers*. Ed. James Vincent. Detroit: Gale, 1982: 534–36.

Byrd, James W., Scott Downing, and Art Hendrix. "McMurtry Circles His Wagons: An East Texas Roundup." *Southwestern American Literature* 14.2 (1989): 4–19.

Campbell, Joseph. *Hero with a Thousand Faces*. New York: Meridian Books, 1949.

Cleveland, Ceil. "Memories of McMurtry." *The Houston Post* 2 Jan. 1991: D1.

Clifford, Craig Edward. *In the Deep Heart's Core: Reflections on Life, Letters, and Texas*. College Station: Texas A&M UP, 1985.

Clifford, Craig, and Tom Pilkington, eds. *Range Wars: Heated Debates, Sober Reflections, and Other Assessments of Texas Writing*. Dallas: SMU, 1989.

Cox, Diana H. "*Anything for Billy*: A Fiction Stranger Than Truth." *Journal of American Culture* 14.2 (Summer 1991): 75–81.

Cowan, Louise, "Myth in the Modern World." In *Texas Myths*. College Station: Texas A&M UP, 1986.

Crawford, Ian. "Intertextuality in Larry McMurtry's *The Last Picture Show*." *Journal of Popular Culture* 27 (Summer 1993): 43–54.

Curtis, Gregory. "The Power of Polite Discouragement: Behind the Lines." *Texas Monthly* 14.12 (Dec. 1986): 5–6.

Davis, Kenneth W. "The Themes of Initiation in the Works of

Larry McMurtry and Tom Mayer." *Arlington Quarterly* 2 (Winter 1989–90): 29–43. Rpt. in Reynolds as "Initiation Themes in McMurtry's Cowboy Trilogy."

Deen, Sue McMurtry. "The McMurtry Family." *Archer Country, Texas 1880–1980 Centennial Family History and Program June 29–July 6, 1980*. Archer City, Texas: McCrain Publishing Co., 1980: 95.

Degenfelder, E. Pauline. "McMurtry and the Movies: *Hud* and *The Last Picture Show*." *Western Humanities Review* 29 (Winter 1975): 81–91.

Dubose, Thomas. *"The Last Picture Show*: Theme." *RE: Artes Liberales* 3 (1977): 43–45.

England, D. Gene. "Rites of Passage in Larry McMurtry's *The Last Picture Show*." *Heritage of Kansas* 12.1 (1979): 37–48.

English, Sarah. "Larry McMurtry." *Dictionary of Literary Biography Yearbook: 1987*. Ed. J. M. Brook. Detroit: Gale, 1988: 265–74.

Folsom, James K. *"Shane* and *Hud*: Two Stories in Search of a Medium." *Western Humanities Review* 24 (Autumn 1970): 359–72. Rpt in Reynolds.

Garza-Falcón-Sánchez, Leticia. "The Chicano/a Literary Response to the Rhetoric of Dominance." Ph.D. diss. U of Texas, Austin, 1993.

Gerlach, John. "Larry McMurtry." *American Novelists Since World War II*. Ed. Jeffrey Helterman and Richard Layman. Detroit: Gale, 1978: 328–31.

———. *"The Last Picture Show* and One More Adaptation." *Literature Fiction Quarterly* 1.2 (1973): 161–66.

Goodwyn, Larry. "The Frontier Myth and Southwestern Literature." *American Libraries* (Feb. 1971): 161–67; (Apr. 1971): 359–66. Rpt. in *Regional Perspectives: An Examination of America's Literary Heritage*. Ed. John Gordon Burke (Chicago: ALA, 1973): 175–206.

Graham, Don. "Is Dallas Burning? Notes on Recent Texas Fiction." *Southwestern American Literature* 4 (1974): 68–73.

————. "*Lonesome Dove*: Butch and Sundance Go On A Cattledrive." *Southwestern American Literature* 12.1 (1986): 7–12. Rpt. in Reynolds.

————. *Texas: A Literary Portrait*. San Antonio: Corona, 1985.

————, James W. Lee, and William T. Pilkington, eds. *The Texas Literary Tradition: Fiction, Folklore, History*. Austin: UT College of Liberal Arts, 1983.

Granzow, Barbara. "The Western Writer: A Study of Larry McMurtry's *All My Friends Are Going to Be Strangers*." *Southwestern American Literature* 4 (1974): 37–51. Rpt. in Reynolds.

Greene, A. C. *The Fifty Best Books on Texas*. Dallas: Pressworks, 1981.

Haley, J. Evetts. *Charles Goodnight: Cowman and Plainsman*. Norman: U of Oklahoma P, 1936.

Harrigan, Stephen. "The Making of *Lonesome Dove*." *Texas Monthly* 16.6 (June 1988): 82–86, 156–59.

Hassan, Ihab. *Radical Innocence*. Princeton, N.J.: Princeton UP, 1961.

Hickey, Dave. "McMurtry's Elegant Essays." *Texas Observer* (7 Feb. 1969): 14–16. Rpt. in Reynolds.

Jones, Roger. *Larry McMurtry and the Victorian Novel*. College Station: Texas A&M UP, 1994.

Kael, Pauline. "Hud, Deep in the Divided Heart of Hollywood." *Film Quarterly* 17.4 (1964): 15–23. Rpt. in *I Lost It at the Movies*. Boston: Little, 1965, 78–94. Rpt. in Reynolds.

Kehl, D. G. "Thalia's 'Sock' and the Cowhide Boot: Humor of the New Southwest in the Fiction of Larry McMurtry." *Southwestern American Literature* 14.2 (1989): 20–33.

King, Larry L. *Of Outlaws, Con Men, Whores, Politicians, and Other Artists*. New York: Viking, 1980.

Lamar, Howard R. "Regionalism and the Broad Methodological

Problem." *Regional Studies: The Interplay of Land and People*. Ed. Glen E. Lich. College Station: Texas A&M UP, 1992.

Landess, Thomas. *Larry McMurtry*. Austin: Steck-Vaughn, 1969.

Landon, Brooks. "Larry McMurtry." *Dictionary of Literary Biography Yearbook: 1980*. Eds. Karen L. Rood, Jean W. Ross, and Richard Ziegfield. Detroit: Gale, 1981. Rpt. in Reynolds.

Lawrence, D. H. *Studies in Classic American Literature*. New York: The Viking P, 1923.

Lee, James Ward. *Classics of Texas Fiction*. Dallas: E-Heart, 1987.

Lewis, R. W. B. *The American Adam*. Chicago: U of Chicago P, 1955.

Lich, Lera Patrick Tyler. *Larry McMurtry's Texas: Evolution of the Myth*. Austin: Eakin, 1987.

Lyall, Sarah. "Book Notes: Shopping Trip." *The New York Times* 2 Feb. 1994: 18C.

Marx, Leo. *The Machine in the Garden: Technology and the Pastoral Ideal in America*. New York: Oxford UP, 1964.

Mogen, David. "Sex and True West in McMurtry's Fiction: From Teddy Blue to *Lonesome Dove* to *Texasville*." *Southwestern American Literature* 14.2 (1989): 34–45.

Morrow, Patrick D. "Larry McMurtry: The First Phase." *Seasoned Authors for a New Season: The Search for Standards in Popular Writing*. Ed. Louis Filler. Bowling Green: Bowling Green U Popular P, 1980, 70–82.

————. "Mental Retardation in *The Sound and the Fury* and *The Last Picture Show*." *Re: Artes Liberales* 6.1 (1979): 1–9.

Neinstein, Raymond L. *The Ghost Country*. Berkeley: Creative Arts, 1976.

Nelson, Jane. "Larry McMurtry." *A Literary History of the American West*. J. Golden Taylor, gen. ed. Ft. Worth: TCU, 1987, 612–21.

O'Keefe, Ruth Jones. *Archer County Pioneers: A History of Archer County Texas*. Hereford, Texas: Pioneer Book Publishers,

Inc., 1969.

Peavy, Charles D. "Coming of Age in Texas: The Novels of Larry McMurtry." *Western American Literature* 4 (1969): 171–88.

———. "Larry McMurtry and Black Humor: A Note on *The Last Picture Show*." *Western American Literature* 2 (1967): 223–27.

———. *Larry McMurtry*. Boston: Twayne/G.K. Hall, 1978.

Phillips, Billie. "McMurtry's Women: [Libido, Caritas and Philia] In [And Out of] Archer County." *Southwestern American Literature* 4 (1974): 29–36.

Phillips, Raymond. C. "The Ranch as Place and Symbol in the Novels of Larry McMurtry." *South Dakota Review* 13.2 (1975): 27–47.

Pilkington, William T. *My Blood's Country: Studies in Southwestern Literature*. Fort Worth: Texas Christian UP, 1973, 163–82.

———. "The Recent Southwestern Novel." *Southwestern American Literature* 1 (Jan 1971): 12–15.

Reid, Jan. "Return of the Native Son." *Texas Monthly* 21.2 (Feb. 1993): 202, 228–31.

Reynolds, Clay. "Back Trailing to Glory: *Lonesome Dove* and the Novels of Larry McMurtry." *Texas Review* 8 (1987): 22–29. Rpt. in Reynolds.

———. "Come Home Larry, All is Forgiven: A Native Son's Search for Identity." *Cross Timbers Review* 11 (May 1985): 65. Rpt. in Reynolds.

———. "Showdown in the New Old West: The Cowboy vs. the Oilman." *Lamar Journal of the Humanities* 6.1 (1980): 19–31.

———, ed. *Taking Stock: A Larry McMurtry Casebook*. Dallas: SMU, 1989.

Sanderson, Jim. "Old Corrals: Texas According to 80s Films and TV and Texas According to Larry McMurtry." *Journal of American Culture* 13.2 (Summer 1990): 63–73.

Schmidt, Dorey, ed. *Larry McMurtry: Unredeemed Dreams*.

Edinburg, TX: Pan American UP, 1978.

Sewell, Ernestine P. "McMurtry's Cowboy-God in *Lonesome Dove*." *Western American Literature* 21 (1986): 219–25. (*CLC* 44: 259–62.) Rpt. in Reynolds.

Slotkin, Richard. *The Fatal Environment: The Myth of the Frontier in the Age of Industrialization, 1800–1890*. New York: Atheneum, 1985.

————. *Regeneration through Violence: The Mythology of the American Frontier, 1600–1860*. Middletown, CT: Wesleyan UP, 1983.

Sonnichsen, C.L. *From Hopalong to Hud: Thoughts on Western Fiction*. College Station: Texas A&M UP, 1978.

————. "The New Style Western." *South Dakota Review* 4 (Summer 1966): 22–28.

————. "Sex on the Lone Prairee." *Western American Literature* 13 (1978): 15–33.

Speidel, Constance. "Whose *Terms of Endearment*?" *Literature Fiction Quarterly* 12.4 (1984): 271–73.

Stout, Janis P. "Journeying as a Metaphor for Cultural Loss in the Novels of Larry McMurtry." *Western American Literature* 11 (1976): 37–50. Rpt. in Reynolds.

———— ."Cadillac Larry Rides Again: McMurtry and the Song of the Open Road." *Western American Literature* 24.3 (Nov. 1989): 243–51.

Summerlin, Tim. "Larry McMurtry and the Persistent Frontier." *Southwestern American Literature* 4 (1974): 22–28. Rpt in Reynolds.

Summerlin, Charles T. "Late McMurtry." *Lamar Journal of the Humanities* 2.1 (1975): 54–56.

Tangum, Marion. "Larry McMurtry's *Lonesome Dove*: 'This Is What We Call Home.'" *Rocky Mountain Review of Language and Literature* 45.1–2 (1991): 61–73.

Thurn, Thora. "McMurtry's Settlers: Molly and Emma." *CCTE*

Studies 47 (1982): 51–56.

Todorov, Tzvetan. *Mikhail Bakhtin: The Dialogical Principle*. Minneapolis: U of Minnesota P, 1984.

Trachtenberg, Alan. *The Incorporation of America*. New York: Hill and Wang, 1982.

Underwood, June O. "Western Women and True Womanhood: Culture and Symbol in History and Literature." *Great Plains Quarterly* 5 (1985): 93–106.

Utley, Robert Marshall. *Billy the Kid: A Short and Violent Life*. Lincoln : U of Nebraska P, 1989.

Willson, Robert. "Which Is the Real 'Last Picture Show'?" *Literature Fiction Quarterly* 1.2 (1973): 167–69.

Wolfe, Tom. *The Electric Kool-Aid Acid Test*. New York: Farrar, Straus, and Giroux, 1968.

Woodward, Daniel. "Larry McMurtry's *Texasville*: A Comic Pastoral of the Oilpatch." *The Huntington Library Quarterly* 56 (Spring 1993): 167–80.

SELECTED REVIEWS

Horseman, Pass By

Minter, David L. "To Live and Die in Texas." *Texas Observer* 15 Sept. 1961: 6.

Poore, Charles. "Books of the Times." *New York Times Book Review* 10 June 1961: 21.

Tinkle, Lon. "Raw and Rough Look at Ranching Texas." Reading and Writing. *Dallas Morning News* 28 May 1961, sec. 5:9.

Leaving Cheyenne

Sprague, Marshall. "Texas Triptych." *New York Times Book Re-*

view 6 Oct. 1963: 39.

Tinkle, Lon. "Of Fate and Doom in Ranch Country." *Dallas Morning News* 13 Oct. 1963, sec. 1: 24.

The Last Picture Show

Bode, Elroy. "The Last Picture Show." *Texas Observer* 20 Jan. 1967: 17–18.

Hickey, Dave. "Elegy and Exorcism: Texas Talent and General Concerns." *Texas Observer* 20 Jan. 1967: 14–16.

Jack, W. T. "Sex Wasn't Everything." *New York Times Book Review* 13 Nov. 1966: 68–69.

Tinkle, Lon. "Critical Spirit in Texas Fiction." *Dallas Morning News* 26 Feb. 1967: 2G.

Moving On

Barthelme, Steve. "McMurtry's *Moving On.*" *Texas Observer* 8 Jan. 1971: 13–16. See also McMurtry's point-by-point rebuttal, "Answer from McMurtry" (*Texas Observer* 26 Feb. 1971: 22–24).

——————. "Barthelme's Response to McMurtry's Answer to Barthelme's Review of McMurtry's *Moving On.*" *Texas Observer* 12 Mar. 1971: 15.

All My Friends Are Going to Be Strangers

C(lemons), W(alter). "Drowning a Book." *Newsweek* 20 Mar. 1972: 110.

Crooks, Alan F. "Larry McMurtry—A Writer in Transition: An Essay-Review." *Western American Literature* 19 (1984): 146–147. Rpt. in Reynolds.

Donald, Miles. "Lone Ranger." *New Statesman* 2 Mar. 1973: 314.

Gordon, Roxy. "McMurtry's *All My Friends.*" *Texas Observer* 25 Aug. 1972: 14–15.

Terms of Endearment

Adams, Phoebe-Lou. *Atlantic Monthly* Nov. 1975: 126.
Deemer, Charles. "A Pro Strikes Out." *New Leader* 15 Mar. 1976: 19–20.
Lehmann-Haupt, Christopher. "A Messy Vehicle That Runs." *The New York Times* 22 Oct. 1975: 43.
Sorensen, Roberta. *Western American Literature* 11 (1977): 356–58.
Towers, Robert. "An Oddly Misshapen Novel by a Highly Accomplished Novelist." *New York Times Book Review* 19 Oct. 1975: 4. Rpt. in Reynolds.

Somebody's Darling

Busby, Mark. "McMurtry, Out of the Chute, Stumbling." Rev. of *Somebody's Darling*. *Zest Magazine, The Houston Chronicle* 14 Jan. 1979: 35.
Landon, Brooks. "Larry McMurtry." *Dictionary of Literary Biography Yearbook: 1980*. Eds. Karen L. Rood, Jean W. Ross, and Richard Ziegfield. Detroit: Gale, 1981. Rpt. in Reynolds.
Lyons, Gene. "Day of the Hocus." *Texas Monthly* 6. 12 (Dec. 1978): 220+. Rpt. in Reynolds.

Cadillac Jack

Browning, Dominique. "The Knicknack Cadillac." *Texas Monthly* 10.10 (Oct. 1982): 177+.
Busby, Mark. "The Junk Man." *Texas Books in Review* 5 (1983): 31–2.

Reynolds, R. C. "Come Home Larry, All is Forgiven: A Native Son's Search for Identity." *Cross Timbers Review* 11.i (May 1985): 65+. Rpt. in Reynolds.

The Desert Rose

Adams, Charles L. Rev. of *The Desert Rose*. *Western American Literature* 20 (1985): 167–68.

Benedek, Emily. "An Author Recaptures His Voice." *The New Leader* Nov. 1983: 18–19. Rpt. in Reynolds.

Busby, Mark. "McMurtry's Cardboard Characters." Rev. of *Desert Rose*. *The Bryan-College Station Eagle* 8 Oct. 1983: 1bb.

Davis, Rod. "A Surfeit of Bimbos." *Texas Monthly* 11.11 (Nov. 1983): 192+.

Mano, D. Keith. Rev. of *The Desert Rose*. *National Review* 25 Nov. 1983: 1495–96.

Lonesome Dove

Clemons, Walter. "Saga of a Cattle Drive." *Newsweek* 3 June 1985: 74. (*CLC* 44: 254.)

Lehmann-Haupt, Christopher. *New York Times* 3 June 1985, late city ed.: C20. (*CLC* 44: 253–54.)

Marvel, Bill. "A Book Larger Than Life Revised a Dying Genre." *The Dallas Morning News* 5 Feb. 1989: 1C+.

Milazzo, Lee. "*Lonesome Dove* Is the Great Texas Novel." *The Dallas Morning News* 30 June 1985: 12C.

Texasville

Busby, Mark. Rev. of *Texasville*. *The Bryan-College Station Eagle* 15 Aug. 1987: 14.

Erdrich. Louise. "Why Is That Man Tired?" *New York Times Book Review* 19 Apr. 1987: 7. Rpt. in Reynolds.

Frye, Bob J. "A Festival of Cynicism." *Fort Worth Star-Telegram* 26 Apr. 1987: 6D.

Pilkington, Tom. "The Last Picture Show—Part II." *Dallas Times Herald* 12 Apr. 1987: 5C.

————. *"Texasville*: A Review of Reviews." *Texas Books in Review* 7.1 (1987): 15–16.

Reid, Jan. "The Next Picture Show." *Texas Monthly* 15.4 (Apr. 1987): 152+. Rpt. in Reynolds.

Film Flam

Bawer, Bruce. "Tinsel Talk." *New Criterion* June 1987: 77–81. Rpt. in Reynolds.

Lenihan, John. "Entertaining Views of Hollywood's 'Ego Zoo.'" *Texas Books in Review* 8.2 (1988): 2.

Anything for Billy

Milazzo, Lee. "'Billy' Misfires: McMurtry's Uneven Dime Novel Falls Short." *The Dallas Morning News* 16 Oct. 1988: 10C.

Pilkington, (William) Tom. "McMurtry's 'Kid' Doesn't Square with History." *The Dallas Times Herald* 11 Sept. 1988: 10C.

Tatum, Stephen. "A Fitting Life for Billy the Kid? A Review Essay." *New Mexico Historical Review* (Jan. 1990): 79–90.

————. "Hopelessly Devoted to You." *World & I* Jan. 1989: 333–42.

Winckler, Suzanne. "The Old West, The New South." *Texas Monthly* 16.10 (Oct. 1988): 146+.

Some Can Whistle

Kingsolver, Barbara. *The New York Times Book Review* 22 Oct. 1989: 8.

Winckler, Suzanne. "Whistling in the Dark." *Texas Monthly* 17.10 (Oct. 1989): 160, 163.

Buffalo Girls

Schaeffer, Susan Fromberg. *The New York Times Book Review* 7 Oct. 1990: 3+.
Loose, Julian. *New Statesman & Society* 3 (25 Jan. 1991): 36+.
Winckler, Suzanne. "Back in the Saddle." *Texas Monthly* 18.12 (Dec. 1990): 64+.

The Evening Star

Busby, Mark. *Southwestern American Literature* 18.1 (1992): 100–101.
Edwards, Thomas R. *The New York Review of Books* 13 Aug. 1992: 54–56.
Plunket, Robert. *The New York Times Book Review* 21 June 1992: 12.
Starr, Mark. *Newsweek* 8 June 1992: 58.

Streets of Laredo

Busby, Mark. *Southwestern American Literature* 19.2 (1993): 93–94.
Draper, Robert. "Mean Streets." *Texas Monthly* 21.8 (Aug. 1993): 40+.
Graham, Don. "Take My Sequel From the Wall." *Austin Chronicle* 13 Aug. 1993: 20–22.
Jones, Malcolm. "The Ghost Writer at Home on the Range." *Newsweek* 2 Aug. 1993: 52.
Perrin, Noel. *The New York Times Book Review* 25 July 1993: 9.

Pretty Boy Floyd

Busby, Mark. *Texas Books in Review* 14.4 (1994): 4.
Graham, Don. *The Dallas Morning News* 16 Oct. 1994: 10C.
Skow, John. *Time* 19 Sept 1994: 82.
Zion, Sidney. *The New York Times Book Review* 16 Oct 1994: 31.

SELECTED FILM AND TELEVISION
REVIEWS

Ansen, David. "Extraordinary People." *Newsweek* 21 Nov. 1983:
    91–92.
Canby, Vincent. "Talented Actors Enrich a Fine Script." *New York
    Times* 4 Dec. 1983, sec. 2: 21.
Crowther, Bosley. "Hurrahs for 'Hud': A Present-day Western
    Drama Has an Apt, Compelling Theme." *The New York Times*
    9 June 1993, sec. 2: 1.
King, Larry. "Leavin' McMurtry." *Texas Monthly* 2.3 (Mar. 1974):
    70–76. Rpt. in Reynolds.
Klein, Andy. *Los Angeles* Jan. 1988: 169.
MacCambridge, Michael. "Trip to 'Texasville' a Disappointment:
    'Picture Show' Sequel Can't Live Up to Original." *Austin Ameri-
    can Statesman* 28 Sept. 1990: 5.
Madigan, Tim. "The Range of Opinion." *Fort Worth Star–Tele-
    gram* 9 Feb. 1989, sec. 4: 1+.
Shales, Tom. "The Splendors of 'Lonesome Dove': CBS Brings
    Larry McMurtry's Western Epic to Television in a Breathtak-
    ing Miniseries." *Washington Post* 5 Feb. 1989: G1+.
Waters, Harry F. "How the West Was Once." *Newsweek* 6 Feb.
    1989: 54–55.
Zoglin, Richard. "Poetry on the Prairie." *Time* 6 Feb. 1989: 78.

Index

ADM-3972   02/18/97

PS
3563
A319
Z59
1995